"Enter the brilliant mind behind *EYES THAT SEEN PLENTY* and become part of Aaron Campbell's world. The author captivates you by describing people in such a way that you feel you know them, and by telling incidents so that you experience them with him.

The young Campbell, wrestling with racial identity and searching for manhood, spirals downward into destructive living. The reader understands Campbell's thinking as he slides into the darkness, grabbing for some type of handhold in Ivy League success, various forms of religion, and even crime. But the despair of this everyman's experience ends in hope!"

—Carl Westerlund; Director of Calvary Chapel Bible College, Graduate School

"*EYES THAT SEEN PLENTY* is a true inspiration for anyone who is journeying for truth and purpose. Aaron's story is one of honesty and humility that helps light the path toward the discovery of healing and salvation."

—Eileen Scott; Senior Writer; *Ivy League Christian Observer*

"For those wondering "What good can come out of Hip Hop?" . . . my answer is *EYES THAT SEEN PLENTY*. This is the recipe for an urban classic! Reading it took me back to when I would hang with DJ Scott La Rock (R.I.P.) at his "Record Pool" and he'd always tell me stories about the youth he counseled at the homeless shelter. (And we all know what resulted from that—Boogie Down Productions!)

With Hip Hop as its "soundtrack," *EYES THAT SEEN PLENTY* takes you on a very personal journey through Campbell's childhood and its winding roads, to his hustling game at the Port Authority Bus Terminal, to the man in the pulpit he is today."

—Louis "BreakBeat Lou" Flores; o-Creator, "Ultimate Breaks and Beats"

EYES THAT SEEN PLENTY

A MEMOIR

AARON W. CAMPBELL

KAATENA
PRESS

Join us at
www.eyesthatseenplenty.com

Published in the United States by: Kaatena Press

Cover Design by: Jude Gavin
Lemonheads Candies ® from Ferrara Pan Candy Company • Used By Permission
Cover Photo by: Merdis Foster
Printed by: Bethany Press International

Music Credits:

"The Breaks": Words and Music by Kurtis Blow • © 1980 Neutral Gray Music/
Funkgroove Music, 405 West 45th St. 4D, New York, New York 10036
All Rights Reserved • Used By Permission

"Wandering Star": Words and Music by Portishead • © 1994 Far Out Music/
Universal Polygram International, 2100 Colorado Avenue, Santa Monica, CA 90404
All Rights Reserved • Used By Permission

"Diary of a Madman": Words and Music by Gravediggaz • © 1994, Ancient
Entities Music/Universal Polygram International, 2100 Colorado Avenue, Santa
Monica, CA 90404
All Rights Reserved • Used By Permission

"The Message": Words and Music, Grandmaster Flash and the Furious Five/
Melle Mell • © 1982, Sugar Hill Music Publishing LTD, 443 Liberty Road,
Englewood, NJ 07631
All Rights Reserved • Used By Permission

"New York State of Mind": Words and Music by Nas • © 1994 EMI April Music
Inc./EMI Music Publishing, 75 9th Avenue, FL 4, New York, New York, 10011
All Rights Reserved • Used By Permission

Tradepaper ISBN: 978-0-9848246-0-1
eBook ISBN: 978-0-9848246-1- 8

For . . .

Natasha Ingrid
my queen, my lioness, my everything

Anni Rebekah
Josiah Aaron
Jonah Matthew
my beautiful children
I thank, love, and so greatly admire each of you

Mom
my smiling, singing lady and first best friend; you're the best of the best

Dad
my hero—so proud to have your name

Everyone has a master plan.
But what do you do when your master plan fails?
Or worse, when it works quite well,
yet you're still found wanting?

What's life all about, anyway?

Join us at
www.eyesthatseenplenty.com

A SIMPLE FOREWORD

What if Joyce had been born in Elizabeth, New Jersey—the portrait of the artist as a young dude.

From Augustine to McInerney, our inherited Western literature often finds a man in a place, in a time, with circumstances that cause him to confront a series of problems. This is literature that takes a snapshot, and gives us a story of the past and present. The future—in the most American of all thoughts and hopes—remains a promise. Inside "Eyes That Seen Plenty" is a promise for our own lives, an inducement to survive, and a reason to try to make sense of it all.

But what we have here substantially is a work of art. The outer limits of the aesthetic universe where the normal abilities of words fail. That is why we love art in the first place, because of the sublime, because of the illimitable, because of the ineffable. The job of the foreword writer then, becomes a game of matching— not outdoing, but like a rug that complements a couch, and brings out it's color. In this case, that rug also has to be some kind of art . . .

Malik Wilson
University of Pennsylvania
class of 2000

TABLE OF CONTENTS

Part II.

Part III.

PART I

STANDING
(ON MY OWN TWO)

I

TERROR BY NIGHT

I was too old to be scared of the dark.

I knew some adults felt that way. I could just tell they did. I felt the same way too; and "dag," I'd often murmur to myself.

But I had my reasons—real good reasons, too. Sometimes I'd wish for somebody to sit me down, pour me some orange soda, and ask me why, so I could answer them from under my favorite Playboy baseball cap, but nobody ever did. That's why nobody got to know my reasons. So while much of the adult world continued getting irked by my sudden "sore throats" and other antics I'd use to wake them up in the middle of the night, they patiently put up with me. I grew up around a lot of adults. They were stressed adults at times, but nonetheless patient.

But I had been through a lot.

It's hard relaying pains from the past, especially when you had an overall "good childhood" with a mother who scorched her very stomach lining to give you nothing but the best. Not to mention a father whose burgundy Monte Carlo would come whenever you called. However, divorce does introduce distance, no matter how you cut it. And when dads don't live at home anymore, well that's just the way it is. So a young woman and her two kids can fall victim to an awful lot while growing up in one of Jersey's trickiest cities: Plainfield.

Now back in the late 70's, there was this disco dance called "the hustle." Mom sure loved to sing and dance, and she was so pretty and did both so well. Whenever a bumpy tune would come on—especially on a Friday or Saturday night at "Momma's" (our grandmother's) house, where things felt so safe and stable in every way—up would go Mom, to whatever part of the room had the least furniture to bump into. And she would proceed to do "the hustle," biting her bottom lip over that smile

3

of hers, just like she always did when she was "gettin' down." It would never be long before I'd jump up and join her. We always loved singing and dancing together.

Whenever we did "the hustle," it reminded me of loud-talking adults always jiving about life itself being a hustle. So I always felt a strange closeness to that dance. For as my little wrists were cutting those unison-circles to the beat, with me and Mom's hips popping out at the same time, it felt like I was dancing out my own life's story. So I'd keep right on dancing.

And life sure was a hustle.

▲ ▼ ▲ ▼ ▲

I hated horror movies. I got teased for it, too. But I didn't care. And while most kids say they don't care about being teased (but really do), this was one area where I truly didn't care. I mean, for the life of me, I couldn't understand why some considered it fun to get scared witless, anyway. Besides, I didn't need to rent some make-believe movie with actors to experience that kind of terror. My own mother's screams could tear the paint off walls. I promise, you only had to hear it once to bear it's scar on both your eardrum and your soul. My soul got scarred before I even knew what a soul was.

One night, in the dead of night, when I was no older than eight, someone started ramming into our back door like psycho murder. It jerk-ed me awake—the whole house was shaking, and my heart was pumping like it could burst. At first, I couldn't even tell where it was coming from. It was coming from our little back door.

Little, like us.

The banging. My brother Brett, two years younger than me, was now popped up in his bed right next to mine. Both of us were in shock, victims of the pitch-black.

The banging. Of course we had no alarm system to sound off. Though we did have Mom's screams, and boy, did she lose it right away.

Only the banging still wouldn't stop. It combined with Mom's screams to make pure chaos—worse than my worst nightmares. She then started screaming my name.

"Aaaaaarrrrrooooooooonnn!"

But what could I do? I mean, sure, she might've called me "man of the house" and all, but wasn't that only to make me feel special when her girlfriends were over? Because this was for real now—calling for a real man to step up and face this thing. And I was just a big-headed kid in cartoon pajamas.

The banging. If there was only some measuring device to gauge the damage being done on my mind at this moment: the fear of nighttime, fear of screams, fear of raging men, fear of demons, fear of fear itself. With no strength and no answers, I hated that all this was happening to me.

Screaming long "pleases," Mom was now begging for our lives. Of course, the Evil at the door could hear her; so why wouldn't it stop torturing us like this? I mean, based on the TV shows, burglars were supposed to flee once people woke up and screamed. However, that wasn't the case in horror movies. So then maybe the Evil just planned to kill us?

The banging. Our little back door ready to break at any second.

The screaming. Mom's hysteria enough to make me hyperventilate. And on this night, I understood that the verge of insanity was more than just a figure of speech.

But then it all stopped. I mean, just like that. Mom stopped screaming, too.

However, the only problem was that this sudden silence was just as scary. Had the Evil really quit and left, or had its rage succeeded in finally breaking inside our bubble? So in this silence, none of us budged.

After a minute or so of zero sound, it was clear that nobody was in our house. We still had no clue where the Evil was—or through which of our ranch windows it might burst through next—but Brett and I took a chance and bolted down the hall for Mom's bedroom, knocking each other over and helping each other along at the same time.

Turning into Mom's room, there she was—the lone, screaming young woman who hadn't even reached her thirtieth birthday. Making out the silhouette of her reaching arms, Brett and I lunged and buried ourselves in her lap. And Mom just squeezed us while sobbing away, and then squeezed some more, with tons of kisses and half-completed sentences like, "Oh, you guys!" Because Brett and I were her "everything," like she'd always tell us while relaxing on a Friday night with a glass of wine and listening to Angela Bofill's, "I Try." However, Angela, Chaka Khan, Brenda Russell, Barbara Streisand, and all our other friends, couldn't be with us during these times. It was "just us," as Mom would always remind us.

The police eventually showed up. One of our neighbors must have heard the ruckus and called them. Though Mom was still so beside herself that she made the cops slide their badges under our door to prove they were the real deal. At first they chuckled, but when they realized how dead serious she was, they quickly cooperated. She finally let them in.

Standing tall, as their walkie-talkie's blasted all the rest of Plainfield's drama, the two black officers asked us lots of questions while jotting our answers in their little notepads. Mom did all the talking, but would look over at me from time to time to make sure her answers were accurate. She and I always worked together.

Man, it felt good having those cops in our kitchen with those big guns on their hips—so relieving not having to worry about the Evil for the moment. In fact, a part of me wished the Evil might try to come back right then, just so it could get its butt kicked and arrested, and perhaps even shot. However, I knew the Evil wasn't that stupid. Plus, I knew the cops wouldn't be in my kitchen much longer—leaving me back to worrying all over again. And sure enough, after stepping outside one last time to inspect our back porch for clues, the officers left their contact cards and then left altogether.

Needless to say, nobody got caught that night. In fact, nobody ever got caught. But you know what? I was used to that. Though at times, it did feel like not getting the one thing you wanted for Christmas.

As Mom locked the back door behind the cops and then triple-checked it, I couldn't believe that our back door had survived such a siege. However, on one of its next visits, the Evil would use some type of axe, leaving our door shredded so savagely that I'd be able to look right through it.

Shortly after that night, Mom started keeping a Louisville Slugger behind her bedroom door. Some male friend who had a crush on her had given it to her. One day at Momma's house, I even overheard Mom mention something about getting a gun. I got so excited to hear that, hoping that she really had, or at least that she would. However, deep inside, I knew that she really hadn't, and that she never would. For Mom may have been tough as any lioness, but she just wasn't the gun type. So baseball bats it remained. Eventually, Brett and I started keeping bats and bars under our beds, too.

Now lest you prejudge, you must know that Mom was raising us to be nothing short of "gentlemen and scholars," like she'd always say. That meant firm handshakes, strong eye contact, cultural exposure, and overall "well-roundedness." However, at the same time, it was a no-brainer that you couldn't perfect your manners in the daytime, if you didn't survive the Evil in the nighttime. So no matter how bourgeoisie we were tempted to be at times, the fact remained that we had crude weapons stashed around our house. And the plan was to be ready to use them.

But of course Mom would always downplay all of this, mostly because it pained her to think about her two boys enduring stuff like this. However, Brett and I didn't brood much over our struggles (not at the time, at least). We saw how Mom sacrificed everything for us, and were just glad that she was okay, and that she always kept that amazing smile that even made famous blues singer Alberta Hunter autograph her album to Mom with "keep smiling, Patricia." Mom was our superhero, our very own Wonder Woman—big bracelets and all. That's why whenever she told us things were gonna be okay, we trusted her.

Well, even after such a night of terror, sunrise still meant time for school: Tom and Jerry cartoons, Pop-Tarts in the toaster, ironing board screeching open, and "hey, who's seen the lint brush?" For it wasn't just any school that we attended. It was The Wardlaw-Hartridge School—one of the most prestigious private schools in this part of Jersey. Mom and Dad didn't agree on much, but our education was the one thing they could come to terms on (and Dad sure hustled to pay that galactic tuition).

Now nobody at Wardlaw knew about these struggles of mine. Mom always taught us that it was none of people's business what went on at home. Besides, even at this young age, I knew that most of my classmates probably wouldn't understand anyway. For although we wore the same blazers and pledged allegiance to the same flag, our worlds were still worlds apart.

But that was fine; really it was, because I wanted to be thinking about other things anyway. I loved my buddies, loved laughter, and especially loved my Star Wars action figures. So whether with my wealthy classmates in their hilly suburbs, or back in my neighborhood with my homeboys and our self-taught acrobatics, all I wanted was to have a ball.

It's so ironic: as kids, we want so badly to hurry-up and become adults; only to one day become "grown" and then find ourselves itching after every drop of our childhoods all over again—clutching memories like an old treasure map as we try to reconnect the dots in hopes of figuring out all that we've become.

So yeah, I loved laughter all right, but I'd still sleep with the lights on right until college. I'd still have recurring nightmares of me, Mom, and Brett being tied and tortured until I was close to twenty. And I'd still be lured into bottles of wino-liquor long before I was twenty-one. And then, like a bad-breath pirate who couldn't be trusted, I wouldn't even trust myself.

The serpent: Who was I anyway?

The game: Like Adam, I deliberately ate it.

The guilt: Like in Shakespeare's *Macbeth*, I couldn't hide it.

Psalm 23: Sweet asylum for my Jude 13.

This is my story. And I've got some onions to peel.

II

THE WARDLAW-HARTRIDGE SCHOOL

We make our salute, to the Green and the Gold,
To the colors of spring and fall.
And striving for gold,
As we watch our lives unfold,
It's the striving together we recall.
To learn and to know, this is what we share,
Cognoscere et conficere.
We fight for the truth, and not just for the rules,
At Wardlaw-Hartridge School.
                    —Wardlaw-Hartridge School alma mater

It was a rainy, spring day, and the big green leaves were drooping wet from the trees. There I was, alone in one of their classrooms and a bit chilly too, writing and doing my best just like Mom had told me. For some time now, she had been saying that Wardlaw-Hartridge was gonna be our next school, and now there I was, taking the admissions test. Then, that following September—on yet another rainy day—there I was again, being lead to my desk to start the second grade. I didn't cry on my first day, either. In fact, I don't remember any kids crying. It was that kind of place.

My second grade teacher was the sweet Mrs. McNish. She was the type who preferred tea over coffee and loved having a shiny apple to place on her desk. Mom loved Mrs. McNish, and Momma—a second-grade teacher, herself—adored her just the same. Mrs. McNish was even close to Momma's age, with white short-cut hair, thick glasses, and the warmest smile that felt like a hug every time.

At Wardlaw, our classrooms were in petite, colonial houses called "cottages," all arranged into a cozy community like something right out of the Berenstain Bears books. Each cottage had its own woodsy name as well, like Acorn, Pinecone, or Mushroom. My class was in the Mushroom, and I loved that name, because it always reminded me of little gnomes with pointed hats and storybooks with happy endings. And during story time, our stories sure did have happy endings. So at Wardlaw, we whistled while we worked, mixed oil paints to Beethoven, enjoyed banquet-style lunches, and made stunning impressions on visitors. This was an elitist school.

Now, story time and happy endings aside, there were plenty of rules at Wardlaw-Hartridge as well; and these rules were meant to be kept.

Rule number one: We had to wear uniforms; yellow dress shirts with grey slacks, while the girls wore yellow shirts with plaid skirts. And our shirts were to always be tucked in, with no exceptions. Lastly, the school's shield bearing the Latin motto, *Cognoscere et Conficere*—"to learn and to know"—was to be sewn onto the pockets of our hunter-green blazers. The girls could have the same done on their green cardigans if they so wished.

And while everyone's blazers, shirts, and slacks were more or less from the same uniform store, it was kids' shoes that really said it all: Exclusive Bass', Clark's, and mahogany penny loafers—that most kids put shiny dimes in—from the elegant shoe stores in downtown Scotch Plains and Westfield. Not to mention the luxury cars that most of these shoes hopped out of every morning, and the way some mothers wore full-length furs so nonchalantly with their sweatsuits. Well, Mom made sure Brett and I had our mahogany loafers to put shiny dimes in as well. The only difference is that after paying for them, she'd have to skip lunch for over a week.

Rule number two: Unless it was gym class or recess, running was strictly prohibited on our campus. Even speed-walking was viewed with contempt. Whenever a kid tried to sneak a sprint between cottages, it seemed like a teacher was always there to rebuke them. And these rebukes were always in the first person plural—"We walk, ladies and gentlemen!"—which had a way of making you feel especially naughty.

Rule number three: Whenever an adult entered our classroom, we were to stop whatever we were doing and rise to our feet in full attention with hands perfectly placed at our sides—not like military academy students, just like some kids with great manners and a tremendous respect for elders.

Speaking of elders, our headmaster's name was Mr. Everett New-comb, a witty older guy with short white hair, a squarish head, and a New Englander smile, who in the spring wore peach and pink blazers with perfect ties to match. Stalwart, and with a sergeant's sternness that he kept on reserve, Mr. Newcomb was the type who could've run our very country.

Once, Mr. Newcomb got really sick, and everyone was especially worried, teachers too. But he eventually came back—like a real general always does—and how we all stood extra tall as he entered our classroom again! He thanked us deeply for the cards we'd made for him, and just before getting teary-eyed about it, he switched topics and told us that while he was home recovering in his backyard one day, a hawk had swooped down and snatched up a rabbit right in front of him. "Wow," we all said.

The dean of students was Mr. Wuest, a tall middle-aged German guy who looked like he was once really good at basketball. Cool as a long-legged cat, he always wore the same broken-in boat shoes and tan corduroy blazer with brown elbow patches. But don't get me wrong, Mr. Wuest still had plenty of class and could hang with Jersey's snootiest at any wine and cheese function. It's just that he had this rugged way about him, too. Like he could also step into any of Plainfield's liquor stores to buy a quart of beer without someone calling him out as a "white boy."

Dean of students: Funny thing was, we students didn't even know what that title meant. Though we kept a healthy fear of Mr. Wuest just the same. I mean, you'd rather step in dog mess a hundred times during recess, than to go to his cathedral-styled office for just one of his "talks." And he knew we all felt this way, so he'd use this smirky, dry humor on us, just to keep us wondering if he really liked us or not. But at the end of the day, Mr. Wuest loved what he did and loved us kids. However, he still preferred to only teach sixth and seventh graders; as if too many of us younger ones on too regular a basis might drive him nuts.

Rule number four: Everyone had to change clothes for gym class, and only Wardlaw-Hartridge gym gear was acceptable. But this was an awesome rule, because right above the gymnasium was our school store. The "Mother Store" it was called, and it had all your heart could wish for. I mean, there were Wardlaw-Hartridge "college banners," book-bags, baseball caps, sweatshirts, sweatpants, and on and on. Those two sweet women behind the counter would give you as much stuff as you wanted.

All they'd ask you to do was sign some measly piece of paper once you were finished. The whole experience was quite intoxicating, almost like being in Willy Wonka's chocolate factory.

Until one day, Brett and I skipped into the Mother Store for yet another one of our shopping sprees, only to see those two sweet women now looking at us with a fresh batch of sternness.

"You boys aren't allowed to get anything from this store anymore, because your bill hasn't been paid!"

Bill? I suddenly realized what signing that measly piece of paper was all about.

"Okay," I mumbled from under my day-old Wardlaw baseball cap. And with that, Brett and I shrank from the store like kids who had just been caught stealing. Meanwhile, the rest of our classmates stayed right at the counter, smiling and pointing at whatever they wanted next—those two women right back to being sweet again. Everyone signing that measly piece of paper like it was nothing.

Now Mom, Brett, and I were used to not being able to afford stuff. (We were even used to hearing people suck their teeth as they waited in line behind us at the grocery store because we were paying with straight coins.) But there was something about that day in the Mother Store that was different: the condescending look in those two women's eyes, the way they blurted my personal business in front of all my classmates (as if to publicly punish me for being less "privileged"), and the burning shame I felt. In fact, that very shame would keep me from setting foot in the Mother Store for years to come—even long after our bill had been paid.

But I still loved Wardlaw.

So while there were lots more rules to be kept at Wardlaw, lastly, Mrs. McNish had her own special rule. At the end of each day, we were to wait in a single-file line at the classroom door so she could take her time in giving each of us a warm handshake while bidding us a great rest of the day. She was the best.

Then it was outside, to where all the other kids would be pouring out of their own cottages as they scurried to their respective Benzes, Jaguars, or spotless Wardlaw-Hartridge minibuses. Everyone heading back to their surrounding suburbs until the next day. Everyone except for us.

Now, pristine as our campus was, there was still one thing that set Wardlaw apart from the other private schools in the Patriot Conference, like Princeton Day School, Rutgers Prep, Lawrenceville Prep, and Stuart Country Day. And this one thing was actually a big thing—a stigma from which Wardlaw tried so hard to free itself. For you see, while all those other schools were located in quaint suburban towns found at the end of rolling highways and such, Wardlaw sat on the edge of tricky Plainfield—which had its own rules, as well.

So Wardlaw's utopia was subject to regular disruptions as local Plainfield kids cut across campus on their way to and from public school. And how Wardlaw shuddered at this constant "leak" in their otherwise sheltered environment. They even tried posting no trespassing signs on the large oak trees around the perimeter of the campus. But little did they know that according to Plainfield's rules, even grown men would cut through people's very backyards in broad daylight! So those signs may as well have been written in Mandarin.

Every day like clockwork, the Plainfield kids would come cutting through Wardlaw like the #114 bus. And they'd take their sweet time doing it too, giving my curious classmates ample time to study them through the window, and our teachers ample time to shake their heads in disgust and wish that Wardlaw was located somewhere else, like Lawrenceville or Princeton.

"Class, just ignore them and get back to your work, please!"

To many of our teachers, the Plainfield kids were just a mischievous bunch looking for trouble. I mean, if Wardlaw was a Monet, then Plainfield kids were graffiti. If Wardlaw's campus was Smurf village, then Plainfield kids were considered Gargamel. However, the truth of the matter was that they really meant no harm. They were just a group of regular kids who didn't feel like walking all the way around Wardlaw's campus on their way to Cedarbrook Elementary. And of course they were more than curious to know about this exclusive, rich world that was right in the middle of their neighborhood.

Cedarbrook Elementary was like a zoo compared to Wardlaw. I knew this because my mother had been a teacher there, where once a troubled eight year-old threw a book right at her face and split her lips open. So it was inevitable that Plainfield's Cedarbrook kids would also come to covet all that Wardlaw had. I mean, what kid wouldn't? Shiny red convertibles parked in front of our cottages, homemade cookies that you could smell every morning, art rooms with giant windows and tons of supplies for all the "mess-ups" your creativity needed, and gyms with the best equipment money could buy.

However, while cutting through and window-shopping, of course they'd wear their best poker faces like they couldn't have cared less. Though that was understandable. For to display how they truly felt would be the same as confessing that they were just some "have nots," heading to their "have not" school. And even the youngest Plainfield kid still had their pride.

Kids usually detect more than adults realize, and it wasn't long before they could detect how the Wardlaw community felt about them, which in turn, made them resentful. That's why many of them transformed from these sheepish passersby into a pack of militant marauders who were feeding off that negative attention they got. Of course, this only made the Wardlaw community look down their noses at them even more; which, in turn, only made the Plainfield kids even more resentful. And on and on the wages of ignorance, fear, classism, and racism continued to pay out.

Sometimes I'd overhear some of my teachers complaining about them:

"Why are they just so angry all the time? What a shame . . ."

As they felt so safe talking about them right in front of me like this, my teachers didn't understand that, minus the green blazer and shoes that made Mom miss a week's worth of lunches, I was just a Plainfield kid myself. We all got our groceries from the same A&P, our candy from the same Puerto Rican bodegas, and our clothes washed at the same laundromats whenever our washing machine broke.

And yes, maybe a few of those trespassing kids were just "angry" and as hardheaded as an inmate's knuckle. (I mean, even the rest of us Plainfield kids tried to stay on the good side of those types.) However, the fact remained that most of those kids were simply acting out in response to being made to feel lesser and ashamed—the same way I felt in the Mother Store that day.

Anyway, as they'd trespass, the ones who knew me from the neighborhood would often spot me out and their faces would light up—as if knowing someone from Wardlaw gave them an instant sense of belonging.

"Yo, what it be like, Aaron?"

"Yo, what it be like, Omar?" I'd get excited and answer right back, even if it was considered disruptive by one of my teachers. It never ceased to amaze my classmates that I actually knew "them." Like I was extra cool for having access to a facet of life that was such a mystery to them.

All of this was when it first dawned on me that I lived in two totally different worlds.

III

THE SCHOOL OF HARD KNOCKS

Third grade was by far my toughest year at Wardlaw. It was as stressful as the stock-market floor.

My third grade teacher was Mrs. Yardley, a short, older woman who was always dressed to the nines: heels, stockings, business-length skirts, blouses with matching scarves, and jackets with antique brooches. Every morning after pledging allegiance, she would lead the class in singing, and her voice was surprisingly sweet on the ears, like something from an old record. Mrs. Yardley taught well and simply adored a classroom of "bright" private-school kids. However, her major handicap was in dealing with kids who may have had slight "handicaps" themselves.

She was nothing like Mrs. McNish.

The summer before third grade, Mom was offered a new job. "Promising," is the word she kept telling her girlfriends over the phone, along with "corporate personnel" and "Macy's." However, there was one drawback. It wasn't the Macy's on Plainfield's Front Street, but the Macy's on West Thirty-fourth Street—all the way in Manhattan and over an hour away by public transportation. However, if it meant more money and thus a better life for me and Brett—enabling Mom to pay for more of our tennis lessons and soccer camps, and even ransom our car back from the shop—then Mom was all for it. So she resigned from her teaching job and got her head ready for the New York hustle.

Well, this meant that Mom would have to start catching a 7 a.m. train out of Plainfield, which also meant that she'd have to start dropping us off at a babysitter before school—and at 6:30 a.m., at that. So Mom began her search for the perfect babysitter, and lo and behold, she found just the one. It was Mrs. Malone, an older Jamaican woman with a sweet, even-keeled nature who kept an immaculate house. Best of all, she lived only a block away from Wardlaw. So Mom and Mrs. Malone worked out the details, and Mom sighed with relief and said that this was all gonna work just fine, after all.

However, as perfect as the plan was, it still didn't make it easier for Mom to part ways with us on those cold, dark mornings.

"Bye-bye, now. You boys be safe today." Fighting back the tears while watching me and Brett climb out of our noisy red Audi Fox, she'd continue watching as we dragged our sleepy feet all the way up Mrs. Malone's brick steps to ring her doorbell.

"Mommy loves you boys!" She'd yell behind us one last time, just in case we needed some last-minute reassurances.

"Love you too, Mom."

Once Mrs. Malone opened her front door and waved, off Mom's car would go screaming away—our fan belt desperately needing to be replaced. Mrs. Malone would then lead us to her small, but cozy TV room, which we understood we were to never wander from. By the time the sun was up and piercing through the TV room's window blinds, it would be time for us to take that short walk by ourselves to Wardlaw. By this point, Mom would still be riding that packed train somewhere between Plainfield and Manhattan.

Then, after school, I'd simply walk over to the Pinecone—the first-grade cottage—and wait for Brett's dismissal, so I could walk us right back to Mrs. Malone's again; our classmates shouting our names from their luxury sedans as they'd whiz by us. And we'd stay at Mrs. Malone's for another four hours or so until Mom's train came back in. However, no matter how dark it was, or how overtired she felt, when Mom finally got off that train and picked us up, she'd come beaming like the sun with that smile of hers. I mean, it was like a family reunion every day; and Mrs. Malone just loved watching Mom shower us with kisses.

Since we only lived four blocks away, we'd be back home in no time. (What a relief it was to pull into our dark driveway and see that our house hadn't been broken into.) Then once we were back home, the evening hustle began: getting our clothes and stuff ready for the next day while Mom threw together a late dinner and asked us a million questions about our day. And if we ate and got ready for bed quickly enough, she'd let us watch a little TV—starring George Jefferson, Black America's comical answer to the racist Archie Bunker. Then, after a few more laughs and cuddles with Mom, it would be time for bed. But of course not before triple-checking the lock on our back door. Then, at 5:30 a.m., off would go Mom's alarm clock, and it would be time to take it from the top all over again.

▲▼▲▼▲

Now Mrs. Malone's house clearly wasn't home, but it's not like we disliked being there, either. Those early mornings were a bit lonely, but in the afternoon her house became the neighborhood hangout. And the reasons were quite simple: Mrs. Malone had the perfect rectangular yard for big football games, and Kenny, her teenage boy, was one of the coolest kids to be around. In fact, he was so cool that he could have joined the reggae group Musical Youth and rocked his own solo on "Pass the Dutchie."

So each day as Brett and I arrived from Wardlaw, the rest of the neighborhood kids would be showing up there as well. Jabaar was always there first. He lived right behind Mrs. Malone's and went to Hubbard Middle School with cool Kenny. And though Jabaar was only in the seventh grade, he was colossal next to the rest of us, almost the size of an adult. Plus, his afro was bigger than Michael Jackson's on the *Off the Wall* album cover.

Then there was Crazy Tommy, another middle schooler, and well, he was just plain crazy. With sleepy eyes, a caramel complexion, and a near-bald haircut, you'd rarely even see Crazy Tommy approaching. You'd just notice him perched on the split-rail fence all of a sudden (having just cut through somebody's backyard, of course). He'd always sit there for a while, watching everyone through his sleepy eyes while sucking his thumb. But don't get his thumb-sucking twisted, because the only thing babyish about Crazy Tommy *was* his wet thumb. Wild enough to punch even a grown man in his face, Crazy Tommy could be another kid's nightmare.

"Yo, ain't y'all Miss Campbell's kids?"

He mumbled at me during one of our first days there. He asked like he was 99.9% sure, but just needed to be certain before drawing any further conclusions about the two brothers in their odd-looking green blazers.

"Yup," I answered, smiling inside already, because I knew what that question meant.

"Thought so," he mumbled again through his thumb, and then looked off to the next point of interest, and that was that.

So while other kids may have needed to watch their step with Crazy Tommy, me and Brett sure didn't, because we were "Miss Campbell's kids." And while Mom was all the way in New York City and worried about us unto ulcers, her sweet reputation on the streets still had us covered. You see, Mom had taught most of these teenagers back when they were at Cedarbrook Elementary. And everyone loved some "Miss Campbell"—I'm sure even that kid who threw the book at her mouth that time. Crazy Tommy especially loved Mom.

I could even remember one Saturday morning when Mom, Brett, and I were walking to the A&P on West Seventh Street, during another long period when our car was down. Perched on the metal rails in front of the grocery store was Crazy Tommy, resting in the early sun like a young crocodile. Now Crazy Tommy may have had a rep for being unpredictable, but whenever he'd see Mom, he was nothing but predictable smiles. So he hopped off the metal railing and started toward us. Though Mom was the only one in his sight.

"Tommy! Hey, baby-cakes!"

Never referring to him as "Crazy Tommy," Mom talked to him like he was one of her own. Just like he was in her second grade classroom all over again, she hugged him, kissed his forehead, and even squeezed his cheeks. Then, as she did with all her former students, Mom started asking him a bunch of personal questions about his home life and all, like only she could get away with doing, simply because she cared that much. Then finally, she smacked him. Though not on his street-scarred, "pretty little face" as she called it; just on his thumb that was always attached to his face.

"Now boy, would you get that thumb out your mouth! You big ol' thing!"

Soaking in every last drop of this motherly affection, Tommy smiled even more now, even leaving his wet thumb at his side until she was finished visiting with him. Mom always had that special touch, which is also why she was able to get some of the toughest kids to do things that even the toughest male principals couldn't. So with just one more pinch of his cheeks and a final "tell your mother hello for me," Mom was finished; and Tommy was glowing.

Now, let another onlooking teenager decide to start teasing Tommy for getting all "soft" in public like that. Crazy Tommy would've probably bloodied the whole side of his face by the time we had come back out the store.

▲ ▼ ▲ ▼ ▲

There was one other thing about Mrs. Malone's. You see, Jabaar, Kenny, Crazy Tommy, and all the other neighborhood kids for that matter, never seemed to have any homework after school. Meanwhile, by the third grade, I already had a bookbag loaded with books. So between Mrs. Malone's house being packed with kids who didn't even own bookbags, and Mom picking us up so late every evening, let's just say that I didn't put much time into my homework (even though Mom had asked Mrs. Malone to sit us down to do it). And how Mrs. Yardley despised this. Now from a teacher's standpoint, that could be understandable. It's just that Mrs. Yardley seemed to have crossed the line into despising me as well.

"Aaron is a bluff! All he ever does in class is daydream!"

The first thing Mrs. Yardley had to say at Mom's first parent-teacher conference. Mom just sat there, speechless. She had taken the entire day off from New York, just to hustle to this half-hour meeting, just to hear another woman call her firstborn a bluff. And being yet another single mother who already felt guilty about everything all the time, this would plague Mom for years.

"Well, Mrs. Yardley," Mom slowly regaining herself, "I am an educator also, and I know that my son is capable. I mean, I did teach second grade, and know a little about . . ."

"Well, *a little* bit of knowledge can be a dangerous thing, now can't it?"

Beyond speechless, Mom was now in straight shock. Clearly, Mrs. Yardley had no respect for her. And you know, maybe if Mom wasn't a struggling single parent and had instead pulled up to the conference in one of those big Benzes with a big diamond on her finger, Mrs. Yardley wouldn't have tried to get away with such a smack across Mom's face. In fact, Mrs. Yardley always reminded me of those two women from the Mother Store.

Later that evening, Mom told me what Mrs. Yardley had said, and I saw the pain in her eyes as she tried to shrug it off. At first, I hated Mrs. Yardley for hurting Mom like this. However, at the same time, I also knew that Mrs. Yardley wasn't entirely wrong. Because it was true, I would wander off in my thoughts during class, and then when she'd call on me, I'd nervously overcompensate by just blurting out something like I'd been paying attention all along. However, those thoughts and daydreams of mine weren't all that voluntary, nor were they recreational. In other words, it wasn't trips to Disney World I'd be fancying.

On a given day, there was no telling where my mind would be. I might be caught in a nasty replay of one of Mom and Dad's vicious arguments—the reason I was actually glad they were separated. Or perhaps, I was remembering one of those nights when Momma had to race all the way to our house in the middle of the night, because the stress was giving Mom another outbreak of those nasty hives that were making her throat swell shut. Or maybe I was thinking of one of the nights when we had spotted the Evil creeping outside our dark house. Then of course, there was that night with the banging at our back door.

I could also have been worrying about Mom being so far away in New York City, and wondering if that mugger was gonna try to flip her down the Port Authority Bus Terminal's escalator steps again. So you see, while Mrs. Yardley was so convinced that the best thing for me was a more focused singing of "America, the Beautiful" or learning long division, a child psychologist would have held a different view.

Lastly, I could have been reliving that night with Big-fat-Ron.

Big-fat-Ron: Brett and I would say it like it was his natural name. And while we liked him, we hated him, too.

Well, Mom may have worked like an "old hag"—as she'd sometimes refer to herself when she was overtired and discouraged—but the fact remained that she hadn't even turned thirty yet, and when buying wine at the liquor store, men still asked her to show some ID and it was obvious that they wanted her phone number, too. Spanish? Sicilian? Black-and-white mix? Indian? Men just loved trying to guess what this stunning woman was. So although she was young to be struggling all alone like this, her face still didn't show it one bit.

Now some of Mom's saving graces were her girlfriends, none of them related by blood, but all of them my "aunts" just the same. There was

Aunt Ronnie, Aunt Charlotte, Aunt Linda, and Aunt Marlene, all of them stylish and pretty, just like Mom. When weekends came around, and another insane work week was over, the music in our living room would go up extra loud, and they'd all laugh and jive and sing the night away—even forcing me to do "the hustle" if I got too close.

On most Friday and Saturday nights, they'd have their good times right in the comfort of our living room. Other times, they'd make plans to go out: New York City, downtown Newark, or maybe even some suburban spot. As long as Mom remembered to bring me and Brett back some Fat Boy burgers from Red Tower on nearby West Fifth Street, we were more than fine with it.

Plus, the other reason Brett and I didn't mind was because this meant that Lance would get to babysit us. A senior at Plainfield High School, Lance lived right across the street from us, and must have been one of the coolest dudes in Plainfield. And since Mom and Dad were so close with his parents—our "Uncle Joe" and "Aunt Louise"—he was the perfect choice in every way. So whenever Mom would hop in the car with her girlfriends, Lance belonged exclusively to me and Brett—and how we loved it.

Lance would show us all there was to know about being cool: how to strut, how to breakdance, how to "pop and lock," and all the latest slang plus the little bit of Spanish he was picking up on the streets. And being an insightful eighteen year-old, Lance could even detect how Brett and I lacked that certain "something" from not having a man in our house. So he took his role in our lives all the more seriously. To make us tougher, he'd punch us in our arms until we'd stop "acting like some punks" and fight him back. Then he'd just smile big, like he was so proud of us, before moving us on to the next challenge—putting a drop of hot sauce on our tongues without making a big deal over it. He even gave us some of our first talks about "being with a girl." Lance loved us, and he made us look forward to growing up and becoming men—just like him.

However, whenever Lance had a date with his fly girlfriend, Felicia, Mom would ask Lance's older brother Ron to watch us instead. Now while Lance was the cool one, the athletic one, and the one the girls whistled at, Ron was quirky, non-athletic, and heavyset, with thick-framed glasses that were always sliding down his big, flat nose. More so, Ron knew absolutely no slang, and instead of Hip Hop, he listened to this weird, foreign music with singers that looked even weirder. He'd even try singing some of those weird songs to me and Brett, but no matter how hard we tried to dig it, we just couldn't. So Ron was nothing like Lance. We still tried to have fun with him, nonetheless.

Until one night, Ron changed, like a werewolf during a full moon. Only this was so real. I have no clue what even set him off that night, but this is what I do remember:

Brett and I running for our lives while hysterically crying, begging him to stop.

"Sorry, sorry, Ron! Sorry, Ron! Sorry!"

We didn't even know what in the world to be sorry for, but we were desperate in trying to make him stop. Only there was no stopping him. Since Ron had been left in charge, there was nobody to save us—not even Lance. We were trapped in something satanic, where our very home was now the altar.

Disoriented, as Big-fat-Ron flung our little bodies like rag dolls, Brett and I bounced off everything, including each other. I mean, we could've been bleeding and not even noticed. I was seven or eight years old at the time, making Brett only five or six.

Time seemed to be at a standstill; running, screaming, crying, and more running is all we did, only stopping to quickly dance in place from the pain of his big, fat hands smacking our butts again—as if he had premeditated how best not to leave any marks on us.

So he continued beating us like two dogs that had turned on the family kids. But again, why was Big-fat-Ron turning on us like this? Why was he so bent on seeing such horror on our little faces? Next, he began whipping us with our very own toy snake. It was baby-blue and green, with this goofy little top hat and an innocent smile.

I'd never look at that snake the same again.

Then, Big-fat-Ron disappeared for some reason. So there Brett and I were, trembling, holding each other tightly under our kitchen table—trying to hide, but whimpering too loud to stay hidden. Suddenly, Big-fat-Ron's yelling face appeared right before us, and we screamed like it was starting all over again. His hot angry eyes blacker than crayons and staining my brain forever. Then to Brett's pure horror, Ron cattle-yanked him from under the table, leaving me there in ongoing shock.

This was maybe the worst night of my life. So surreal, even as I write about it.

But it wasn't over yet.

Well, Big-fat-Ron must have put Brett to bed. All I knew was that I was now alone with a much calmer Big-fat-Ron. Except for the glare from our big TV, all the lights in our house were now turned off as well. As I was made to lay in his lap—still sobbing and hyperventilating away—I had been conquered for sure. So it was at this point that Ron began to rub and feel all over my body while slobbery-kissing me all over my mouth like I was his own mini-version of Lance's Felicia. And though I didn't yet know a thing about homosexuality or pedophilia, I definitely knew I was being violated. I knew that Ron wasn't making me feel like a man the way Lance always did. No, he just made me feel like a fat man's little girl.

Now as for how far Ron went with me that night, well to this day, my mind has completely blocked it from recollection. It just fades into black, in an almost unsettling kind of way. I mean, it's as if kids' brains have some built-in sanity-response-team that kicks in during such moments and blocks all recall to keep a kid from possibly losing his mind. Brett and I never told Mom a thing about that night—to keep her from possibly losing her mind. For although we were "just kids," as adults would say, we still knew that she was already carrying too much.

So there was no telling where my mind would go that year in school—while Mrs. Yardley was busy pitying me for the wrong reasons. And while I knew her assessment of me was bogus, at the end of the day, I was still her little student who craved her approval, just like all kids do. After that nasty meeting she had with Mom, I found myself trying to please her more than ever, just to earn that same smile I'd watch her give so freely to my other classmates. (And if I really impressed her, maybe I'd even get that same hug?) So I worked even harder to guess the right answers, strove harder to be the first one to finish a test, and tried my best to obey (though a side of me still loved the attention I got from sometimes misbehaving). And you know, maybe if Mrs. Yardley didn't act like she was so perfect, I wouldn't have felt like I needed to be so perfect to earn her acceptance.

Until one day, I saw the light. It happened while our class was in the dining hall having lunch. As usual, Mrs. Yardley was sitting at the head of our table, and while eating my hot lunch, I couldn't help but notice as she struggled to blow her nose. Now of course, in keeping with all the etiquette for blowing one's nose, her Kleenex was perfectly folded, her hands perfectly positioned, her head perfectly lowered, and her volume was perfectly low.

However, all her best etiquette was now powerless. Because as she pulled her perfectly folded tissue away from her face, there was the most stubborn string of mucous stretching from her nose and growing longer the more she pulled the Kleenex away. She was so embarrassed, and rightfully so, digging around in her purse like she might find a hole to crawl into.

I just smiled and went right back to eating my lunch, for everything had just become clear to me: Mrs. Yardley could look down at me and Mom, like we were less than her, all she wanted. At the end of the day, she was still just another gal with nasty snots, just like the rest of us.

And that was no bluff.

IV

Dr. Prince and the Revolution

Could you hear that funky sound?

"*PSYCHOALPHADISCOBETABIOAQUADOLOOP!*"

In fact, our next door neighbors wouldn't even need to play their own stereos, because on Saturday mornings, Mom loved nothing more than having all our windows opened so the breeze could carry the fresh smell of Pine-Sol through our house while she cleaned.

"*PSYCHOALPHADISCOBETABIOAQUADOLOOP!*"

We could even hear our stereo while playing kickball up the street. And if you listened closely, you might even hear Mom snatching the needle back on the record so she could hear that bizarre but super-bad intro just one more time. And what a super-bad intro it was. Why, I'm talking about Parliament's "Aqua Boogie," by Plainfield's very own George Clinton.

Based on the lyrics, along with the animation on the album cover, the song was about this cool, little jive man who's fighting off this giant squawking bird that's trying to snatch him up and drop him into the water, "The Funk." Throughout the song, this cool, little jive man maintains his hatred of both the water and the obnoxious bird. However, by the end—once he finally gets snatched up and thrown into the water—the cool, little jive man stops whining about how he can't swim, and now he doesn't even want to get back out! He's become addicted to "the Funk." The song was as silly as could be, but then again, I loved silly stuff. And it's funkadelic rhythm was so funky that even a toddler would have to bop its little head.

Now Mom may have mushed like a sleigh dog, but music was definitely her massage therapist. On Saturdays, she'd play records all day—dancing, singing, cleaning, cooking, and the million and one other things that single Moms do on their "days off."

"In or out, you guys, while I'm mopping this floor!"

Next to neighborhood kickball, running in and out the house seemed to be me and Brett's other favorite sport.

"What'cha cooking, Mom?"

"Didn't y'all hear what I just said?"

"Sorry, Mom." (Though still not obeying.) We may have been into Mom like there was no tomorrow, but we could still be some thickskulled rascals. "So what'cha makin,' though?"

"It's banana bread! Now, get out!"

Now you wouldn't find any loose quarters between the cushions of our couches, nor would you find any surprise dollar bills in our laundry, but Mom still knew how to siphon a reservoir from a puddle when it came to giving us the best. And more important to Mom than our mahogany loafers for school was the food we ate. So even when times were "lean," you could still count on there being some homemade banana bread, zucchini bread, granola, and other healthy stuff that always had the word "farms" somewhere in their brand names. "Weird stuff," as a lot of my friends would call it, but to us it was normal.

I mean, even alfalfa sprouts were normal. I'll never forget the time Mom sent me to the store to buy some, and the way the stock-boy laughed at me like I was drunk when I asked him where I might find them: "Man! I don't know!"

"Mom, don't make me go to the store for alfalfa sprouts no more . . ."

"You mean, 'any more'!"

Quick to pounce on my bad grammar, Mom always worried about me and Brett making habits with our slang outside of school, and then it backfiring on us while we were at Wardlaw. And her concern was valid because it was already challenging enough at Wardlaw being a minority with perfect grammar. However, Mom didn't need to worry; because just like she and Dad knew how to turn their slang "on" and "off," depending on time and place, Brett and I were already mastering that same skill.

"Mom, those older kids at A&P make fun of me when I go in there askin' for stuff like alfalfa sprouts."

"Just ignore them, Aaron!"

Sucking her teeth, Mom couldn't have cared less about some stock-boy's opinion of her grocery list. Plus, I could tell she wished she had been there when he had laughed at me like that. She would've checked him right on the spot—making him forever embarrassed for not being more "open-minded" (one of Mom's favorite terms). Then, she'd probably realize that she had taught him back at some point—or at least one of his siblings—and then really start lecturing the mess out of him.

However, it wasn't too long after that day with the alfalfa sprouts that two older teenagers mugged me as I was walking home from the store. So she didn't send me on grocery runs for quite some time.

So though you wouldn't find any delicious pineapple soda or Wonder Bread in our house, Mom's philosophy was simple: If you were truly hungry, then you would in fact start munching on a bell pepper and some raw spinach. She was right, too; because you sure would catch me riding my clanky BMX bike down the street with a mouth full of raw veggies. But the whole time I'd just be waiting for one of my friends to offer me some of their "red" Kool-Aid—so sugary thick that it would be halfway turned into Jello.

▲ ▼ ▲ ▼ ▲

828 Field Ave.

Right off of West Eighth Street, our house was the light-green, two bedroom ranch with the big front yard. Like Mrs. Malone's, my yard was also a top-pick for neighborhood football games. When our lawnmower was broken, the grass got way too high. When Mom couldn't afford to pay someone to rake, the leaves got way too high. During winters with our busted gutters, the ice on our front steps got way too dangerous. However, throughout all the seasons—the sighs, the tears, and the screams, too—it was the laughter, the love, and the wonder of our great life together that still made 828 "home sweet home." Our sanctuary. And if you saw that pretty young woman lugging those groceries down the street with a big tear in her stockings, you might not have guessed that the place where she was headed looked so classy.

Now you didn't need an educated eye to see that our house was teeming with culture; though back then, I didn't even know what "culture" meant. However, I could tell by the way adults used it, that it referred to something "deep"—like the exotic photos in those fancy books at the used bookstore on Park Avenue, where Mom loved to browse and converse with the two older, white women who owned it.

When you first stepped through the double-front doors of our house (though one of the doors was jammed shut and hadn't been fixed since my parents separated), on the atrium wall was this large woven tapestry, so thick that you'd need a baseball bat to beat the dust out. Needless to say, it never got dusted. Opposite the tapestry was the framed print of a starving Ethiopian boy squatting on the dusty-red ground that looked hard as brass. Always "aware," Mom had that piece hanging up even before Quincy Jones and Michael Jackson put out "We Are The World."

Next was our living room. And if it wasn't one of those super-rare days when our electricity was temporarily shut off (the bill simply getting too high, at times), then of course music would be playing through our tall, handsome speakers, everything from Chicago to the Commodores. Though don't let all the upbeat, dance music mislead you. Because just as if there was some clock in the corner of the room that could suddenly strike "refined time," the vibe could quickly switch to the reflective piano keys of Keith Jarrett, Chick Corea, or Japanese synthesizer-legend, Kitaro.

Before you could even admire our Ethan Allen couches—with leather too thick for a cat's claw to puncture—your eyes would immediately be drawn to the gallery of Native-American and African art that adorned our walls and shelves. There were carved masks and hats (that Brett and I loved to dress up in), exotic instruments carved from wood and stone, a giant framed print of ancient Egypt's boy king—Tutankhamun—on an immense wooden easel, and above our marble fireplace was a large Chinese abacus.

Lastly, with all types of hanging plants in our huge windows, and stacks of pricey hardcovers on Native-American and African art on almost every flat surface, our living room was the perfect blend of "home" and "another world," and I'd spend countless hours exploring the wonder of it all. Then whenever Mom played Chick Corea's "Leprechaun's Dream," my imagination with my Star Wars figures would really blast off.

Next was our dining room. If our living room was the exploration room, then our dining room was the heirloom room, because on the large, dark oak hutch were all of Mom's choice family photos—crusty black-and-whites preserved in antique frames that Mom searched high and low for. She had them arranged on a perfect spread of white lace, and I could always tell which visitors Mom considered special guests, when I'd see her walk them over to the hutch for a rundown of our family history.

The first photo Mom always started with was of her late father, William Hicks, or "Bozo" as he was nicknamed as a boy. From South Hill, Virginia, William was the son of a hard-working, but illiterate mechanic—"Daddy Mack"—a black man who worked with his hands and bootlegged moonshine on the side. William's mother was a blue-eyed Cherokee woman, who had taught her husband to read and became blind in her later years. Next to Mom's picture of her father William was a photo of her mother, Annie—our grandmother, the one we called "Momma." And like Bozo, Annie was also a half-Cherokee Virginian. However, Annie's father was Jewish.

As story has it, Annie's maternal grandfather was a Cherokee who just popped up one day in a Virginia town, arriving from some Indian reservation with his brother. They were said to have arrived on a white horse, wearing moccasins and with hair down to their waists. His name was Macklin and although Mom didn't have any pictures of him, we imagined that he was a strong man with the stature of a chief.

Macklin soon settled in that Virginia town, and it was there that he married a Cherokee woman named Rebecca—they were Annie's grandparents, and Mom's great grandparents. It was said that no matter how acclimated Macklin was, he still refused to wear "white man's moccasins." More so, he warned the whole town that if anyone dared set foot on his property, he was gonna shoot them. And sure enough, when one of the white men decided to test him, Macklin shot him without a second thought. Then standing over him he said, "Now didn't I tell you I was gonna shoot you?" In fact, it was said that the white men in that town feared and hated Macklin so much, that when he finally died they threw a party.

So back to my grandparents now, William and Annie. Well, they met as fellow students at Virginia State University. After graduating, they moved up north to Newark, New Jersey to start a family. However, before they could get married, William had to convert to Catholicism for the Catholic Church to acknowledge their betrothal. For as Annie grew up in the South as an Indian-Jewish "mulatto" rejected by her Jewish side, it was the Catholic nuns who embraced her. Hence, she became Catholic at a young age. So Annie and William married right away and had three daughters—my mother was the eldest.

Annie and William were teachers in the Newark area, and William was especially noted for teaching science as he just loved dirt and nature. So much so, that after moving his wife and three daughters from Newark to a three-bedroom house in the neighboring city of Orange, one of the first things he did was plant an apple seed in their new backyard—making it clear that it was for his future grandkids to one day enjoy.

Now, as a kid, William had a severe bout with rheumatic fever which damaged his aortic heart valve. He enlisted in the army right after high school and got sent home because of it. Then one day, when my mom was eleven years old, she looked out the window of their new house and saw him lying face down in the middle of the street—this was his first heart attack.

Well, [my grandfather] was then one of the first five people in the country to have open-heart surgery. Groundbreaking for medical science and beyond risky, the procedure was performed at The National Institute of Health, in Bethesda, Maryland. And while the other four patients supposedly died soon after their surgeries, my grandfather's procedure was a tremendous success. And while the medical community was rejoicing, nobody was happier than Mom and the family.

However, seven years later (after William's artificial heart valve had been damaged in an accident), Mom woke up in the middle of the night to the sound of her own mother's screams. She ran to her parents' bedroom, only to see her daddy having another heart attack—this time, in his sleep. And this time, he died—right in front of them all. William was forty-two, leaving Momma widowed at forty. And though Mom was only seventeen, she had to ready herself to help raise her two younger sisters, my Aunt Carol and Aunt Cecilia, or "C.C."

Now, whenever Mom was giving someone the family history, she never mentioned her dad dying in front of her. And of course she still missed him; I could tell by the babyish way she'd still say "Daddy" whenever talking to me and Brett about him. Matter of fact, on the night he died, the last thing he ever said to her (after tucking her in) was "Good night, my love." So while I never got to meet "Grandpa" (I guess that's what I would've called him), I sure loved climbing that apple tree in Momma's backyard that he had once planted, just for me.

Well, after our dining room was our den. Although the tall stereo speakers stood in the living room, it was the den that housed our stereo—

our "mother-ship" as Parliament might say. And this was back when stereos were much more bulky and metallic. Ours was a Fisher brand; it was silver with big shiny knobs and a large blue dial-screen that would illuminate the room like a baby moon after sundown. Our stereo was stacked in a huge entertainment unit that was typical of the 1970's: sleek and square, with wooden doors that swiveled open to reveal upside-down wine glasses, mirrored walls, and shelves lined in forest-green velvet, the same color as our drapes.

So even the most hurried walk through our home made one thing clear—when Mom and Dad had furnished this place, they never planned to part. But by the time I was four and Brett was two, they were separated. Then by the time I was seven, they were divorced. Then things changed. And as for that sweet Fisher stereo, with its cool blue screen and tall speakers that kept Mom grooving while she cleaned and cooked and then relaxed with Angela Bofill, the Evil eventually came and stole that from us as well.

"*Dag!*"

▲ ▼ ▲ ▼ ▲

Dad.

Even though Dad wasn't around as much as a father who lived in the same house, and even though he wasn't there to stop the Evil on those dreaded nights, he was still our hero. If Mom was Wonder Woman, he was Superman. And whenever we saw him, Brett and I would run and jump into his arms just as if he did live with us. He'd hug us tightly with that happy laugh of his, and then go right into making up more words to his special song for us, called "My Two Sons."

Then, like every other 80's kid, Brett and I would get right down to business—begging Dad to drive us to Toys "R" Us to replace whatever Star Wars figures we had broken or lost (he must've replaced Darth Vader seven times, alone). And if he couldn't take us himself, he'd reach into his pockets and give us the money for someone else to. Yeah, he was nuts about his boys. Like I said before, he was the one who paid the thousands of dollars every year for us to attend Wardlaw. And by the way, if we had ever told Dad about that night with Big-fat-Ron, he might've killed him.

With a Kent Golden Lights cigarette and a lukewarm coffee in his hand, Dad was a sheer businessman—a true jack of all trades. Whether the task involved academics, a hammer, or a microphone, he always seemed to be right at home. I guess growing up in Jim Crow's South had instilled in him at a young age that no task was too small and every opportunity had to count.

Dad was born in a bedroom of his family's small farm, delivered by the community nurse (since nobody could afford a doctor) on a dirt road in North Carolina's swampy backwoods: home to rattlesnakes and alligators, tobacco and cotton fields, catfish and hogs. Wearing potato sacks for diapers while his older siblings used the outhouse, Dad knew what poor (or, "po'") was before he could even pronounce it.

Now this part of Carolina's backwoods was both "black country" as well as "Indian country." The Indian side of the community was called "Down Below," while the black side was called "Up Ahead," with the two separated by a single dirt road. And while there was always racial tension between the two sides, that still didn't stop many of them from mixing over the years. So in time, strangely enough, you had Indian cousins acting racist towards their own black cousins, and vice versa.

There were two Indian tribes in this area. The tribe "Down Below" was the Waccamaw Siouans. The other, and more famous tribe, was the Lumbees from Robeson County, just a short drive up the road. History credits the Lumbees as being the same tribe into which the famous "lost colony of Roanoke" may have been absorbed. This was also the tribe of the legendary Henry Berry Lowry—the Indian who hid out in the swamps and single-handedly drove the entire KKK from Lumberton after they had murdered his father and brother. The Lumbees were also the first tribe in the entire U.S. to have their own four-year college, which today is North Carolina State at Pembroke.

Now while almost everyone with family from the South claims "some Indian in their family," to look at my Dad was to look at an Indian man, for sure. He was tall and well-built, with brownish-red skin and silky black hair that would've made for the perfect ponytail. Though back then, Dad was hardly the ponytail type.

Additionally, just the way Mom's family history had my great-great grandfather mysteriously popping up from some Indian reservation, Dad's family tree had some mystery of it's own. Only this particular "mystery" was an evil that nobody ever wanted to discuss. For truth be told, my great-great-great grandfather was a white man named "Ol' Man

Chauncey." He had this large farm with a main farmhouse where he, his white wife, and white children lived. Chauncey also had a cabin on his farm where his Indian indentured-servant lived (my great-great-great grandmother). Well, he ended up taking his pleasures with her, and she bore three girls for him, one of whom was my great, great grandmother. Then, on top of that, "Ol' Man Chauncey's" white son would later take his own pleasures with one of his father's three daughters (his own half-sister), impregnating her as well. Sick stuff from sick men. Thus, beautiful North Carolina, home of the sweetest bacon and blueberries, was also a cauldron of some of the most racial evils. This was also why our family contained almost every racial dynamic: Indians, whites, blacks, "Free" issues, and of course, Ol' Man Chauncey and his sons. However, with all these different flavors, my nearest family was predominantly Indian.

Anyway, while some Indians and blacks took turns shunning each another, both sides remained just as shunned by the "White Only" signs that were posted everywhere in the downtown area of the city of White-ville (yes, it's actual name). In fact, Dad attended segregated schooling from first grade all throughout high school—"separate," but never-ever "equal." Because even though the Supreme Court had declared school segregation unconstitutional in 1954, the white folk in Carolina's backwoods (as in many other places) didn't feel like making the switch yet. So in these parts, there was a school for whites, a school for blacks, and then another school for Indians—a three way segregational system.

Well, Dad was the top student in all his classes, as well as the teacher's favorite. Though even that couldn't buffer him from Jim Crow's nasty blows. For as much as Dad loved books, he still had to wait until the white schools had finished abusing them. One of the saddest instances of racism was the time in high school when Dad had written the perfect physics research paper on "The Origin of the Atomic Bomb." When Dad went to his teacher to see why he had received an "A-" (when there wasn't a single red mark on any page in the paper), the teacher began berating him like he was crazy. "Aaron, that was an inappropriate topic for you. That's the kind of topic someone would choose who's interested in nuclear physics!" And when Dad then asked him, "How do you know I'm not interested in nuclear physics?", the teacher retorted, "Just how many colored nuclear physicists do you know?" Hence, the nuclear explosion of Dad's dream career.

Well, Dad still graduated as valedictorian, and by eighteen years old had already become an academic legend in his community. So when he decided to head north to New Jersey to matriculate at Seton Hall University, he had more people rooting for him than he could feed at any pig roast. He was the first person of color from that part of the country to attend an all-white undergraduate college or university. More so, there were only four blacks in his incoming freshman class of more than 1,200 students.

However, even with the culture shock and it being his first time sitting in class with whites, Dad's genius soon amazed his college professors just the same. He had the sweet, rare mixture of pure brains, great work ethic, and country wit. As a case in point, one time when preparing for his anatomy and physiology final exam, Dad was in the same pickle as every other classmate: how do you reexamine a whole semester's worth of the cat's musculoskeletal, nervous, and circulatory systems when the specimen was already dissected to bits?

Dad came up with the perfect solution—one that would also solve his problems with the alley cat that kept getting into his trash. He simply took some solutions from the lab, set a chemical trap in his garbage can, asphyxiated the alley cat, and then gave his lab partner a call to rush right over. Then, staying up all night, they got to reexamine the cat's musculoskeletal, nervous, and circulatory systems, after all. Well, out of a possible 100 points on the final exam, Dad shocked everyone with a 104, while his partner got a 102. And though Dad's "solution" wasn't all that fair— not for the cat, nor for his classmates who loved alley cats—Dad hadn't left the Jim Crow south to fail.

Well, Dad graduated from Seton Hall in only 3 1/2 years, and then became the youngest person in the university's history to serve on the president's cabinet. It was from this position that he did more for creating job opportunities for minority and poor students than anyone in the school's history: developing and implementing educational programs in pre-law, pre-med, and pre-dental, along with minority scholarships, internships, and so much more. Thus, Dad had literally gone from being a "po' boy" from the country to an unbelievable enabler. This was also why stories about men like W.E.B. DuBois and Booker T. Washington were always so easy for me to believe. Because to me, my dad had paddled up the same river and scaled the same waterfalls.

Then one day, as Dad was teaching one of his courses at Seton Hall, he couldn't help but notice this one new student—a shy and pretty girl who, story had it, was only driving that big Cadillac around town because it was her father's who had just died of a heart attack. So Dad began tutoring Patricia, then he began courting her, and in just a short time, he and Patricia were getting married in the Catholic church right on Seton Hall's campus.

Dad then bought them their dream house: a two-bedroom ranch with a big front yard (ideal for perfect football games) in a city called Plainfield, about twenty miles from Newark. They were one of the first minority families to move onto the block, which back then was mostly Jewish. For although Plainfield's race riots had driven a lot of whites from the heart of the city, you still had blocks such as these that were mostly white.

Well soon after the move, I was born, and Dad just loved having a baby boy to take his very name, "Aaron." Though I wasn't a "junior" exactly, because Mom made sure to give me her daddy's name, too—making me "Aaron William." And since Dad was making such great money, Mom enjoyed the life of the stay-at-home mom of the 70's—taking me to Bloomingdale's for lunch, making my yogurt from scratch, and dressing me in Osh Kosh back when you could only find it in the most quaint boutiques. She also worked on her fashion modeling career. Then two years later, my brother Brett was born. And when Brett came home from the hospital, Dad lifted me up to the crib and said, "Y'all are gonna look out for each other. That means if one of you has fifty cents, the other one gets a quarter!"

However, before I'd even know what fifty cents was, Mom and Dad had separated. But even as a little kid, I'd sometimes look through the ornate photo book of their big wedding day at Seton Hall—studying the adoration in their faces as they looked at each other. Sometimes, Mom would even tell me and Brett: "Your dad and I may argue and fight, but there was still a time when we were very much in love."

As a matter of fact, I did have one, lone memory of their intimacy: I couldn't have been older than four, and there we were, cruising somewhere in the big, green convertible Thunderbird with white leather that Dad had just surprised Mom with. It was a sunny day, and as they sat in the front seat, I was in the back, but leaning forward with my elbows propped on the armrest between them. They were holding hands, and I can remember feeling so complete . . .

But that was it. Because other than that were the overshadowing memories of arguments that always left Mom crying, Dad lighting a ton of cigarettes while fighting back his own tears, and other family members asking me and Brett for the hundredth time if we were okay. And as for that big, green convertible, it was rusting away in our junky garage—the white leather now browned by dirt, debris, and tons of spider webs.

▲ ▼ ▲ ▼ ▲

So then, here's the question: Did all this post-divorce drama and such qualify 828 Field Avenue as a "broken home?" Well, let's see, there were indeed parts of our house that were broken from all the burglaries. (Iron bars bolted over our laundry room window.) And no doubt, I had seen hearts broken, even heard voices broken from long arguments. Not to mention that the toilet handle in our small bathroom stayed broken, since more than one plumber claimed to have fixed it, but was really just taking advantage of Mom being single and clueless about that type of stuff. By the way, I'd sometimes wish for the water company's long, shut-off tool to be broken. However, that never broke.

There was one last thing that was never broke, either: Mom's will to see her boys "through the fire," like Chaka Khan sang about. Through the ice, too. Because those times when Mom would be forced to carry armfuls of groceries through the rough, winter blizzards up to her knees, I'd have to chip her frozen laces loose with a butter knife before being able to pull her boots off her numbed feet, as she'd just lay back on her bed, moaning in pain.

So you see, this was why years later, when I'd first learn of this socio-logical buzzword, "broken home," I'd almost have to chuckle. Because up until that point, I just thought that it was a basic thing called "life"—of which every household on the planet has it's own sobering yoke to bear. And aren't we all just an eensy-weensy bit broken, ourselves?

▲ ▼ ▲ ▼ ▲

Then there was one morning I'd never forget. There I was, getting ready for school, as Mom's puny clock radio was now standing in for our Fisher stereo that had just been stolen. As always, we were listening to New York

City's 98.7 Kiss FM when this song caught my attention like never before. For as I listened, it felt like someone was singing about my very life.

I'd quickly learn that this song was "When Doves Cry," by Prince, the same one who sang "1999" and "Little Red Corvette." Well, instantly beating out Michael Jackson's "Billy Jean," this was now my favorite. For beneath its bouncy drumbeat and keyboard melody, there was this underlying sadness and pain to it. Kind of like my own life, you could say. Because underneath Parliament's silly "Aqua Boogie," my Star Wars collection, and tons of family fun, I too had this underlying sadness and pain. A pain that I was already learning to suppress a little too well. That is, until I found this song to relate to.

"This is what it sounds like when doves cry."

I'd sing the chorus over and over in my head, dissecting it more every time. I mean, it was the most unorthodox form of counseling imaginable, but here this song was teaching me something precious. It was letting me know that it was completely okay to cry, even if only on the inside—just as I imagined a dove would. So, at nine years old, "When Doves Cry" became my introduction to "the blues," even though it was a pop song.

I was a bona fide Prince fan by now, and I even begged and twisted Mom's arm until she took me to see his emotionally turbulent movie, *Purple Rain*. Mom eventually grew weary of constantly having to put her hand over my eyes, but I was looking for so much more than naked girls. Munching away on my popcorn in that dark theater, I was in deep study of my new hero Prince as he acted out his own true-to-life story of growing up in his own "broken home" with his own "jacked-up" issues. And so introspectively aware of my own issues, I studied his every move.

Well, towards the end of the movie, Prince gets buried in a whirlwind of woes. To make things worse, he feels like nobody understands him. (I could relate to that.) The stress keeps rising in his life, and it's obvious that he's getting really close to simply writing everyone off and retreating into aloofness forever. (I could relate to that, too.) However, by the end of the movie, everything works out wonderfully! And as I sat there, watching him close out the movie with his performance of "Baby I'm a Star," I could've shed tears of joy—a billion times happier than when Daniel-San defeated Johnny with that crane kick in *The Karate Kid*. Prince had made it through, after all—which meant that I could make it, too!

Man, I loved Prince. Plus, he looked like he was just as ethnically-mixed as I was. So I just went ahead and adopted him as an older brother. And just like a big brother, he was letting me know a lot: that you can be crazily misunderstood, and even endure the craziest stuff, without having to go completely crazy yourself.

So I still rarely cried as a kid (though my heart stayed pretty heavy beneath all my jokes and antics). But whenever I played "When Doves Cry," I'd do all the crying I needed to for the moment—on the inside. So during my next annual check-up, when Dr. Cho, my pediatrician, routinely asked me how I was doing, I just smiled and told him I was doing fine. Because I had my very own child psychologist now—cool, big brother Dr. Prince.

V

THE FUNKY-FRESH 80'S

No matter what was going on in my life, or what might've just happened the night before, once I ran out our back door on a sunny, summer morning to play with my homeboys, all was "fresh." In fact, it was better than fresh; it was "funky-fresh."

It all started with whoever woke up and got dressed first. Then it was straight outside, to where the locusts made their racket high up in the trees and the inchworms descended on silky strings. And whoever made it outside first wouldn't have to run and ring the others' doorbells. We had our own official, "come-outside-and-play" call.

"*Ooooooh-ooooot!*"

Launched at full blast, it was prepubescently high-pitched enough to penetrate doors and windows—your morning cartoons, too. Then, after one of us had made the call, all we'd have to do was wait and listen. Because without fail, the same response would come back in no time.

"*Oooooooh-oooooot!*"

And like a pack of wolf cubs, we could even discern each other's tones. For instance, if I made the first call, and one of my homeboy's responses came back with the same energy as mine, that meant, "Hey! I'll be outside in a minute!" However, if their response was much slower and even sullen-sounding, then that either meant, "Dag, I can't come out right now" (maybe because of chores, punishment, or both), or "Dag, I gotta go somewhere." Yup, we knew each other that well. Just like best friends are supposed to.

Greg was my first friend ever, going all the way back to the crib days. He was only a few months younger than me, and his house was directly behind mine, with our backyards separated by a chain-link fence that we had trampled to the ground over the years. Greg and I got so close

41

because our parents had become like family before we were even born. So naturally, his mom was my Aunt Jackie, and my mom his Aunt Pat. And though both our moms had the unspoken right to spank the other's kid, that never had to happen.

Now our dads hit it off so sweetly because they had so much in common. I mean, they were both "colored boys" from the South, they had both come up north and "made it big," and they were both raising their families on a nice, Jewish block. In fact, the night Greg was born, our dads got so drunk celebrating, they had to cling to the huge oak tree in Greg's backyard to keep from falling off the planet. The very oak tree Greg and I grew up ducking behind during dodgeball.

There was one last thing our dads had in common: They both moved out early on, and at about the same time, too. Pretty soon, it seemed like there were no dads living in my neighborhood; just single-parent homes with mommies carrying the load of a mommy and daddy. This is why when meeting other kids from the neighborhood and maybe asking, "hey, where's your mom," it would never cross your mind to say, "where's your dad?" And by the way, our block didn't stay Jewish for long, either. In fact, the four-story house next to Greg's soon became a "group home" for troubled kids from New York City.

Greg also had two teenage sisters, Sheri and Jamel. And though they were too old to build forts with us, they'd still join us by tying their jump ropes to the trampled fence for some endless rounds of "double-dutch." And whenever Mom spotted them from our kitchen window, she'd come skipping outside to see if she still had "the touch" from her early Newark days. And shockingly, she most surely did, and "wow," we'd all say.

Remi Batson was my other homeboy. He lived on West Eighth Street directly across from Greg, in a humongous Victorian house that had long since been converted into apartments—the way much of Plainfield was now going. Now as to where Remi and his family were originally from, none of us knew much about him. It just seemed like one day Greg and I were playing, then along came Remi, and that was that. Miss Batson was really nice, too. She just never socialized much with Mom or Aunt Jackie.

So all this being said, once our little posse—Brett, Greg, Remi, and me—had been reunited once again by our "come-outside-and-play" call, we'd be ready for another full day of running, sweating, and laughing, where someone always got hurt and either called time-out or just cried it out and then continued. And while an adult might've thought our days looked the same, to us each one was incredibly different. For these were our wonder years, in our own little world of wonder: watching how water twisted around the bends of our newly-dug "rivers," baking mudballs in the sun as we prepared for a game of war, and climbing trees so high while studying every critter along the way. Yeah, everything was new to us. Even how far a ball could go when you kicked it with different parts of your foot.

And once we got tired of running around outside, we'd simply run into Greg's basement, where we never got tired of listening to our favorite record: Roosevelt Franklin, Sesame Street's only black puppet. I mean, you could tell just by his lingo:

"Peta' Pipa', picked a peck of pickled PIGSFEET! But my name is NOT Peta' Pipa', it's Roosevelt Franklin . . ." And let it be said that Roosevelt Franklin was so cool, that if Elmo were around back then, he would've had to wait until Roosevelt Franklin and his crew had finished their songs.

But whatever activity we were engrossed in, if it was Saturday morning, it all came to a screeching halt at 11 o'clock. Because that's when WWF wrestling came on, featuring Jimmy "Superfly" Snuka, and our all-time favorites, Rocky Johnson (Dwayne "The Rock" Johnson's dad) and Tony Atlas—the first black tag-team champions. This was even before Hulk Hogan's "Hulkamania."

Now Remi's favorite was the Iron Sheik. And after watching him, he'd always try to put one of us in the Iron Sheik's infamous "camel clutch." The only problem was that Remi always applied way too much pressure, leaving someone writhing in pain while sucking their teeth at him. "Dag, Remi!" Then, laughing all the more because we were now hurt, that was Remi. Which is exactly why one time, when Wardlaw didn't have school and I had to go with Mom to Cedarbrook Elementary, and spotted Remi "sitting out" for bad behavior and sulking, I just pointed at him and laughed right back.

So these were the best of times. And by the way, Greg's house had plenty of "red" Kool-Aid and Wonder Bread, too. Plus, if we put lots of butter and garlic powder on the bread, he'd put it in this crazy new thing called a "microwave" so we could have ghetto garlic bread. It was mushy beyond words, but you couldn't tell us it wasn't gourmet.

▲ ▼ ▲ ▼ ▲

The early 80's were fly for sure. The coolest cars were the Corvette, the Datsun 280 ZX, and the Trans-Am. The coolest dog was the Doberman. The coolest cologne was Brut or Aramis 900. The coolest football team was Tony Dorsett's Cowboys or Lynn Swann's Steelers. Buckwheat was the life of The Little Rascals, and Eddie Murphy's Buckwheat was the life of Saturday Night Live. The best chicken on the planet was Kentucky Fried, and Red Lobster was like a five-star restaurant.

Then there was the Jheri curl, the hairstyle invented by Chicago hairdresser, Jheri Redding. And unless you just loved your afro, everyone had "the curl"—profiling around with some big, mirror-lens shades while keeping their "do" extra-shiny with that spray "juice" that you could smell in your sleep.

Speaking of sleep, if your "do" was official and moist, then you had to sleep with a shower cap. So a good, glistening Jheri curl required some work, for sure. But once Michael Jackson got his, all that hard work suddenly became a pleasure for everyone. All except for Mom, of course. Her Indian hair wasn't the texture for it.

Then came another phenomenon: playing nothing but your favorite music videos all day, it was called "MTV"—Music Television. People said it was "out of this world," and even their ad campaign featured an astronaut sticking an MTV flag on the moon. Now if you couldn't afford cable to watch MTV, then you had to find a household that could. Our spot was Greg's den, and how we'd sit there for hours in hopes of seeing just one Michael Jackson video. And during those periods, we'd end up knowing them all: Pat Benatar was the toughest; Cyndi Lauper, the silliest; Billy Idol, the angriest; Talking Heads, the craziest; and Sting, the coolest. Then along came a comedian named Weird Al Yankovic; and since he spoofed Michael Jackson's videos, we'd settle for his stuff just the same.

Then another meteor struck. And if MTV was "out of this world" then this one was "out of this galaxy." Plus, this one was strictly an urban thing. Originating with some black and Puerto Rican dudes in the

Bronx, it was called breakdancing—or breakin'. And from New York to North Jersey, this meteor's "radiation" suddenly had everyone doing the most bizarre stuff, like spinning on their backs, and "poppin' and lockin'" like their limbs had an electric current going through them. And even though adults were already warning us with stories about kids snapping their necks from head-spinning, that didn't stop us one bit. In fact, the less friction between your head and the carpet, the better; so we always ripped the glossiest pages from Mom's fashion magazines.

Now if breakin' was this new baby on the scene, then Hip Hop was the nursery. Way more than just breakin,' rappin', and taggin' (graffiti), Hip Hop was the entire culture—our culture. I mean, it was a whole new attitude (cold chillin'), a whole new way of speaking ("that's stupid-fresh"), and the effect it had on us was bananas. So no longer needing to snatch crumbs from the grown folk's table of Disco, Hip Hop was like our very own "kids' menu"—and it was tastier than Aunt Jackie's ribs and collard greens.

All you had to do was watch what happened whenever Afrika Bambaataa's "Planet Rock" started playing. Random kids would all but stampede to whatever source the beat was coming from, usually someone's "box" ("boom box" and "ghetto blaster" being corny terms that evolved later). And if it was a really nice "box," best believe the person would have it perched high on their shoulder as they strutted down the street, draining their D-sized batteries and loving every minute of it. All for the sake of the neighborhood enjoying it with him. For that's just how this whole Hip Hop thing was—communal. So whether trading breakdance moves with total strangers, or just giving passing cars the thumbs-up for blasting Newcleus' "Jam On It," Hip Hop had us all in bliss together. A much needed escape from life's stresses.

But it went even deeper than that. In a nutshell, Hip Hop was for us what the "I Am Somebody," Civil Rights Movement was for our parents and grandparents. I mean, perhaps for the first time, urban youth actually had the authority on something that everyone else wanted to learn about, officially making us "experts" in something. And how good it felt after finishing our breakdancing routine at the nearby roller-skating rink, to see a bunch of suburban kids trying so hard to imitate us. And mind you, this was eons before any dance studio would be caught dead teaching a breakdancing class. That's also why it was nothing for me to be at one of my wealthy classmate's houses and have their parents beg me to show them my "moves" right on their spacious kitchen floor.

So while *The Brady Bunch, Different Strokes,* and the rest of material society tempted young urbanites to feel like they had nothing, they now had Hip Hop. Therefore, so what if your phone was disconnected for a minute? And so what if your refrigerator was empty? And so what if your "Adidas" had one extra stripe because they were really just "jeepers" from the Dollar Shoe Outlet on Route 22? Because of Hip Hop, you could still flex your millionaire attitude like you "Ruled the World," just like Kurtis Blow's rap. And whenever someone pulled out a Polaroid camera for a group shot, our poses summarized it all: hands on our hips like we were the sheriffs in town, baseball caps worn on the tippy-top of our heads like crowns, our "Adidas" loosely-laced like royal slippers, our leather spiked belts and bracelets shining like armor, and of course, our coolest grimaces that said, "cold chillin'!"

And while Cazelle glasses, Kangol bucket hats, and gold chains were the ultimate in Hip Hop accessories, we were too young and broke to have any of that stuff yet. Though my babysitter Lance certainly had enough to "rock it" for our entire neighborhood. And speaking of "Rock It," once Herbie Hancock came out with that hit song, turntable scratchin' was immortalized.

So officially ditching Roosevelt Franklin and WWF, Hip Hop became our new world of wonder.

▲ ▼ ▲ ▼ ▲

Now in the same vein of Hip Hop giving urban youth that needed boost of confidence, the lyrics in many of the raps served the same purpose. For this was back when rappers called you a fool for doing drugs or dropping out of school! Back when even "party songs" would relay serious messages about "the struggle." Some songs even did it in a comical way, giving people that needed moment to simply laugh at the fact that they were broke beyond their control. That's why everyone loved Kurtis Blow's, "The Breaks:" It made struggling a bit easier for the moment:

> And the IRS says they want to chat . . .
> (That's the breaks; that's the breaks)

> You can't explain why you claimed your cat!
>   (That's the breaks; that's the breaks)
> And Ma Bell sends you a whopping bill . . .
>   (That's the breaks; that's the breaks)
> With eighteen phone calls to Brazil!
>   (That's the breaks; that's the breaks)
> And you borrowed money from the mob . . .
>   (That's the breaks; that's the breaks)
> And yesterday you lost your job!
> Well, these are the breaks!
> Throw your hands up in the sky,
> And wave 'em round from side to side,
> If you deserve a break tonight, somebody say, "ALRIGHT!

And you could always tell who really needed that "break" by the way they'd holler "Alright" at Kurtis' command.

Now as large as Hip Hop was to the urban world, believe it or not, this was still when MTV would never play it. Except for when this cool, white gal named Blondie busted a rap in her song, "Rapture." But Hip Hop hardly needed MTV's approval. Besides, Don Cornelius' dance show, *Soul Train*, played more than enough Hip Hop, and you didn't need cable to watch *Soul Train*.

Then came the day when I got my very first record. Delivering more of that "Hip Hop blues" to let you know you weren't alone in the struggle, it was "The Message" by Grandmaster Flash and The Furious Five. And you could hear people reciting these lyrics almost everywhere:

> The bill collectors ring my phone,
> And scare my wife when I'm not home . . .
> It's like a jungle, sometimes it makes me wonder,
> How I keep from going under . . .

And whenever I jammed to it, the part about bill collectors always made me think about the little Asian man who ran the garbage disposal company in our neighborhood, and how he'd kick our front door with his big boots whenever our monthly payment was way late. Since he'd do nothing but yell at Mom anyway, she'd always make me and Brett duck beneath the window ledges, so he wouldn't see us when he put his face to our windows to look inside. And like lyrics in the song, this "bill collector" thing was a bit scary, but not really because of the little Asian man. It's just that I was still scarred over anyone banging on our doors.

It's like a jungle, sometimes it makes me wonder,
How I keep from going under . . .

VI

BODEGA BLUES

Then there was one of the sweetest moments of my childhood, all puns intended. It was the day when Mom and Aunt Jackie decided to let us walk to the store by ourselves. But not just any store. I'm talking about "the candy store"—the Puerto Rican-owned bodega on West Fourth Street, four blocks up Liberty Street and right across from Plainfield's housing projects. The same projects we always figured the ones who'd rob us came from.

Having already raised two daughters, sending Greg into the streets like this was a piece of cake for Aunt Jackie. However, not so with Mom, since I was her firstborn. Mom was always conflicted about the whole thing: wanting to keep me and Brett close to her, but at the same time, knowing that for us to become "strong men" (as she'd say), we'd have to learn to handle ourselves. So while churning in her million-and-one mommy fears, she forced herself to think like a daddy and decided to cut me loose. However, she didn't hesitate to tell Brett that he was still too young. Leaving our predictable back yards, we embarked on our next exciting chapter of wonder. We were nowhere near hitting puberty, yet this made us feel like men, for sure.

We looked like some street-walking pros from the start, but only because we were imitating how we'd seen others do it: walking in the middle of the street and taking your time to move for a honking car, yelling over each other's voices even though we were right next to each other, and being ready to chase the ice cream truck at the drop of a dime. Lastly, we cheered for every driver whizzing by in their souped-up car, and then argued over who had "called it" first.

"Yo, that's my car!"

"No, that's my car! I been called that car!"

"Greg, Greg, didn't I call that car first? See! See!"

"Okay then, okay then . . . That one's my car then! That's my car then!" And for some reason we'd always say everything twice.

Now even though the bodega was only three blocks away, it took us every bit of forty-five minutes to get there. And we'd get excited whenever we bumped into some of our homeboys from little league baseball, like Quani, Altereek, or even short, Puerto Rican Tito—the pitcher for the Pirates who'd have more gorgeous cousins and aunts clapping for him than you could count.

So by the time we finished yet another debate—like who was the flyest between Real Roxanne, Lisa Lisa, or Sheila E—we'd finally reach the bodega with its freshly-painted, but already graffiti-scribbled walls. And on a hot summer day, there was always a crowd out front: grown men standing around smoking Kools, someone on the busted payphone trying to get on a payment plan for some bill, and of course, swarms of other kids laughing, loud-talking, and riding bikes with the smallest ones on the handlebars. And you could tell which kids had already been inside the bodega by whose tongues were candy-stained.

Now the bodega itself was the epitome of cramped quarters. For the bodega had just about everything from Spanish coffee, to paper towels and mouse traps, all stacked in the skinny aisles that could really only fit one person at a time. And as for sugar, whatever you craved, it was there: Krimpets, Honey Buns, BBQ corn chips, Little Hugs, Kool-Aid packets, and more. And while the 20 oz. Tropical Fantasy sodas was the best use of 49 cents, we tried to steer clear of them, since there was an urban rumor that the KKK had put the sodas only in the hoods to make black men sterile.

And yes, the bodega had candy for days. It was all kept behind Plexiglas where you had to point and ask for it by name. But even with the Plexiglas, the fat Puerto Rican man at the counter still had to watch like a hawk. Because while a lot of these loitering kids didn't have a penny to their name, they already had lots of thievery in their game.

If walking to the bodega felt manly, the greatest manhood moment was when you stepped to the counter to order your candy. A pocket full of pennies, nickels, and dimes was all you needed. Quarters were considered like gold. And if you were lucky enough to get picked by some older dude to guard his ten-speed bike while he ran in the bodega real fast, then you could suddenly have an extra two or three quarters like nothing.

So as the Puerto Rican man yelled "whaddya want" over the Salsa coming from his little box, it was time to make your order, and it was all about ordering fast. But then again, "fast" for us was still quite slow, indecisive, and frustrating.

"Lemme get ummmm, two Now & Laters. No, not 'dat one, uhh, yeah 'dat one! Yeah, two a' 'doze . . . Then lemme get uuuuuh, two Fire-balls . . . ummm, lemme get fifty-five Swedish Fish. Uhhh, 'dem green Jingles . . . uhhh, two 'a 'dem Whistle Pops . . . ummmm, three Lem-onheads, a Johnny Appletreat, two Cherry Clans, and a Dip Stick . . . No, no, forget the Dip Stick . . . Just gimme that much in Swedish fish, instead. Fish a penny each, right?"

It was all about spending your very last penny. Besides, living in paycheck-to-paycheck households, what did any of us know about actu-ally saving money? As you dumped your sweaty change on the coun-ter, it was obvious that the Puerto Rican man did this for a living—the lightning-fast speed with which he slid the coins into some box that was nailed against his side of the counter. And if your change added up—be-cause again, kids were in there trying every hustle imaginable—the man would finally fork over your candy in a small brown bag. And this be-loved brown bag was your personal treasure sack, security blanket, mid-day snack, and lunch too—all wrapped up in one. And surprisingly, it's paper wouldn't even get soggy from the constant sweating of your hands.

Stepping back outside with your trusty little brown bag in hand, the sun would seem brighter, the busted concrete smoother, and you were just in a fantastic mood all of a sudden. Then, while meandering back down Liberty Street to our backyards again—sucking, chewing, and drooling, as we littered wrappers left and right—Remi would begin tell-ing us some of the "tales from our hood." Since he was the one with the two older brothers, he just knew this type of stuff.

"Yo, y'all know Miss Girty-Girt lives in the cemetery next to the bodega, right?"

Miss Girty-Girt: she was the neighborhood bag lady who would all but crawl up and down West Eighth Street, wearing a black garbage bag as a cloak while pushing her tottering grocery cart. In fact, the garbage bag she wore was so big, with her hunched back and head hanging so low, that people were always shocked to learn that Miss Girty-Girt was actually white.

And boy was she rugged. We learned that one day as we were throwing rocks at her from the edge of Greg's yard. Suddenly, she stopped pushing her cart and began coaxing Greg over to her with her bony finger. And almost hypnotized with curiosity, Greg slowly headed towards her. But then Remi noticed that she actually had a brick in her other hand behind her back. So we quickly pulled Greg back; and then we really let her have it with rocks.

Anyway, Remi continued telling us his story.

"Do y'all know who lives in the cemetery with Miss Girty-Girt?"

"Nope," we all said.

"The Killer Clown!"

The Killer Clown? What in the world? We had never heard of him before! So we now hung on Remi's every candy-slurping word.

"Well, the Killer Clown is this clown, right? They say he lives next to this one tombstone in one of those underground army-type tents. And some people know where the tent is because once they found this chopped-up dead dog next to it."

And of course I now wanted to go back and look for the dead dog's remains myself, but it was like Remi was already reading my mind.

"But you can't go in there lookin' for the Killer Clown. Because if you do, then later that night, your doorbell will ring and when you answer it, there'll be this clown just standing there. And he'll kill you on the spot!"

Believing every bit of it, we all walked in silence for a while. This marked the day when the Killer Clown became our true boogeyman. None of us ever set foot in that cemetery, either—no matter how much we'd double-dare each other. Though we still pegged Miss Girty-Girt with rocks every chance we got.

▲ ▼ ▲ ▼ ▲

Aside from the Killer Clown, there was other stuff we got exposed to on these manly journeys for the sweetest candies. Only it was hardly sweet at all. In fact, it was super sour, and super stressful, too: I'm talking about the unseen "dog-eat-dog" pressure of the streets—from which we learned that even kids weren't exempt. So while Hip Hop culture was pumping that much-needed confidence into us, that dog-eat-dog pressure had a way of snatching it all away just as quickly.

Most of the time, as we walked or rode our bikes past some other posse of kids, we'd just exchange harmless, curious glances—maybe even a few "wassups." However, that definitely wasn't the rule. For we could just as easily end up exchanging random glares of contempt, along with the sudden feeling that you needed to somehow assert yourself right on the spot. I mean, instead of "guilty 'til proven innocent," it was like everyone was "uncool and corny 'til proven cool and tough."

There was even one time when we started arguing with this random group of girls for no reason. It was four of us and four of them, and as loud and bold as they were, they looked like they even enjoyed getting bloody elbows from fighting boys. It all started as we walked past each other in the middle of the street. First, it was the contemptible looks back and forth, then it became insults—again, for no reason at all.

"Ugly punks." One of them mumbled loud enough for us to hear.

"Man, y'all the ones who's ugly!" Remi fired right back like he just knew they were about to try something. But then the alpha of the girls—the fattest and roughest one—came right back, ready for ruckus.

"Man, shut up before I go get my older brother to punch you dead in your stupid mouf'!"

"Man, go get 'em!" Remi had heard enough by this point. "I got older brothers too, and they'll SERVE your punk brothers!" And Remi had a point there, because Monty and Yon, were super muscular and wore tank-tops to prove it. But the girl still wasn't phased one bit.

"Okay then, bet! Bet! I'mma get my brother and his boys on you, you, you, and your brothers! N*gg*h!"

"What! You 'da n*gg*h! You dummy!"

N*gg*h: And the crazy thing was, this was actually before we had reached the age of using that word as a term of endearment. So it still stung almost like a curse word.

Now by this point of the argument, we were all throwing so much hate back and forth that a passerby would never have guessed that this started just over some petty eye exchange. But that's precisely how the dog-eat-dog pressure was—constantly oppressing you, and making you feel like every single instance was some all-defining test of whether you "passed" or not. And boy, when you felt like you had "failed," the pressure could sure make you start hating yourself pretty badly, too.

Now since I didn't have any older, muscular brothers of my own, I always backed down whenever someone mentioned getting older people involved. I longed to have someone in my corner like that, because sometimes I would picture myself walking out the bodega and some random older dude punching me dead in the face, and nobody there to take up for me. And although I did have older, muscular cousins on my dad's side who were just as big as Monty and Yon, I only saw them once or twice a year at family cook-outs because of the divorce and all.

I watched the way Remi walked the streets with his chest out like his brothers were his bulletproof vest, and I couldn't help but covet that. Meanwhile, my chest felt weaker than an ugly turtle with no shell. But of course, I would never share this with anyone. In fact, none of us dared to share any of our fears or weaknesses with each other. The code of the dog-eat-dog simply had no place for that.

So in much the same way as a moose will start displaying its rack by dipping its head from side to side when another bull appears, subconsciously, we now understood that it was all about showcasing our own "racks"—with any cool or tough thing you could think of doing on the spot; just to send the message that you weren't some "soft punk." (The worst thing you could be called in the hood, by the way.) And since you could never be cool or tough enough, everyone tended to go overboard at times. Stressful? No doubt. But it was so pervasive that it was normal to us.

So for all sociologists and ethnographers out there, this was the very germ of black-on-black crime, already incubating in our little hearts. This was also why years later, when I'd come to hear of case studies of black men having higher risks of hypertension at a much younger age than other groups, it was as if I knew that already.

Not to mention how this dog-eat-dog even began affecting—or rather, dictating—the way we'd sometimes relate to each other. Because even after returning to the safety of Greg's backyard, we would sometimes start picking on each other for no reason: attacking each other's weaknesses, and refusing to let petty offenses roll off our backs like we normally would. In our constant preparation not to fail on those mean streets, sadly, sometimes everything was expendable—even your childhood friends.

And quite interesting how we never felt that same need to assert ourselves when passing by some crew of random white kids. (Even though in this part of Plainfield, the remaining white families rarely let their kids walk these streets.)

▲▼▲▼▲

Then along came a big blessing, easing more of that dog-eat-dog stress than I realized. For as Aunt Jackie soon remarried, not only did Greg acquire a stepfather—a Muslim man named Mr. Lynch—but he also gained a handful of stepbrothers and stepsisters. Among Greg's three older stepbrothers was Jalil—just as cool as Lance the babysitter. However, Jalil was cool in a different way: He was sheer "loco"—our very own Evil Knievel.

Mr. Lynch and Jalil pretty much became a stepfather and stepbrother to us all. They were both expert motorcross riders, the ones who'd fly as high as our houses on those jumps at the racetrack. More so, Greg's garage was now the hub for over twenty mud-covered Kawasakis and Yamahas. And if Jalil wasn't in the garage slimed in motor oil, then he was teaching us tricks on the BMX bikes he had built for each of us from scratch. And he enjoyed us as much as we enjoyed him. That's why even after breaking his leg in multiple places in a motorbike accident, he still defied the doctor's orders and hopped after us all day.

He even took sheet metal and built a BMX quarter-pipe against the trampled fence between our backyards. Then pedaling up it as fast as he could, he'd fly so high in the air that Mom couldn't help but gasp while washing dishes at our kitchen window. But that was nothing compared to the time when he made us lay on the ground so he could jump over us. And when he miscalculated and his back tire came down on the edge of my belly flesh, Mom really screamed her head off. Jalil just hung his head, smiled, and apologized a million times.

Mom still trusted Jalil, although she had to put her foot down the day he had all of us hold onto the back bumper of his souped-up race car as he dragged us down the icy street. Because while he was the craziest twenty year-old she might've known, she knew that he had been raised by a good father, and that in the face of danger, Jalil would lay down his life for us without a second thought. Not to mention that he was also a black belt in martial arts. So one day, when I asked Mom the biggest question of all—if I could ride bikes with Jalil to the BMX bike trails, two cities over from Plainfield—she hesitated, but eventually said yes. Though she didn't hesitate to tell Brett that he was still too young.

Now while Greg, Remi, and I already knew that Jalil was "the man," we still had no clue how much he was "the man" across so many neighborhoods. As we pedaled to the trails—block after block, and hood after hood—it seemed as if every kid in front of every bodega would notice Jalil, yell out his name, then quickly jump on their own bikes to join our growing swarm of riders. Before long, there must have been over thirty of us—ghetto BMX'ers. And yes, almost everyone had their trusty brown bag of candy. But no matter how many tagged along, Jalil kept his eyes solely on Greg, Remi, and me—his little brothers.

Well once we got to the bike trails—in some distant park behind these run-down basketball courts—I could see what a motley crew we were. Some of the top dogs from the different hoods we had just passed through had obviously joined us. Greg, Remi, and I were probably the youngest. So we all did our share of races and jumps while working on new bike tricks in between. And of course everyone stopped what they were doing to watch Jalil. Without fail, he'd go flying through the sky every time, even close to some of the branches. No wonder those police couldn't keep up with his acrobatics the time he came racing up my driveway to hide until the coast was clear.

So it was another sunny day in the concrete jungle. But towards the evening, as everyone had pretty much gobbled through their brown bags and now looked to head home, this older dude started bugging out. For not only had someone ridden over his beloved yellow T-shirt on the ground, but there was now the deepest tire tread across it. And while I'd never seen this older dude, since his shirt had "Juice Crew" on the back, I just assumed it meant he was down with big-time New York City rappers M.C. Shan and Marley Marl.

"Yo, I'mma ask one . . . more . . . time! Who rode on my shirt?"

And since nobody was confessing, the dude actually began going up to each person on their bikes and holding his shirt to their tires to find the match. And with veins sticking out his neck, he was dead serious, too.

However, since I knew it wasn't me, I just sat back on my bike, sucking on a green Jolly Rancher stick. Besides, even if it was somehow me, I knew that Jalil wouldn't even let anyone raise their voice at me. And if it had to boil down to fists, blades, or whatever else, Jalil was too tough and too loco, and everyone knew it. That's also why, many years later, when he'd become a Hollywood stunt-double for big actors like Jamie Foxx, Don Cheadle, Wesley Snipes, and even alongside stunt-legend, Jackie Chan, none of us were the least bit surprised.

So no matter how much he might've used us as crash-test dummies for his latest stunts, he was nuts about us. And that day at the trails helped me realize that I finally had an answer for when other kids started threatening to get their older brothers: His name was Jalil Jay Lynch.

VII

YEAH, I'MMA WHITE BOY

Just as nothing could beat some fried chicken with hot sauce, or Lemonheads from a hot bodega that softened those joints just the right amount, well nothing could beat a blue oxford shirt with some pleated khakis. I mean, with or without spray starch, the combo could never lead you wrong. Then add to that one of those knitted ties (the kind Michael J. Fox wore in *Family Ties*) and a navy blazer, and you now had "classy" in the palm of your hand. And if you loved argyle socks too, then you were most likely a "prep." And after five years at Wardlaw, best believe I had become one. And all the breakdancing, brown bags, and street feuds couldn't stop it from happening.

Now of course Hip Hop, my box, and baby-blue suede Pumas were all in my bone marrow (even though Mom couldn't work the Pumas into the budget). It's just that after all this time, Wardlaw was deep in my bones as well. So not only was I was more than comfortable on "that side" of things, but it was growing stronger now with every passing, fancy Bar Mitzvah.

Well the year was 1987, and as a seventh grader, Wardlaw had us immersed in everything from George Orwell's satires to the names of the nation's top universities. I had even started playing the flute. And although someone from my neighborhood might have called it girly, it was really no different from a man wearing a pink oxford shirt—of which Mom made sure I always had one, since it looked so sharp with a navy and green tie.

Speaking of oxfords, Mom had long since stopped working at Macy's in New York and now worked at the Ralph Lauren store in uppity Short Hills Mall, where she even used her store discount to make sure Brett and I had the same Polo as everyone else at school. Even if some felt she

59

had no business considering Polo because of how much we struggled financially, it was that important to her that Brett and I never felt "second-class" at school. Besides, by now we weren't struggling nearly as much. Especially not since Mom's boyfriend moved in with us.

Raymond was his name: a fashionable, athletic brown-skinned man who was originally from Teaneck in North Jersey by the George Washington Bridge. And even though Raymond and Mom never married, he became like our stepfather just the same; he really loved me and Brett. He and Mom first met at a party one night, where after some convo, he invited her to dance to George Michael's "Careless Whispers." Things took off from there, and Mom seemed happy. We dug him, too. So months later, when she sat me and Brett down and asked us how we'd feel about him moving in with us, we said yes without a second thought.

Then a couple of weeks later, Raymond walked through our front door to stay, with his chocolate-point Siamese cat named Leo and a 150-pound Bullmastiff named Joker. And boy, did I love Joker. Another thing I loved was the fact that I'd no longer have to worry about the Evil anymore. Because there was finally a man in our house—a scary dog too—and I'd sleep soundly for the first time in years, like every kid should.

Now Dad, on the other hand, had remarried some time ago. My stepmother's name was Joyce, a slightly shy and consistently sweet woman who gave the best hugs. Originally from the Newark area just like Mom, Joyce loved us just like Raymond did. In fact, whenever we spent weekends at Dad's—since he still lived in Plainfield, too—he'd always cook us the biggest country breakfasts while Joyce religiously made my favorite mac-and-cheese dish like only she could. Then by the time I was ten, Joyce had given me and Brett the best gift ever: a baby brother named Kyle.

By the way, Raymond also worked at Ralph Lauren. He was at the store in the Hackensack Mall, about an hour's drive from where Mom's store was. And Raymond sure knew how to throw some threads together. So while Mom took care of our Polo for Wardlaw—our oxford shirts, khakis, and blazers—Raymond took care of our social side, if you will—our rugby tops, sweaters, and plaid short sets. Basically, when Mom and Raymond were through, Brett and I looked like two boy models from one of Ralph's catalogs. And as Raymond also made a point in stressing how these clothes weren't for neighborhood "rough play," he wouldn't have to worry much about that. For as I said earlier, my other world— "that side" of things, the Polo side of things, the less stressful side of things—was now wooing me over.

But don't get me wrong. Bodega candy was still the best, Greg was still my homie, his mom still my Aunt Jackie, and Jalil still my everything. I mean, whenever me and Brett had forgotten our "latch-key" at home (by fourth grade, I was walking us home and locking the door until Mom came home), if we couldn't "break in" the house ourselves, Aunt Jackie's was the first place we went. However, it's just that at this point in my life, I was wrestling with a lot of identity stuff—wondering where in the world I really belonged.

More so, as much as I adored my hood, I still hated how a peaceful walk to the bodega could always devolve into some dog-eat-dog drama at any second. The way older kids could be so quick to prey on you (and if your football or BMX bike was nice enough, they might take that, too). Just like when I got mugged that one time coming home from the grocery store. Or even the time when this fat, older thug-girl randomly walked up to one of my friends and slapped her hands over his ears, almost bursting his eardrums and making him scream as if he was the girl. So this was also why—in my subconscious search for some peace— I started gravitating to Wardlaw's stress-free atmosphere. And the more my young mind stressed over whether I was really tough enough for my hood, or whether I had withheld enough mercy from the defenseless Miss Girty-Girt, or whether I'd ever be crazy enough to just punch some random kid in his face for no reason at all, the more I found myself desiring "that side" of Wardlaw's "greener" grass.

Now, let it be made clear that even pristine Wardlaw had its own shortcomings, and even its own refined version of dog-eat-dog that could be just as damaging. But at this point in my life, the humid streets still proved no match for Wardlaw's air-conditioned extracurriculars. So as we mud-covered sixth graders stood chanting "We Will Rock You" in our locker room after finally beating The Peck School in soccer for the first time in Wardlaw's history (with me as the star goalie), my mind had been made up: Wardlaw would be my new ice-cream sundae with extra "everything" on it. And the shiny red Ferrari in one of my classmate's garages would serve as the cherry on top.

"Ooooooh-ooooot!"

So now when I'd hear my homeboy's making our come-outside-and-play call and wouldn't answer back, it was nothing personal. I was probably just on the phone, planning my next trip to the sweet suburbs away from Plainfield for a while.

▲ ▼ ▲ ▼ ▲

Recalling some of those after-school sleepovers, or "play-dates" as our moms liked to call them: I'd pack a bag like I was going on vacation. And once that special Friday arrived, it was hard to concentrate during class as I'd count down the hours. Once school was finally over, there would be no walking home on these days—worrying if the older Plainfield High kids were gonna pick on me again for my "nerdy" school uniform. Instead, I'd be in a shiny big Benz, cruising to a galaxy far, far away. And how sweet it felt as some of those very high schoolers now had to jump out of the middle of the street as we honked and zoomed by. Maybe they saw me sitting pretty, and maybe they didn't; I really didn't care.

Out of all my classmates' homes, Craig Weisman's was probably my favorite. Craig and I grew close back in fifth grade, when he was new to Wardlaw and one day I was venting to him about how I hadn't been invited to some big sleepover with our other classmates. I even confided in Craig (who was Jewish) that I felt it was because I was black. Well, not only did Craig invite me to a Richard Pryor movie right on the spot, but he even had his mother pick me up at my house. After that, I was at Craig's house all the time, and his parents were as sweet as could be. Plus, he lived near so many of our other classmates that we all ended up running through Scotch Plains' stress-free acres together.

So on Friday sleepovers, the first thing Craig's mom would do was take us to the video store so we could rent as many movies as we wanted. Next, she'd take us to the Jewish deli, and walking into that place was like walking into a scene from a movie: the smell of hot pastrami and giant pickles, the "easy listening" playing over the speakers, and the nicest old man who made you feel like a prince by the way he took such pride in making your sandwich. And though the place was never packed, there'd always be some other moms in there with their own kids, in their own private school uniforms.

Then with our big, late-afternoon lunches and even bigger movie selection, it was off to Craig's home that sat high up on a hill. And upon entering his atrium—where the ceiling was too high to even notice it—we'd quickly shed our ties, unbutton our shirts, and head straight for his den with its exquisite Asian decor. So relaxing, I'd feel no stress at all. His spacious backyard was trimmed to perfection with a greyhound that took majestic laps around the pool and bubbling-warm jacuzzi. And the first time I saw the life-sized arcades and pinball machine in his basement—requiring no quarters for play, at that—I felt like I was dreaming.

So this was my new world of choice. And as this was also around the time when we started "liking" girls, was it any surprise that I now desired white girls over girls of color? I mean, just the thought of them singing Debbie Gibson with their hair-sprayed, highlighted hair had me ready to pull out my best Polo and mousse my own hair until it was spiked. More so, since there were already those in Plainfield who'd diss me as "white boy" anyway, I just started wishing I were white, altogether.

So as for that BMX bike that Jalil built from scratch for my birthday, it was now collecting rust in my backyard. No offense, but "we" suburban kids were more into skateboards.

▲ ▼ ▲ ▼ ▲

"Hey Dad, can I have fifty dollars, please? Me and my friends are all pitching in to buy Brian Bosonac a skateboard for his Bar Mitzvah."

"Now you know, son . . ."

Whenever Dad began with those words, it was lecture time.

". . . you're gonna have to realize that even though you go to school with those rich kids, that you're simply not rich like they are! Now look, I'mma do this for you this one time, son, but fifty bucks is entirely too much for a gift at your age."

Though giving Dad my best listening face, all I could think about was not letting my buddies down. But Dad was right. And while he loved that I was getting along so well at the school he worked hard to pay for, he still wanted me to know my limits—for my own good. But it would take years for me to appreciate such wisdom. Because once I set foot in Brian's Bar Mitzvah, I forgot our talk ever happened. Just like Madonna's song, I was living in a material world; and I had crushes on material girls.

Well for starters, seventh grade was all about the Bar or Bat Mitzvah—the name, of course, depending on whether you were a boy (Hebrew word for "son" being "*bar*") or a girl ("daughter" being "*bat*"). This was the ceremony when our Jewish classmates would formally take their own stand before "G—d," no longer abiding under their parents' covering. However, as solemn as this was, none of us invitees really went to that part of the synagogue service. We just counted down the hours until sundown, when the big, fancy party would start and not end until after midnight.

Now for Brian's Bar Mitzvah, those of us who received the fancy invitation were to report to Wardlaw's parking lot where a chartered bus would take us to the destination. The bigger the Bar Mitzvah, the more of a statement the family was making, and Brian's family made a huge statement by renting out the Livingston Country Club. It was close to an hour's drive from Wardlaw, but only right down the road from Short Hills Mall where Mom worked at Ralph Lauren.

Anyway, once we stepped off the bus—with girls looking like future fashion models and us guys looking like future tycoons—we could hear the music already. Stepping inside, it was set up like a giant carnival: rides, cotton candy, clowns, you name it. Meanwhile Brian, the man of the hour, stood like heir to the throne, thanking everyone for coming and reminding us to please enjoy ourselves. And as the DJ played Expose's, "Let Me Be The One," it suddenly made you start scanning the room for that classmate you had a crush on, perhaps to find her already looking at you while giggling with her friends. Better than any happy scene from any 80's movie, the whole thing felt magical. But the party was just beginning.

Well this carnival room was just a warm-up, as we were soon ushered through some double doors into a banquet room with fancy tables, multi-colored lights, a giant disco ball, and a smoke machine for the dance floor. There the DJ gave us the rules for the night—simply to party our heads off. To top it off, he even had his own dancers to entice us fellas onto the dancefloor. Grown women, super pretty of course, dressed in black heels, tights, white blouses, and black suit jackets with tails. And it worked too, because in no time we were all dancing the night away with our suit jackets tossed over the chairs at our dinner tables.

Just like kids love playing "house," now in the wave of all these fancy Bar and Bat Mitzvahs, we seventh graders loved playing "ladies and gentleman." For as Brian's family and friends of family stood around the perimeter of the banquet room, with women wearing large stones around their necks, wrists, and fingers, and the men holding Cognac glasses and cigars, we'd just imitate the sophisticated stuff we'd see them do. So at the end of the night, I'd be more than honored as one of the girls asked to wear my suit jacket over her chilly shoulders.

Then finally—sometime before midnight—it was time for everyone to head back out those country club doors to hop on the chartered bus where the engine was already running. More than a bit of a bummer, it was almost like waking up from a dream. But we'd sure keep it alive by talking about it in school—right up until the next Bar or Bat Mitzvah. Then we'd start from the top all over.

▲ ▼ ▲ ▼ ▲

Well no longer did I have that "bluffing" problem that had so disgusted Mrs. Yardley back in third grade. For while I was always still deep in my thoughts, I was now at the age where I wanted this thing called "success," and my grades beautifully reflected it as well. So of the three possible seventh grade classes, I had been placed in the topmost, or honors class. Now since most of my friends I hung with were also in honors, I never gave much thought to how students in the lower two classes were making along—minority students, especially.

The lowest of these seventh grade classes was 7S, which the honors kids mocked as "7 Stupid." And sadly, if you were both black and in "7S," then that could be like a double wammy, as you would not only be subject to the occasional, dumb racist stuff, but also to the subtle yet painful forms of classism, which for these students often translated into no Friday play-dates in the suburbs, no close-ups of mansions or Ferraris, and not many Bar or Bat Mitzvahs, either. Hence, an entirely different Wardlaw experience. And no, they'd never get that dreamy feeling in this world the way I did, because for them it was like a world with a lowered ceiling. So meet the three types of Plainfield kids: the trespassing, public school kids curious about being "in," the honors Wardlaw kids who were "in," and the 7S Wardlaw kids who probably wanted "out."

This also explains why a couple of years down the road, when most of us minority students would end up resenting Wardlaw (during our militant days), I'd notice how some of my homeboys and homegirls would have this deep, abysmal anger. I'd almost want to tell them to chill out a little, just for their own peace of mind. But I didn't fully understand that they had never been afforded much peace of mind while they were there.

Now along with my honors classes, I'm sure the fact that I was so light-skinned played a part in my being embraced by some in this world. This also may have explained why some parents seemed to have no qualms about me "going out" with their pretty little daughters. So then, did all this make me a "lucky one"? Well, I guess that would depend on the angle from which one viewed it. For while many black students might not have always enjoyed the same acceptance at Wardlaw because of their darker skin color, I, in turn, didn't experience the same unanimous acceptance on the streets because I didn't look "black" enough. So the bottom line was that it really wasn't "win-win" for any of us—as we all paid some type of price and had our own blues to sing. It was really just a blessing that none of this drove any wedges between any of us, as we always remained unified, encouraging each other to succeed and never give up, and ready to demand a handful of Lemonheads anytime one of us had brought some to school.

▲ ▼ ▲ ▼ ▲

The end of seventh grade marked our big graduation from the lower school; where we'd now be heading to Wardlaw's upper school campus two cities over.

As expected, our graduation was as fancy as could be. And of course my huge family was present—Mom, Mom's two younger sisters who helped raise me as well, Momma, my little cousins, Dad, my stepmother and her parents, my two brothers, and Raymond. Every family packed into the same auditorium where I had done so much running, laughing, and developing over the years. Even where in fifth grade I once so disrespected our new gym teacher from Scotland, that he lost control and flung me into the wall. Only to quickly realize how badly he'd messed up as he begged me (as I was in complete shock) not to report him, which I didn't.

Now the thing that had my family most excited about my graduation was that I had just become the first minority student in Wardlaw's history to win the annual public-speaking contest. My speech was on Dr. Martin Luther King, Jr.—my absolute hero—and I had even been asked to deliver it at the ceremony, and how honored I was. For just as this life of digging white girls, the suburbs, and Bar and Bat Mitzvahs hadn't subverted my love for Hip Hop, it also hadn't subverted my love for Dr. King and all he had accomplished for me to even be where I now was. And I wasn't even nervous when the time came for me to approach the lectern. Quickly scanning the audience and seeing my family taking up almost two rows and beaming with joy, I smiled back and began.

"Mr. Newcomb, Mr. Wuest, fellow graduating class, parents, and friends . . ." Looking at each one as I named them, Wardlaw had taught me well. Wardlaw taught very well, period. And lo and behold, there was my third grade teacher, Mrs. Yardley, sitting in the front row with the rest of the teachers, smiling so proudly. Looking at her now, you would've never guessed she was that same teacher who had so disrespected me and Mom. Well, I had obviously earned her approval now! And as I was still just a kid, I must say it felt good.

Well in a matter of four engaging minutes, I recited my entire speech from memory without a single word misspoken. Then as it was time for my closing, I decided to do something for the first time. For as I highlighted Dr. King's famous "I Have A Dream" speech at the end, and realized how even with all the dumb racist stuff, that times were definitely way better than they used to be, I extended my arms towards the audience and said, "as I look across the auditorium this evening, I can see that Dr. King's dream has come true. Thank you!"

Oh, the explosion of applause! As I descended from the lectern, there was Mr. Newcomb, hopping to his feet to shake my hand in that classy, pink sports jacket. I was sure going to miss him. Mr. Wuest, too.

Speaking of Mr. Wuest, just before we got our graduation certificates, it was his turn to give out three of Wardlaw's most historic and prestigious awards. Each award had its own fancy name, and each recipient would get their name immortalized in gold-leaf calligraphy on the large wooden plaques that hung high in the school's largest foyer.

Well the first award went to the two valedictorians: Nick Zagorski and Jackie Co. This didn't come as a surprise to anyone, but we still gave them a big applause, nonetheless, because they had really earned it. Next were the awards for the best in athletics. Applause, again. Then finally, it was time to announce the winners of the Kirkpatrick Award, awarded to the "best all-around student" for academics, athletics, leadership, and extracurriculars.

So there I sat among my peers, already more than satisfied with being the first minority student to win the public speaking contest—and on the enlightening topic of Dr. King, at that. That's why as I now noticed how Mr. Wuest was looking my way before announcing the winner of the Kirkpatrick Award, in a flash I wondered, *"What in the world is he looking at me for?"*

"Aaron Campbell."

The applause all but shook the steel beams above us, but I was in such shock that I could barely hear a thing—not even Mom's shrill screams. And mind you, this was one of those rare times when Mom just loved to cry. Because not only would she be overwhelmed with joy, but times like these had a way of reminding her just how much we had suffered over the years to get to this point. How much she had suffered to always give her boys the absolute best of everything.

So along with my public speaking award, that evening I had also become the first male minority in the school's hundred-year history to win the Kirkpatrick Award. I say "male" because to everyone's pleasant surprise, Raissa Maynard—a Caribbean girl who had been at Wardlaw with me since second grade—was called up right after me.

What a night it was!

And as I walked up to receive my award, where Mr. Newcomb was clapping away like a firecracker, all of Wardlaw's teachers rose to their feet to honor me. And just to think, here they were honoring the likes of *me*—the charming, witty black kid in Ralph Lauren's finest, who was really just a single-parent kid from around the corner, scarred by the Evil and desperately searching for love and acceptance from two totally different worlds, while looking to racy Prince films for tips on socializing. But despite the true enigma that I was, I was now Wardlaw's best all-around student!

Receiving my award from Mr. Wuest while giving the best handshake Wardlaw and Mom had taught me, I couldn't help but remember the last time he and I had shook hands. Why it was last year, when I was in sixth grade and had gotten busted for selling Playboy and Penthouse magazines in school. Knowing I could've easily been expelled, with tears in my eyes, I looked an angry Mr. Wuest square in the eye, sincerely apologized, and then extended my hand like a crushed gentleman. Man, I felt so dirty on that day, so much so that I never bothered telling him which of my rich classmates was actually supplying the whole operation from their father's secret collection.

So that's why, as Mr. Wuest and I stood at the lectern, we shook hands and smiled at each other a little longer than normal. I had come a long way since that day, and he never gave up on me. So, with the ceremony now over, we all made our way over to the old auditorium for some refreshments. At times like these, Mom and Dad got along extra fine, even taking a moment to step aside and share words like, "wow, we really made something special there."

Lastly, there was one more happy moment for me. A few days after my graduation, Dad took me over to his buddy's big, annual cookout. Jackie Steele was his name, one of Plainfield's black millionaires who lived in a mansion way up in the rich, hilly section of Plainfield known as "Sleepy Hollow." For even though Plainfield had more than enough hoods, it also had this luxurious part that bordered Scotch Plains. And there were more than a few black families living in Sleepy Hollow, and professionally, they stuck together like glue. Their bond made especially strong by the fact that this was still when society at large refused to acknowledge people of color having such power and influence on the "finer side."

Well of course I loved these cookouts, mostly because Jackie Steele's backyard was like nothing you could describe without a camera. His rock garden stream winding down from his house to his bathtub-warm pool, with its underwater lights making it glow against the starry sky. Blues was playing through the speakers in the large cabana, and Dad had just finished grilling another batch of his addictive chicken and refilled his glass with only the best of scotches. He and his friends sat by the poolside while I just kept diving off the diving board.

"Come here, son. I need you for a minute."

Dripping wet as I climbed out the pool, I shuffled over to where they were sitting. Dad was so relaxed and happy—this Jim Crow farm boy-turned-educator, businessman, and county-wide political person— reclining in the backyard of his buddy's mansion. And as the men around him sipped their own scotches, Dad continued.

"You see my boy, here?" He took his sweet time like he was reliving every part of it. "Well, he just gave his speech on Dr. King at The Wardlaw-Hartridge School's graduation." All the men encouraged him on, as everyone knew about Wardlaw, and its price, too. "Now not only was he the first minority to ever win the public speaking contest in the school's history, but then my boy won their Kirkpatrick Award, given to the best all-around student in academics, athletics, leadership, and extracurriculars. He was also the first minority to ever win that award!"

And I'll never forget that look on Dad's face. Just like Mom had stuff that only she could rejoice in because of the single-parent sacrifices she had made, Dad also had stuff that only he could rejoice about—from his own seventh grade in a segregated school, to his own financial sacrifices so that Wardlaw always got their money.

"Ok, go on back in the pool, son." He dismissed me with the proudest head nod.

"Sure, Dad." And as I turned and dove my best dive back into that glowing pool, I couldn't help but smile big underwater. Times like these had a way of making up for the all the times he'd missed. No matter how early or how ugly the divorce, the bond between a father and son can still be divine.

VIII

NAW, I AIN'T WHITE!

Tiffany, Erika, Jennifer, and so on. These were some of my blonde and brunette Wardlaw gals who loved talking like "Valley girls," watching Molly Ringwald movies, and dancing to girl band The Bangles. And I dug that stuff, too. However, all "that stuff" came to a screeching halt the summer after seventh grade—when I first saw her.

I was riding bikes through Plainfield with my homies one day when I saw her. And man, how love songs started running through my head! Half-black and half-Puerto Rican, she might've been the flyest girl I had ever seen. I'm talking about Melinda.

My homies already knew her. See, it was just me—"the private school kid"—who was late as always. However, at that moment, I felt right on time. And as far as Wardlaw, I almost didn't care if I never saw that place again.

She was sitting on her front porch with her girlfriends as we cruised by on our bikes.

"Waddup, Melinda?"

"Waddup, Deuce." Man, even her voice was fly. I mean, if Cupid were real, he would've skipped arrows and just stabbed my heart with a Rambo knife instead.

By this point, my neighborhood crew had expanded as well. (After all, it's not like I wasn't hitting the streets at all during my suburban vacations, just much less than normal.) So along with Chico and Donaldo, Deuce was my other homeboy. Originally from Brooklyn, Deuce lived right up the street from Melinda, and they both went to Hubbard Middle School. And yes, all of us were in the same grade.

But back to my heart with the Rambo knife in it. Well, we stopped our bikes so she and Deuce could catch up a little, while I just played it off like she was nothing special. But it was impossible to play it off for long, because after that day I was "coincidentally" riding past her house at least once a day. And in no time, I was sitting right on her porch with her. Lisa Lisa had just come out with "Lost in Emotion," and best believe I was—and for the first time in my life, too. Man, I could really see why they called it a "crush"!

That high-noon sun felt especially warm on her brick porch (my Lemonheads tasted sweeter, too). Plus, I realized that my Uncle Mike, my father's older brother, had built Melinda's very house (as I could spot he and Dad's designs anywhere). Thus I felt even more entitled to be there. However, as random fellas would ride by on their bikes and mopeds and stare at me—like who in the world did I think I was to be sitting with fly Melinda—instead of making me feel even more like "the man," such looks would often have the opposite effect: making me feel like some out-of-towner or weirdo because they didn't know who I was.

See, with all of us getting older now (and evermore consumed with being "cool" and accepted), Wardlaw was becoming more of a problem for me in my neighborhood. Because while my homies knew me, those in city sports knew me, and those around the bodega by the projects knew me, because I went to private school, there were still many who didn't— thus making me a stranger to them. And how I detested that. Why, I even tried asking Mom if I could go to Hubbard instead of Wardlaw; but she just looked at me like I was on drugs and that was the end of it. Not to mention that Mom had taught at Hubbard back when I was younger, where not only were there fights every day, but one day this kid had bitten part of another kid's face off! (It still messed Mom's head up to even discuss that gory event.)

But again, back to me and Melinda. She had her little box playing L.L. Cool J's new single, "I Need Love"—the song that made every Hip Hopper want to be in a relationship. And could it be that "fly" Melinda was now liking me back? Man, I got giddy just thinking about it; though I still couldn't get cocky. But if I was butter, best believe I'd be in liquid form!

We had even planned our first kiss. It was the night when I sang Levert's "Casanova" to her, and she then sang the Temptations' "My Girl" back to me. And as she sang, I could've dropped the phone and run around my block faster than Ricochet Rabbit and Speedy Gonzalez combined—never minding if she could really sing or not.

Forget puppy love; this must've been dinosaur love!

But then, something happened. After a couple of months of me being at her house almost daily, it was like out of nowhere, she was suddenly "busy" all the time. And whenever she did decide to chill with me, it definitely wasn't for the whole afternoon anymore. She'd just talk to me from her screen door. No more box, and definitely no more L.L. Cool J's "I Need Love." Pretty soon, she just stopped answering my phone calls altogether.

Curtains.

Well, Deuce was always the one who got to the bottom of stuff. He was even the one who had spotted Melinda smoking Newports after school one day and said, "Yo, I'mma tell Aaron, girl!" (even though her response was, "So what? You can!"). And since we had all returned back to school by now, Deuce asked Melinda about the situation as they walked home from Hubbard one day.

"So what's up with you and my man, Aaron? Y'all ain't been chillin' no more."

"Deuce, do you really think I'd talk to a boy from Wardlaw-Hartridge?" She dropped it on him like he had just asked her to trade in her L.A. Gear and gold chain and dress like a Valley girl.

"A boy"—that's all I was to her now.

And it was bugged, because when people from Wardlaw said the school's full name, it always sounded powerful and elitist, as if Harvard and Princeton were just waiting with open arms. However, when people from my neighborhood said it, it sounded repulsive and corny, almost like a curse word.

Well, Deuce told me all that she said. And though I played it off like I didn't care, I felt smooshed like a bug. Plus, I knew that Melinda hadn't really been feeling this way all along. I mean, I had an entire summer on her porch to prove it. But I wasn't dumb; I knew the real reason; someone must have been teasing her about liking a "Wardlaw boy"—a Wardlaw boy with zero fly, Hip Hop clothes, at that (because this was before Ralph Lauren was popular in the hood). And believe me, as much as Wardlaw got dissed in our neighborhood, it only needed to be one or two people teasing her. Even Melinda had her reputation to protect.

So although I knew all about that great "road to success" Wardlaw had me on and all that jazz, the fact remained that now at thirteen years old, I didn't care nearly as much about success as I did about identity and acceptance. And as amazing as my classmates' homes and such were, I once again realized that "my world"—my neighborhood and all that was in it—was still my everything, and where I needed that acceptance the most.

On the streets it was much deeper than a popularity thing. It was a manhood thing. While being a "man" at Wardlaw meant showcasing your ambition, intelligence, and great resources, on the streets it was all about showcasing your bravado—achieving that balance of being cool as ice and tough as rocks—and getting that R-E-S-P-E-C-T. And as I now felt that I lacked both "ice" and "rocks," I couldn't help but conclude that I wasn't a real man, no matter how well I was doing at Wardlaw. I may have looked like everyone else as I rode my wheelie down the street, busted the latest dance moves, or "busted out" in the latest North Jersey slang, but the truth was that inwardly, I often felt like a square among circles.

So with all this being said, as we began reading Nathaniel Hawthorne's classic, *The Scarlet Letter* (the story of a woman who'd been ostracized by her community for committing adultery and was forced to wear a scarlet letter "A" as a badge of disgrace), I had come to recognize Wardlaw as my own scarlet letter. That's why, as nice as Wardlaw's athletic gear was, you couldn't have paid me three hundred dollars to wear that stuff near the projects. Not to mention that whenever people asked me where I went to school, I tried to change the subject.

For a school that was giving me so much, it sure felt like it was taking so much away. To me, Wardlaw was taking away my street identity that I so freely relished back when I was younger and it didn't matter where you went to school. So where did I truly belong, then? Because at the same time, there were definitely enough subtle instances of racism at Wardlaw that painfully reminded me that I wasn't fully accepted there, either.

So there I was, searching for identity and acceptance while trapped in this limbo between two worlds. And in my mind, it was all Wardlaw's fault. So "that school" is all it became to me—even after my name had just been immortalized in gold-leaf calligraphy as the school's "best all-around student." Besides, with more trips to the assistant headmaster's office than I could count, pretty soon I wouldn't be much for Wardlaw to be bragging about, anyway.

Eighth grade marked some major changes for me, as there were major changes going on all around. For starters, there was this brand new drug on the
scene called "crack." And the way it hit the streets, you would've thought the
ground might crack. I mean, just its cryptic name alone made the craziest
images come to mind, like giant snapping jaws or coffins with rotting bones.

I can even remember when Mom first told us about it. Since Mom
taught night-classes for high school dropouts as a second job from time to
time, she usually knew the latest news on the streets before other adults.
So one evening, as Brett and I were watching TV in our bedroom, Mom
poked her head in like she had just received an intelligence briefing.

"Boys, watch out! Because there's this new drug on the streets called
crack, and it's making people act crazy! Don't go anywhere near it!"

"Making people act crazy?" I couldn't help but revisit some of our
home robberies: like the time our back door got shredded to splinters
with an axe or hatchet, or that day when it felt like someone was staring
at me and Brett through the slits of our closed closet door before we ran
out and got Jalil. Was crack responsible for those times?

However, my thoughts mainly went to that shady-looking, bony
dude who we always kept an eye out for; and not just because he walked
up and down our block all day long, either. There was something weird
about his every move: the unnecessary fast walking, the way he was so
jittery and paranoid, the perpetual sheen of sweat on his dark-brown
face. Then there was that night when he was fast-walking back and forth
in front of our dark house. Mom, Brett, and I stooped down below
Mom's bedroom window, studying him like our lives depended on it.
And Mom's scream almost burst my eardrum when he suddenly veered
across our lawn as if heading straight for our front door, only to veer back
towards the street again as if something were controlling him. Well if that
wasn't crack, then I didn't know what was.

More so, it wasn't too long after Mom had briefed us that night before I was standing on the corner of our "nice" block, using the tip of my
sneaker to investigate something I'd never seen before. It was an empty
plastic vile with a little red cap on it, almost looked like the missing piece
to a toy. But this was crack—the devil's toy; something that made even
the toughest men start whining like babies.

And beyond our own home invasion drama, crack's effects were
spreading everywhere. For one, the types of cars my homies and I grew

up coveting were now getting fancier, with rims and "kits" that made them flashier. Their stereo systems were getting much louder, and the ones buying all this stuff were getting much younger. And as for that dog-eat-dog pressure that always gnawed at us? Well, crack would now escalate everything to pitbull-eat-pitbull—ushering in a degree of fast money, covetousness, and selfishness that the streets had never seen before. Crack was the new thermostat, and we could all feel the heat.

In fact, Deuce's mom was on crack. But since this was still in the beginning of it all, nobody even knew what to do about it. All we knew was that Deuce sure missed his mommy, and that before becoming an addict on the streets of New York, she had enjoyed a successful career at ABC News.

▲▼▲▼▲

It was also around this time that Greg's stepfather (Jalil's dad) took us to see a movie like nothing we had ever seen. For while *The Karate Kid* had everyone exiting the theatre with this dose of happy adrenaline, this movie had everyone leaving the theatre with a rush of evil adrenaline, and a bit of gloom, too. The movie was *Colors*—a raw story about South Central L.A.'s notorious Blood and Crip gangs.

Well from the opening scene, where two warring gangs are "bum-rushing" the bars of adjacent jail cells to get at each other, it was clear that this would be like no other film. For South-Central was like no other place. And until this point, we "East coasters" thought California was just a place full of multiracial, breakdancing parties like in the movie *Breakin'*. But *Colors* was depicting nothing short of an urban Vietnam.

At the same time, however, we still loved it all. Because even though this was taking place on the other side of the country, it was still part of our beloved Hip Hop culture. I mean, even famed, Queens rapper Roxanne Shanté was on the movie's soundtrack. So we just nodded to the beats, cheered for the bad guys, and booed the cops like normal. However, with scene after scene of these young dudes in their red or blue plaid shirts getting blasted in cold blood, and with guns in more shapes and sizes than I had ever seen, a sobering fear started creeping over me. It was a fear similar to what you felt when you thought about Russia and the threat of a nuclear war.

"Man, what if this gang-war stuff comes over to Jersey one day?" I began wondering. Because here I was, watching how even kids my age were gang banging. And it wasn't kids from some far away place like Africa or India that I couldn't relate to, either. These were American urban kids, just like me. The very ones I would've grown up riding bikes and swapping candy with if I had been raised in South Central, myself.

There was plenty of crack in the movie, too. And while the whole movie was drop-dead serious, the scenes with the "crackheads"—as we had already learned to call them—had the whole theater cracking up. For we were already learning to laugh at the craziness of Plainfield's crack addicts as well. Needless to say, we left the theater that day changed in a lot of ways. Without even realizing it, we had become even more calloused to fighting, more calloused to bloodshed, and more calloused to crack. Saddest of all, we had become even more calloused to seeing our own die senselessly.

Then, around the same time as *Colors*, South Central's first major rap group hit the scene, bringing more of their West Coast streets to life. Demanding everyone's attention, the rap group's name was N.W.A.— "N*gg*z With Attitude." And though we all knew of the gang-bangin' by now, and had even heard of the injustices of the LAPD towards minorities, we all got shocked and charged as N.W.A. had the nerve to come out with a song called "$#*! the Police." So we'd listen to them from time to time, and couldn't help but get a little angry. (Even though their lyrics had so many curse words that no adult walking by would even let us play that for a minute.) But that was quite all right, because on the East Coast, there was a whole different thing emerging.

For starters, one must understand that this was when the East coast—meaning New York City and North Jersey, in particular—was still the absolute "ground zero" of Hip Hop. In other words, it was the place where Hip Hop's latest trends were invented and etched in stone. So while South Central was busy with its gang banging stuff, and a rapper named Luke Skywalker and the South was busy with their strip-dancing stuff, East Coasters were getting into this thing called "conscious rap." Heavily intellectual, but yet still as fly as any Marley Marl party song, it made you want to dance and study at the same time. It made some want to protest against racial injustice. And then for others, it even made them want to start a race riot. Basically, "conscious rap" would become the black nationalist music of Generation X.

Among the pioneers of this "conscious rap" were the Jungle Brothers, debuting with their first album *Straight Out the Jungle*. And while rappers like Big Daddy Kane and Kool G. Rap would continue profiling in their Gucci jumpsuits and thick rope-chains, it was revolutionary how the Jungle Brother's came on the scene wearing nothing but white undershirts, khakis, and safari-hats. And there was one last thing they wore, too: a black-stringed necklace with a palm-sized black leather circle that had the African continent on it in red, green, and yellow strips of leather. "The African medallion" it was called, and it became the symbol of this entire movement. And for this "conscious" medallion, many playboys were now putting away their flashy jewelry. So now you had some of the roughest dudes walking down the street suddenly talking about being "Afrocentric" and "knowing thyself," and even deep stuff like "Revisionist History."

Then, almost in the same month, came another group called Public Enemy with their bold-titled album *It Takes A Nation of Millions To Hold Us Back*. Unapologetically raw, and looking like they were ready for a revolution (their crew stayed dressed in army fatigues), Public Enemy's brutal honesty towards everything was letting our generation know that if you felt like racial injustices of the past were being glossed over, you actually had the right to talk about it. And of course Public Enemy's music videos only added more fuel to the fire, showing black and white footage of blacks getting blasted by fire hoses as white officers dragged helpless women down the street by their hair—just for demanding equality.

Then, in that very same year, there arose another herald of "consciousness"— some homeless man turned rapper, who every Hip Hopper immediately started calling a prophet. His name was KRS-One (an acronym for "Knowledge Reigns Supreme Over Nearly Everybody). And bringing that same militance as Public Enemy, on his album cover he imitated the famous photo of Malcolm X peeking through his window curtains while holding a gun. Only KRS-One was holding an uzi.

It was groups like these that ushered in what became known as the "Knowledge of Self Movement," and how quickly this wildfire raged across America. It even had blacks in the suburbs getting militant! And once Spike Lee dropped his highly controversial film, *Do The Right Thing*—with Public Enemy's, "Fight the Power" as the soundtrack—even

The White House began paying attention to what was brewing in America's young ghetto minds.

However, as certain as a lot of this stuff was, the Knowledge of Self Movement would also cause some blacks to become racist themselves. Because once all this awareness and righteous indignation had been stirred up, some had no clear-cut, positive avenue to channel such strong emotions. So pent-up hatred would just come naturally—as can happen to anyone from an unjustly oppressed people group.

Not to mention that many whites were scared stiff over this whole thing. And Public Enemy knew this too, and even flaunted it right in people's faces with the title of their next album—*Fear Of A Black Planet*. And once Brooklyn rap group X Clan dropped lyrics asking "how could polar bears swing on vines with gorillas," Afrocentrism in Hip Hop took off to a whole new level. Needless to say, 1989 and 1990 were some heavy years.

▲ ▼ ▲ ▼ ▲

Now as much as I loved jamming to the Jungle Brothers and Public Enemy, I had this dilemma that I couldn't stop tussling over: how to reconcile this new surge of "pro-blackness" all around me, with me being so light-skinned? Not to mention that by this point in my life, if anyone on the streets had asked about me ever dancing to pop music at a Bar Mitzvah, or liking white girls, I would've denied it. For I was a burgeoning black militant now, and the hood could never know that I enjoyed that other world. But back to this issue of my skin tone.

Well, all this "Mother Land" talk with everyone around me so rooted in their blackness all of a sudden, had me wishing that I looked different. And how ironic that while slavery and even post-slavery society once put such a premium on lighter skin, this Knowledge of Self Movement now had some light-skinned blacks wishing they were darker. Because there were now many rhymes in our music inferring that the darker your complexion, the closer to Africa and more "down" you really were.

And for me, it went even beyond my skin tone. Because while there were tons of light-skinned blacks who at least still had "black people hair," my dark-brown, straight-but-curly, thick "Indian hair" had me looking more like the sixth member of Latino boy-band Menudo or *The Karate Kid's* Ralph Macchio. But man, how I'd dream of looking more "black" sometimes as I stood gazing in the mirror. I mean, this Knowledge of Self Movement was so powerful. What a chance to cash in on some tremendous racial pride—and most of all, establish some hard-core identity?

Not to mention how this movement seemed like the perfect fit for me in every way. For unlike blasting guns the way they did in South Central (which I clearly didn't do), or rocking the freshest Nikes with a row of shiny gold teeth (which I clearly couldn't afford), this was finally something that was all about studying our people's true history and using your intellect—my strong point, for sure. Plus, thanks to Mom and the books she always kept around, I had been learning about African-American history ever since I could read. However, be that as it may, I still felt that without that darker skin tone—or at least "black people hair"—that my smarts just weren't enough. Thus, these were my burdensome reasonings as I walked my neighborhood streets at thirteen and fourteen years old.

Well for starters, I never paid much attention during those times when Mom gave guests that journey through our family's history. So no surprise that it never registered with me that my great-grandfather was Jewish, or that so much of Mom's family was Cherokee. So now that I finally wanted to know my "roots," one day I asked Mom.

"So Ma, what are we?"

"What?" She asked like I was speaking a foreign language. "What do you mean, what are we?"

"I mean, what are we? You know, what *are* we?"

"Oh, well Aaron . . . ," she paused to think, but then as if on second thought, stopped her pause short, "You're just black." And simple and plain was how she said it, too. As if we looked like every other black person.

"But we don't look 'black' though."

"Well, that's because we're mixed with Indian. But if anyone asks you, just say you're black." And that was that.

So next, I tried asking Dad. During one of our weekend visits with him, we were eating breakfast at one of our favorite diners, when a clothing tag happened to come off one of our coats, and coincidentally the brand name read "Cherokee." I spotted it and got excited.

"Hey Dad, we're Cherokee too, right?"

"Well son, on your momma's side, you're Cherokee, but on my side, we're from the Lumbee tribe." Then he cut it short in the exact same way Mom did. "But if anyone asks, just say you're black."

Thus, there I was: this knowledge-thirsty kid with two parents who always knew so much about so much, but yet on this one topic, they both suddenly had the same, little amount to say. Now to their credit, they probably thought that I was still at that young age where the best explanation was often the easiest explanation. But if only they knew that as a young teenager in such a "pro-black" neighborhood as ours, I needed this talk even more than the birds and the bees!

So therefore, with no satisfying answers, I'd resort to suppressing it all—even suppressing this ever-so-slight trickle of self-hatred that was germinating from me not having that solid sense of identity that everyone else seemed to enjoy. So I just continued drinking down Public Enemy and studying my blackness, even though the man in the mirror looked like a straight Puerto Rican. And mind you, this was even back when Puerto Ricans were still considered a strange phenomenon in much of urban America (along with Africans too, for that matter). And unlike today's multi-cultural, "brown" society, this was still a time when you were either black or white, period. Nothing in between. So I felt quite alone and often misunderstood.

But I must say that it was sweet how I could count on Plainfield's cluster of Puerto Ricans to make me feel special. I mean, they were so convinced that I was one of them, that they'd never even bother asking me what part of the island my family was from. And as the tough ones on the corner would call me over to them, wink at me like some big *hermanos*, and even offer me some money for my pocket, the thought would cross my mind of just going ahead and joining them. I mean after all, a lot of blacks had begun lumping me in with them, anyway. Like the time that one black girl walked by me on the street, looked at my shirt with Africa on it, and mumbled, "You better take that off and get the one with Puerto Rico!" However, deep inside, I knew it would've been too much faking on my part to go Puerto Rican.

So back to the big question: Why might my Indian-looking dad and Indian-looking mom both be so quick to tell me I was "just black?" Well, though I had no idea why back then, perhaps there were a couple of reasons: For one, centuries of "Manifest Destiny" ideology and distorting historians had mangled and erased so much of Native Americans' history—particularly tribes from the Southeast, because of slavery and all. With the advent of an economy built on African slave labor, Indians quickly became viewed as nothing more than "weeds" to be driven to infertile reservation lands to live or die on—nobody cared. Case in point, in the 1830's, President Andrew Jackson personally authorized thousands of civilians to take up weapons and force the Cherokees and other tribes to walk a thousand miles from the Carolinas to Oklahoma— where countless women, children, and the elderly died as they were refused by every town they passed through.

Therefore, in light of this legislated genocide of sorts, is it any surprise at all that generations later, you'd have Indian descendants (like us) having to say stuff like, "Well we really don't know where our relatives came from exactly; [so-and-so] just showed up from some reservation one day"? Quite a frustrating brick wall to hit when you're supposed to be proudly relaying your family history. And this was also why, if you happened to have a good amount of black lineage as well, it could be easier to just follow that one instead.

And perhaps there was another reason why both Mom and Dad could so easily resort to saying we were "just black." Back in these same times, the entire East coast had become even more polarized between whites and blacks with the infamous "one drop rule"—that said if you had even one drop of "Negro blood" then you were black, no matter what. And this applied even if you were Indian. So in the South you were really either white or "colored," period.

But, the bottom line was that I looked more Indian than black. So when I claimed to be "just black" on the streets (as someone pretty much always asked me), some would look back at me like I had two heads.

"C'mon man, you can't be all black!"

"Yup, I'm just black, man!"

"Man, you can't be all black! Stop lyin'!"

"Man, I ain't lyin'!"

And more than just having two heads, they'd also look at me like I was the most confused person on the planet, and man, that hurt. And though this hot topic wouldn't even come up that often, when you're just a vulnerable kid looking for identity, even a mere few occurrences can sting like two hundred.

But then came one of my favorite discoveries. In fact, it came on a day when I was so bored that I was actually up in our squirrel-plagued attic snooping through old, dusty boxes. Well as I opened one of the last ones, to my sheer joy, I stumbled upon all of Dad's black history paperbacks from his civil rights days at Seton Hall University. He had obviously forgotten they were there. And there were scores of them, too—many even in their original printings when they were sold for as cheap as fifty cents. There was *Black Power*, by Stokely Carmichael, *The Autobiography of Malcolm X*, Henry David Thoreau's *Civil Disobedience*, and almost every book Dr. King had ever penned.

So that was the day I started sitting in our attic and reading for hours on end. And whenever I'd come across anything Dad had underlined or scribbled a star next to, I'd read it over and over before underlining it again with my own pen.

And so my search continued.

▲ ▼ ▲ ▼ ▲

Then, there was Black Gold—Plainfield's "Afrikan Kultural Arts Center" (spelled with "K's" instead of "C's" to connote thoughts of strength) on the corner of Plainfield's West Fifth Street and Watchung Avenue. Not only was Black Gold where you could get those black African medallions like Public Enemy and the Jungle Brothers wore, but it also had all the cowry-shell necklaces, incense, books, and essential oils your heart desired. And if you had the money to spend, you could even buy authentic African masks and hats, like the ones hanging in our living room.

Black Gold's owner was Brother Hassan, an even-tempered man who looked the same age as Mom. While his store also had every dashiki tunic and walking staff you could imagine, you never knew what you'd see Brother Hassan wearing on a given day. More so, with Afrocentrism experiencing the boom that it was, it was nothing to open our local newspaper and see a huge photo of Brother Hassan in the Arts section, holding a Zulu warrior shield and spear with no smile, only the confidence of a man who looked like he just killed a lion.

In fact, Brother Hassan got so much respect on the streets that, whenever he was out taking his usual 2,000 paces after a meal—the same way Egyptian pharaohs once did—all he had to do was just look at guys on the corner using foul language, and they'd start apologizing on the double. Then, after staring at them for a moment longer, he'd finally nod "peace" and continue counting his paces, his evenly shorn dreads swaying from side to side as he walked. He had this lightness on his feet that showed that he really was an expert in African martial arts (the other proof being the muscular black men with gym bags that were always going into Black Gold's basement).

Now Brother Hassan rarely gave more than a pleasant nod to people in passing, but that all changed once he could see that you sincerely wanted to learn something. So as I started going to Black Gold in my hunger for knowledge, Brother Hassan would come alive every time. Plus, he already knew Mom from all the things she had bought from him over the years, and he had a lot of respect for her. Black Gold was like a museum. And with the number of hours I began spending there, you would've thought I was a museum employee. I mean, if I was Daniel-San then Brother Hassan was Mr. Miyagi.

"Hassan, who's Marcus Garvey?"

"Ah," he'd smile like my question was a refreshing tonic, "my young brother, you need to know about him and his movement in the 1920's. And he was straight out of Harlem too! Yes, I want you to read that!" And of course I'd read anything he recommended.

Then there was the defining moment I had been waiting for! It was when Hassan handed me my first African medallion. But not without first giving me an invigorating explanation.

"You see, young brother, the African continent on this medallion bears the three colors: red, yellow, and green. The red is for the blood that's been shed through injustice!" He paused for a couple of seconds with pain in his eyes and then continued. "The yellow is for all the gold the Mother Land has in the ground. The green is for the lush vegetation and beautiful rain forests that still exist there. Now the white man and Hollywood call it "jungle" and whatnot, but that's an ignorant term. It's called rainforest, my brother . . . rainforest! So you see, all of this is why Africa is called the 'Mother Land.' Then lastly, my young brother, the black all around this medallion is for the color of our people."

And as his verbal "rite of passage" was now over, he handed me my medallion. Hence, Brother Hassan—Plainfield's leading authority on "blackness"—was showing me full-fledged acceptance, and it felt super. Not to mention that he had never once asked me about my racial make-up, the way some others curiously did. It was as if he understood all the complex facts already.

So needless to say, I felt safe in Black Gold. And while it was definitely a place where "cool" people browsed in and out, it was more so a place where serious intellectuals came. Even whites were more than welcome there. So as I'd be sitting there studying something deep, it was nothing for some random adult to look over and smile at what this "young man" was doing. Many would even assume I worked there and start asking me about all the books and regalia.

"Now, my young brother, you're also Native American, right?"

Whether Brother Hassan knew that from just looking at me, or from having talked with Mom before, or both, I didn't know, but he continued schooling me. "Well, my brother, you'll notice that I said 'Native-American,' and not 'Indian.' Because there was nothing Indian about America! You see, 'Colombo' thought he was in India when he got here, so he started calling the natives 'Indians.'" And Brother Hassan always stressed his purposeful mispronunciation of Columbus' name, making it clear that he didn't respect the venerated explorer one bit.

"Well, anyway, young brother, are you aware that whites purposely gave blankets that they knew were infected with smallpox to your Native American people?" This was the first time someone had ever shared anything about my Indian people's history with me, so I was all ears. So we'd talk and talk, and I'd learn and learn, and Mom loved it that I was choosing to chill in Black Gold as opposed to playing Nintendo with my homies all day.

So talk about complex! Here was this Puerto Rican-looking urban kid walking down Wardlaw's hallways, decked in Ralph Lauren's preppiest tie while wearing two or three African medallions around my neck, chewing on some kosher lox from one of my Jewish classmates. Call me whatever you wanted, but thanks to Brother Hassan, I still had a head full of knowledge that even my history teachers didn't know much about.

▲▼▲▼▲

Now completely unbeknownst to me, there was something much deeper going on here than me just wanting to know so much about history, kinship lines, and where I came from. There was this insatiable hunger for something more; that's why I'd sometimes look at all the books on Brother Hassan's endless shelves and just wish I could gobble them down in one, impassioned bite. Deeper than racial identity, it was like my very soul was looking for identity.

IX

"God . . . ?"

I was walking home from the projects one evening, and I couldn't help but sing. And at the top of my lungs, too.

> I've got this joy, joy, joy, joy, down in my heart,
> (Where?) Down in my heart,
> (Where?) Down in my heart,
> I've got this joy, joy, joy, joy, down in my heart,
> (Where?) Down in my heart to stay!

What got into me? Had I finally lost it? I mean, nobody did anything like this on the streets, not unless they wanted to get picked on, or maybe even jumped. But yet, for one of the first times in my life, I didn't care what anyone else thought, and it felt so freeing. So at the top of my lungs I continued:

> And I'm so happy, so very happy,
> I've got the love of Jesus in my heart.
> And I'm so happy, so very happy,
> I've got the love of Jesus in my heart!

Something supernatural was going down. I mean, here I was sincerely singing about God, and to God, right in the middle of crazy Liberty Street—the same strip where every drug dealer cruised and every knucklehead cussed. And I still wasn't done:

> And if the devil doesn't like it he can sit on a tack,
> Sit on a tack, sit on a tack,

And if the devil doesn't like it he can sit on a tack,
Sit on a tack to stay!
And I'm so happy, so very happy . . .

I didn't know much about the devil (though I swore I'd seen demons in our front yard before), yet the words of this song felt even bigger than the Evil. And at this moment, I was so very happy. For as surely as Plainfield urban life had baptized me into burden-hood, I now felt burden-free. Even Miss Girty-Girt would've gotten a nice hello if she had scooted past me.

Now I wasn't just making up the words to this song; nor had I learned it from Public Enemy, The Jungle Brothers, or Brother Hassan. Actually, I had just finished learning it in my catechism class at St. Mary's Church, right across from the bodega and the projects. Although we only went to church once a year on Easter, we were in fact Catholic, or "Roman Catholic" as I'd hear adults say. And the reason I was now going to these catechism classes was that it was time for that huge event that came in every young Catholic's life: Confirmation.

It would be fitting to ask if I even believed in God. Well, of course! I mean, didn't everyone? Plus, wouldn't God strike you dead with lightning if you said you didn't? And what did I think God was like? Well, I wasn't really sure. But for one thing, I knew He wasn't like Zeus, Hades, Ares, Aphrodite, or the rest of those human-like Greek gods we learned about in fifth grade. Rather, I always imagined God to be much more loving, even-keeled, and consistent. In fact, I sort of pictured Him being something like Dad during those rare moments when he'd get tickled all over and just hug me tight for no reason at all.

But even with all this singing down Liberty Street, believe it or not, I still had no clue what my Confirmation was about. All I knew was that it was something really "holy," as they'd say. Though it wasn't my nun's fault that I was so ignorant; because that sweet, little Puerto Rican nun was all business when it came to teaching us our lessons. Neither was it Mom's fault; because she always made sure I dropped whatever I was doing when it was time for my evening classes. Lastly, it wasn't any of the Puerto Rican girls' fault, either; because although this was still when Puerto Ricans only occupied a small part of Plainfield, my catechism class was full of them. And some were so pretty that I could just stare at them for the entire hour without getting bored.

So then, whose fault was it that I didn't know diddly about my Confirmation? Well, it was all my fault. For while Mom could at least attest that I'd always head up Liberty Street for my class, I'd rarely make it inside St. Mary's. In fact, I'd usually end up right across the street. And I wouldn't be out there sweet-talking one of those fly Puerto Rican girls, either (though I would've loved too). Actually, I'd be engaged in something else: "crackin'."

Having nothing to do with the drug, crackin' was when you and another person would take turns making fun of anything and everything about each other—especially each other's "mommas"—and it was best when conducted publicly, loudly, and most arrogantly. And even though the old folks would sometimes yell out their windows for us to take all our "fighting" someplace else, crackin' was hardly fighting. It was pure hood entertainment, and one of our favorite pastimes. Plus, all the laughter acted as both a stress reliever and even a type of community builder. I mean, when else would total strangers stand huddled together on a street corner and laugh with one voice for over an hour? Best of all, crackin' was absolutely free, so anybody could afford front row seats.

Now with all that being said, there was one major condition: with all these people giving you their undivided attention, your behind had better be hilarious. Because while being known for your crackin' skills could be just as cool as being known for your fighting, on the flip side, being known for stinking at crackin' could be the same as being known for getting your butt kicked. So while I wasn't known for being a fighter, I was definitely gaining respect for my crackin'. And on these hard-to-earn streets, that was no small deal.

So while the nun was teaching the rest of my class in that second floor classroom, I'd be right across the street—working on my street "confirmation." And as a swarm of people gathered around once again, it was time for yet another battle in the ongoing saga between me and my arch rival, Jay Jordan, a fellow fourteen-year-old from the projects. With this Eddie Murphy candor that had you ready to laugh before he even opened his mouth, Jay was hardly an amateur. In fact, as the crackin' prince of the projects, he could verbally body-slam you so badly, that for years to come, people might still only refer to you by the butt of one of Jay's jokes about you.

However, I was no amateur, either. I had long since discovered the use of comedy as a way to keep my mind off things that were too weighty and crazy to be dwelling on. And the more stressful my life became, the funnier I got. I'm sure it was a similar thing with the secret behind Jay's funniness as well—along with most other hood comedians, for that matter.

So as the streetlight above the corner of West Sixth and Liberty began flickering on, and the crowd stood poised and all ears, "ding-ding" went the bell.

Jay: "Yo, yo, check this out y'all! Yo, this n*gg*'s mom is SO dumb, she called me up and asked me the recipe for ice!" Everyone laughed.

And the thing that made Jay's cracks so funny was how he'd keep this straight face like everything he said was true. I mean, you would've thought my mom had really just finished pestering him about some ice.

Me: "Okay, okay . . ." The crowd really on the edge of their seats now. And I'd better be funny, or it would be "boo" for sure. "Yo, yo, this cat's so poor, that I went to his house for dinner, right? His momz put just ONE bean on my plate. So I ate it, and asked for another. She said, 'Dag Jay, your friend is greedy!'"

"Yo, yo, your momz got glass legs, talkin' 'bout, 'pass the Windex, I'm ashy!'

"Man, your momz' be chillin' in that big black bag in Miss Girty-Girt's cart, talkin' 'bout, 'Yo Girt, we need to put a knockin' [stereo] system up in this piece!" That line brought explosive laughter.

Then after the momma-jokes, we'd always go right to each other's clothes.

"Yo, Remi, Remi! Man, look at Jay's shiny-behind *Courier-News* delivery jacket! Yo, he got on a Courier-News starter jacket!"

"What about you, man? Look at them blue Burger King slacks you be rockin'!"

And because Remi had the craziest laugh of all, he's the one you wanted to win over. I mean, the right joke would have Remi convulsing like someone was riddling his body with bullets. Then after sprawling across the hood of some random car, he'd stumble over to whoever the joke was on and fall over just in time to force the person to catch him, just so he could jab his pointer finger into their cheek while still fighting for his breath. When Remi laughed, everyone laughed.

But as I said, Jay wasn't the crackin' prince of the projects for nothing.

"Okay, okay, Aaron's real funny, right? But yo, look at this n*gg*'s hair, though. Yo, don't this cat look like Ricky Ricardo from 'I Love

Lucy,' out this piece?" (As he then began imitating Ricky Ricardo coming into his apartment from a day at work.)

Well, the whole block went bananas off that one, me included. And while there were plenty of times when crack-fights escalated into fist-fights, that really only happened when one person wasn't funny and started getting extra sensitive from having others laugh at him so much. But Jay and I were both too skilled for that to happen.

So after more than an hour of the crowd voting back and forth with their laughter, we finally stopped and gave each other a pound; but not without publicly warning each other about what was gonna happen the very next time we saw each other. Sometimes Jay and I would bump into each other while we were alone and still tossed a few jokes back and forth, just to keep our tongues razor sharp. And believe it or not, crackin' was pretty much the extent of our friendship. But what a true friendship it was. We had this deep respect for the other's wit and humor, and no instigating crowd ever came between us.

So I'd always keep my crackin' game hilarious. And as I'd walk into the bodega after another showdown, it was nothing to overhear two older dudes who I didn't even know saying, "Yo, see that kid right there? Yo, that's one funny n*gg*h! Wassup, my man? Yo, you be keepin' us rollin', man!"

"Thanks." I'd nod back to them before ordering my brown bag of candy. In this world of the dog-eat-dog—where disrespect could be lurking around the corner at any moment—every bit of encouragement helped. Especially when it came from older dudes from the projects.

However, there was nothing at all funny when I soon learned that the sweet, little Puerto Rican nun wouldn't allow me to participate in the confirmation ceremony because I had missed too many classes. Forgetting all about crackin', it was now time for beggin'!

"You gotta let me get confirmed! Please? Sister, my whole family's been waiting for this . . . My grandma even bought my gold chain and crucifix already!"

And as I said that, she softened a little, because every Catholic knew how serious it was to get that crucifix from your grandmother.

"Please? I'll do whatever it takes!"

She looked at me some more, and then finally smiled and said okay. *Whew!* Mom would've had a heart attack if I told her that I wasn't getting confirmed. The nun just told me that I couldn't miss any more classes, and that I'd have to come on the special retreat she had planned for the following week.

So the following week, we all met outside of St. Mary's, where we packed into two large vans and drove off; away from the corner where Jay and I earned our claims to fame, away from the other corners where other young teenagers were already selling crack, and away from Plainfield altogether, as we headed into the mountains of Berkley Heights thirty minutes away. We pulled into the long driveway of what appeared to be a very special place—a sacred place, even. There was the most amazing view, and acres of gorgeous greenery in every direction. And since it was spring, every flower was blossoming to make the whole thing like a mini paradise.

The feeling of the place was serene, and we climbed out of the vans like we already knew to be super quiet. After taking in more of the scenery, our sweet, little nun led us into a large building in the middle of the grounds. It was set up almost like a church, with pews, kneeling benches, and all, just no statues, no crucifixes, no altar, and no priests. Only a large glass wall at the front providing you with a view of that same gorgeous greenery.

I always knew there was something special about this sweet, little nun; and I would never forget what she had us do next. She addressed us in a reverential but excited tone, and began talking to us like God was right next to her.

"Now, class I want you to spread out and find your own place in here. Then I want you to kneel down and pray to God for a while. Tell Him whatever is on your heart."

Telling God what was on my heart? Wow, this was the first time anyone had given me instruction on talking to God. I mean, all I had ever known was stepping into the little confession booth with its red velvet and frankincense, where I'd then mumble through the black screen to the unseen priest about how many times I had talked "fresh" to Mom; only for the unseen priest to then tell me how many Our Fathers and Hail Marys to recite and that I was forgiven. So now, was I really being permitted to talk to God—just me and Him, without Mary's, or any saint's or priest's help? This was revolutionary! Yet for something so revolutionary, it felt so right and beautiful.

So as the sweet little nun excused herself from the large room, I got down on the kneeling bench, placed my forehead against my hands, and began. Surprisingly, it flowed so naturally—especially as I had never really prayed before, other than saying "grace" before a meal.

"God, I just really, really, really want to know You! I just want to know You, that's all. I really want to know You! I really want to know You so bad! I really just want to know You!" And as repetitive as my prayer was, it was coming straight from the heart; my pathos matching the most tender moment of any movie.

Well, after we all prayed some more, it was time for us to head back to Plainfield. (I almost didn't want to leave.) And though we took the same route back, my heart was now ready to head in a different direction. I wanted to be a new man now.

And why did I now want this change, anyway? Well, if you had asked me back then, I wouldn't have known how to put it into words; but the reality was that I had been through enough by now, to know that I needed some type of healing and wholeness. More so, I knew that beyond how mean and perverted I could be, there was something about myself overall that simply "wasn't nice." (Basically, my same "jacked-up" issues I had related to Prince's character with in *Purple Rain*.) So at fifteen years old, some sweet change sounded like a great idea. And what a better place for change than church?

So a week later, there I was again, interrupting my ninth grade English class like a jerk. Only this time, I actually wasn't trying to be a jerk.

"Hey Mr. Vozar! Mr. Vozar? Listen, I got something to say."

Now by this point at Wardlaw's upper school, I was quite popular. But mainly because of the popular black upperclassmen from Plainfield, who had long since spread the word that I was their "little brother." Then along with being popular, I was cocky, too, earning a reputation among my teachers as one who was smart, but overly-social and prone to obnoxious outbursts of comedy, all of which kept my classmates rolling, and me and some teachers butting heads over whose classroom it was anyway.

So there I was, interrupting English class. But at least this time I wasn't getting up and breakdancing like I had done in the middle of Mr. Biddle's history class.

"Well Mr. Vozar, guess what?" I was making the announcement for my entire class to hear as well. "You're not gonna have to worry about me giving you a hard time any more!"

And what I was saying was so different from my usual banter that Mr. Vozar just had to know where in the world this was going.

"Okay, Aaron. Now please tell me, why might that be?"

And with zero sarcasm, I said it like I could taste it already.

"Well, Mr. Vozar, this weekend is my Catholic Confirmation and it's gonna make me a new man! So I'm not gonna be misbehaving anymore. Come Monday, you won't hear a peep out of me!"

"So, not a peep, Aaron, huh?" He was definitely curious, but doubtful still.

"Nope, not one." I wasn't doubtful at all. He'd see it.

▲ ▼ ▲ ▼ ▲

That momentous Sunday finally arrived. And of course, Mom was up extra early, dressed in her best and smiling big. And of course, she had gotten me a new Ralph Lauren oxford to wear with my blazer. We may have only gone to church once a year, but my Confirmation was just as big a deal as my seventh grade graduation at Wardlaw. Momma was the first one to pull into our driveway in her dark blue Mercedes with its 80's dark blue interior, and she so proudly pulled my gold chain and crucifix from her trench coat pocket. So after taking a few pictures in our front yard, Momma drove us all to St. Mary's Church. Everything felt special already. I mean, even Liberty Street and the projects seemed more peaceful.

We met up at the church with all my aunts, my faithful godparents, and of course, Dad. Some of my neighborhood friends had decided to come as well, I guess curious to see what this talk about me changing was all about. In no time, the ceremony was underway, and it was more than your usual mass. The organs played extra long, the priest read extra Latin between songs, and you had extra people dipping their hands in holy water and genuflecting once they found a pew to cram into. And in the front pews of the church were me and my mostly Puerto Rican classmates, all of us dressed in our best.

But amidst all the hard-to-follow liturgy, and even my own distracting thoughts of all the money I knew my family would be giving me in those envelopes, I hadn't forgotten what I was there for. In fact, I was now wanting this change more than ever. So as the main part of the mass finally arrived, we rose to our feet just as we had practiced beforehand, and formed a line in front of the priest who was now standing at the base of the altar.

I stood tall—nervous, but more so excited. I even studied my classmates who went before me so I wouldn't do anything wrong when it was my turn. I mean, this was it!

However, I quickly found that there was nothing for me to do wrong. Because when it was my turn, the priest simply smiled, repeated something to me, and with no room for me to do anything but smile back, he put some fragrant oil on my forehead. And that concluded my Confirmation. But that was okay, I guess, because it still felt like something special had happened. I mean suddenly, I felt more mature and austere. And afterwards, as my friends ran up to me wanting to be silly as normal, I had this new disdain for unnecessary silliness. So change really was mine, after all!

And where was this new power coming from, then? Well, I figured it must've been the fragrant oil that was still shiny as ever on my forehead. Therefore, I figured that to let more of this power in, all I had to do was let the oil fully absorb into my skin. Simple enough, right? So as I hugged all my relatives, I just made sure to keep everyone clear of my forehead.

But then, out of nowhere, my homie Chico, the one who always succeeded in being goofier than me, snuck up behind me, and as if he had been reading my mind, wiped the oil clear off my forehead with his stupid hand.

"What'cha doin', man?!"

Never mind keeping my composure in a holy place, I was mad enough to cut him off from being my friend for a whole year.

"Dag."

To be purely honest, however, the painful reality had been slowly setting in anyway: nothing had really changed in me after all. Not one bit. I was still the same old Aaron; and Chico's obnoxiousness only confirmed the inevitable.

I was crushed.

So I would still wear that gold crucifix Momma gave me. But when it got lost during one of my school football games, I wouldn't sigh much at all. And as for the Bible Mom had given me to commemorate the day, apart from the sweet words she penned on the opening page, I never bothered reading a single verse from it. Besides, hadn't I heard some-where on the streets that Christianity was just some "white man's reli-gion" anyway?

But little did I know that it was only non-biblical traditions that had failed me on this day—not the beautiful Bible itself. A classic example of "so close, but yet so far." If someone had only told me that in that very Bible (that I was now tossing to the back of my closet) were endless songs even sweeter than what I had sung so loudly on Liberty Street that day; how in that very Bible it spoke of true change and power, and how that power was actually a Person; and how in that very Bible, it gave proof of how that Person never lets anyone down when they look to Him. And that was my problem, I wasn't looking to Jesus, I was looking to religious tradition.

But again, all I knew was that I was crushed and now calloused to the whole thing. None of which was my fault, by the way. And boy, did Mr. Vozar get a headache and a half the next time we had class.

"Hey Aaron, I thought you said you were gonna be a new person come Monday?"

It was like he was talking to someone else. And ironically, we had just started reading William Golding's classic, *Lord of the Flies*—the novel about a bunch of British private school boys who got stranded on a de-serted island and slowly turned savage because of the evil that had been dormant in their hearts all along.

▲ ▼ ▲ ▼ ▲

So what would I do now? Well, the same thing I had learned to do with other letdowns in my life: I'd suppress it. I'd simply put my fragile heart back into my journey bag and continue my search for change and some type of answers for life, elsewhere. However, I wouldn't be alone on this lonely journey. For as I walked out of St Mary's large doors that early afternoon, it was as if this subconscious gang of allies latched onto me unawares. The "Isms" was who they were.

First, there was Deism, the view that there is a God, but that He simply made everything—including the laws of physics and biology and all—and now just sits aloof like an absentee landlord while the laws of science order everything, along with a capricious blend of luck. Then there was Deism's close cousin, Existentialism, the view that since there are no substantive answers to life's biggest questions—and since you only go around this merry-go-round once anyway—you should live it up to the fullest and then spit right in death's face. (Basically, Prince's ideology in his song, "1999.") And of course, Existentialism was never without his daughter, Hedonism, the view that all meaning to life is to be found in living for pure pleasure, by every stretch of the imagination. Lastly, there was Hedonism's tough, older brother, Humanism, the view that within man lies all that man needs to solve every problem and dilemma. Thus, "man" is man's own personal lord and savior.

So from that day forward, I'd be more open to the "Isms" influences than ever before. And the weirdest thing about them was that they didn't need to be understood or "believed in" to still have a major effect on your beliefs, thoughts, and actions—namely your worldview. But one thing was for certain, when they were all combined, what a "cocktail" they proved to be! A real "high on life" is what some might have called it.

And speaking of being "high," at fifteen years old, it wasn't long before I'd gain some other "friends" as well: And of this gang of wino-liquors, Mad Dog was the funniest; Brass Monkey, the craziest; Cool Breeze, the zaniest; and Cisco (the one called "liquid crack"), the slickest. And as for my young liver, it would be the sickest. Doggone stomach aches, feeling like someone had stabbed me dead in the belly.

And of course, none of the adults in my life knew about any of this. I was too good at playing the part of a "good kid." In fact, I was so good, that at times, I even ended up fooling myself—the heart being deceitful above all things. And what nobody would have ever imagined, was that long before my first buzz from that sweet poison, long before sucking in my first Newport, and long before I had fallen so much in love with the darkness, the course of my heart had already been set. And how scary that a kid can be doing all the right things, smiling all the right smiles, and answering with all the right answers, but yet still be enchanted by the Evil.

And speaking of "good kid," I soon got a job at Plainfield's Dairy Queen. Quite the thing to include on your college applications, as it displayed that "well-roundedness" that everyone looked for in a promising student. However, even while working hard there and earning raises left and right, it was still mainly about saving enough money for my first gold rope chain. And unlike that chain and crucifix I had gotten from Momma, I would guard this rope chain with my life.

So the time I was rocking my chain at a house party in Newark and caught word that the notorious South Orange Ave Posse ("SOAP") was planning to rob me, I quickly slipped it to this girl for safe keeping while the posse kept circling around me. I was playing with fire, but it still felt great to have a gold chain that others wanted so badly. Plus, as tricky as that night may have seemed back then, in retrospect it was like hiding a rattle from a newborn. Because I'd get a hundred times slicker than that. A hundred times darker, too.

But anyway, didn't I have some big test at Wardlaw to be studying for? Because Mom had been talking about Princeton and Yale since I was little (especially after the summer where she worked at Princeton in their admissions office).

Part II

Slipping
(into darkness)

X

THINKIN' OF A MASTER PLAN

Veni, Vidi, Vici: the Latin words bearing the simple but sufficient message that Caesar sent back to his senate and to his pregnant wife, Cleopatra: "I came; I saw; I conquered!"

Mrs. Cook, our Latin teacher, was a small, older woman with white hair and dated glasses. She was even one of the "originals," meaning she had attended the girls-only Hartridge School back before its merger with the boys-only Wardlaw. Mrs. Cook was consistently sweet, but she was also consistently naive. She just loved telling us about the good old "Hartridge days," back when they had such an honor system that they took their tests unsupervised across the campus lawn. But the only problem was that these simply weren't those days anymore, and she was far too trusting of us young success predators who stayed paranoid over our grades.

Well, it was my junior year now, and in Latin class we were translating Ovid's *Metamorphoses*, which described a "Golden Age" when righteous people had no need of law to restrain them from their sinful actions. In contrast, while translating these very pages of Ovid, we often cheated so badly that we should've been tarred and feathered right in the school parking lot.

Almost the entire class was in on it, too. After four years with Mrs. Cook, we had the whole thing mastered. We used the Xerox machine in the library to shrink Ovid down to palm-size, and perfected our coughs to cover the sound of passing cheat-sheets; and major thumbs-up to the one who'd zip through their test, walk up, and let Mrs. Cook correct it, then sit back down and pass it around like the holiday turkey. And like Nile crocs fighting over one wildebeest, we wouldn't hesitate to snatch it from another's desk if they took too long with it.

101

It was all about getting into the top universities. Along with senior year's first semester, junior year was when your grades mattered most. So while tennis, golf, and other extracurriculars like horseback riding and music were wonderful to toot your own horn about, at the end of the day, it all boiled down to your grade point average. So while our notebooks came in all different sizes and colors, there was one thing they all had in common: random spots in the margins where we were always calculating our current GPA in light of some test score. It was stressful at times (afternoon headaches, recurring nightmares of oversleeping for major tests, and bending our ears to overhear anything that might be added to our growing resource list), but we had long-since learned that if it wasn't stressful, then something wasn't right.

For Wardlaw had succeeded in making us into secular soldiers—soldiers with an appreciation for literary classics and iambic pentameter. Wardlaw never taught us to cheat; as our teachers checked our papers for even the most camouflaged plagiarisms. But somewhere along the stressful way, we just became soldiers in that area, too. Though we definitely knew when to cheat and when not to. Which is why in most cases we never even bothered. So in classes like advanced placement biology with Mr. Gould, the only solution was to study all night until you were delusional and giddy on only 60 minutes of sleep.

▲▼▲▼▲

By this point, my grades were in great shape. I was in all honors and even a few advanced placement classes, giving me the chance to earn some early college credits. And though my behavior in class was still wild from time to time, it was much more controlled than when I was in eighth and ninth grade—back when I was getting kicked out of class and suspended for a fight.

I had already checked with the assistant headmaster about whether colleges saw your high school detentions and suspension records. He assured me, "No, Aaron, they do not." Though I could tell a side of him wished they really did, just so he could have a quick fix for the nutty things I'd still do at times—like sneaking onto the school microphone and doing the "beat box" until all the black students came running into the auditorium like a party was starting.

By now, the teachers and administration came to the realization that just as some Wardlaw students were "metal heads" (with their long black trench coats, long dyed-black hair, and Iron Maiden and Metallica blasting from their cars in the school parking lot), I, in turn, was a "Hip Hop head," rocking my RUN D.M.C. Adidas jacket in place of a blazer, poofing my hair into the curliest "high-top fade," and strutting the hallways sucking on a baby pacifier, courtesy of Public Enemy's crazy trendsetter, Flavor Flav. And I must confess that I loved having that baby pacifier in my mouth.

Speaking of pacifiers, I was feeling rather pacified with my life for the moment as well. For starters, I no longer wanted to swap Wardlaw for Plainfield High, and now appreciated my private school education and all it was preparing me for. I mean, there were still those in the hood who might've viewed me as an "Uncle Tom" or a "sell-out"—because I was well-educated and could speak properly, like "Properly" was some foreign language like French or Swedish—but for the most part, I was able to ignore it.

Because I knew the deal by now. In a society where slaves were once forbidden to read under punishment of getting their thumbs chopped off, I was now reading some of the best literature in the world. And in a society where countless young urbanites were going AWOL as far as education was concerned, I was an endangered species for sure. And I could be more than a bit cocky about all this too, sauntering into study hall with my biology book as well as Dad's copy of *The Narrative of the Life of Frederick Douglas*, the escaped slave turned abolitionist and lecturer who had taught himself to read.

And by this point, I came to terms with my racial identity as "mixed" (Indian and black), and with great pride in both, I wouldn't hesitate to tell anyone who wanted to know. However, by now, the whole Knowledge of Self Movement had taken a back-burner to that classic, braggadocios, girl-gettin', money-makin' rap business that we were originally accustomed to. So while Afrocentrism and knowing your "roots" would never be considered corny, once again it was your clothes and your crew that defined you, with skin color and hair texture not so much.

Speaking of fashion, bye-bye to those days when my street wardrobe (or the utter lack thereof) was mandated by Mom's leftovers after spending all she had on our private school clothes. (Back when I was sweating bullets in some corduroy pants on fly Melinda's porch.) I had been working at Dairy Queen for some three years now, and had definitely copped some nice, urban wear.

More so, just like anyone who knew about cars knew it was all about the shine on the hood, well anyone who knew about the streets knew it was all about the shine on your sneakers. Which is why everyone could relate to how "Buggin' Out," the key character in Spike Lee's *Do The Right Thing*, was so outraged when the white guy mistakenly put the tiniest scuff on his brand new Jordans. So of scuff-less sneakers, I now had plenty. And all without spending a penny.

You see, one of my classmates at Wardlaw was a nationally-ranked tennis player, who was sponsored by Nike. He'd allow me to order every pair of fly Nikes on the market. It was like a dream come true! All he wanted in return was free ice cream from Dairy Queen. So I kept him gobbling enough ice-cream to give him brain freezes, and he kept my feet getting more attention than I'd ever gotten in my life. No more "Adidas" with the extra stripe from the Dollar Shoe Outlet. Yeah, this is what we called a "come up."

Now if you factored in everyone I knew from working at Dairy Queen over these years, then my crew was quite large. Almost every drug dealer and fly mommy who loved ice-cream knew my baby-face by now, along with all the tastiest concoctions I had invented to make a summer evening extra chill. And though it was nothing but superficial how I could now roll up at parties and get love from the most random and roughest dudes, my ego loved it just the same. Besides, wasn't "being known" all it was about anyway? All the while, my footwear looked just as fly as any of the drug dealers who leaned against their fly rides.

But as far as my true and immediate crew went—meaning the ones I regularly chilled with—I was now running with some of Plainfield's most popular, from wild Starski, to Keell and his cool brother, "Billy D. Williams" (so named after the actor in the Colt 45 commercials). Then there was Fat Greg, who had broken Plainfield High's weightlifting records and could dance his behind off like he wasn't fat. He was so crazy that one time he faked a heart attack right in the middle of class at Plainfield High—an ambulance raced to get him and everything—just because his classmates had sworn to give him $300 (even though they only ended up giving him like $30).

In fact, back before Fat Greg and I even knew each other, I was walking to Wardlaw one fourth grade, winter morning, when suddenly a snowball just missed my head. And as I looked across the street, there was this light-skinned, fat kid looking at me with the fakest innocent face, saying, "Yo, I swear it that wasn't me! It was my friend right here!" So years later, we were a crew now; and even our moms called him "Fat Greg."

As for my original backyard homies, Remi was now dodging trouble in a nearby city called Franklin, while the other Greg was busy working towards a basketball scholarship to college and making headlines in every local paper. Lastly, along with Chico and Donaldo, there was Deuce—probably my best friend of all by this point—who was just as tight with "Billy D. Williams," Fat Greg, and everyone else.

Well, not only was Deuce's mother still on crack, but Deuce was now selling crack himself at the projects right across from our favorite bodega. And though he and I never discussed it, I figured that the knowledge of how his own mother was getting served by drug dealers in New York made it easier for him to justify serving someone else's mother in Plainfield. So rain or shine, sunburn or winter windburn, Deuce would be out there on the corner making money. In no time, he was just as addicted to selling it as the fiends were to smoking it.

The late 80's was the era of the crack dealer. And as rap song after rap song glorified it so much, "clockin'" became the status symbol and secret fantasy of almost every impressionable Hip Hop mind. Even if you knew you'd never sell crack yourself, you still wanted to be close to someone who did. I mean, the alluring hype of it all: the wads of money stacked in shoe boxes, the close friend who'd stash viles in their basement for you, Jetta's in neon colors like "goofy grape" with the newest rims, and girls breaking their necks to peep your style, no matter how ugly you were. I mean, being connected to it all made you feel tougher—like you were somehow more of a man.

Crack was now transforming countless dusty-behind dudes into crispy-clean celebrities overnight, which is why many began dropping out of high school to sell it. And even though some famous graffiti writer had just finished this huge mural in Plainfield saying, "Crack Is Wack," and even though our boxes of Lemonheads now had "Say No To Drugs" stamped on the inside flap, it was too late. The fever was simply too high now for mere "cold compresses," as we all snidely chanted Jamaican rapper Shinehead's single, "Gimme No Crack."

This was also when the smash-hit movie *New Jack City* had come out, featuring Wesley Snipes as he played the chilling role of a ruthless, rags-to-riches drug kingpin named Nino Brown. Deuce and I would watch *New Jack City* at least once a week; and we felt especially connected since Jalil—our eternal "big brother"—was the stunt double in the opening scene when Crackhead Pookie flees a drug robbery by jumping flights of steps on a BMX bike.

And though the director of *New Jack City* would say that the movie was in no way meant to glorify drug dealing and its lavish lifestyle—even pointing at Nino Brown's disgraceful death in the end as a case in point—the reality was that Wesley Snipes had made Nino Brown's life look so powerful and tantalizing that nobody cared how he had died. Many even said that his death was a great way "to go" after "livin' large."

So almost every late school night, Deuce would tap on my bedroom window on his way home from clockin'.

"Yo Aaron, wassup? Y'all got some food to eat? I'm starvin'!"

"Man, you the one makin' the money, man. You need to order me a pizza! It's just Deuce, Mom, it's cool. You can go back to sleep."

"Hi Deuce, baby," Mom would call from her bed.

"Hey, Mom!" And she really was his mom in so many ways.

"So whatcha' studyin', man?"

"Man, doin' a paper for this teacher. I be tryin' to do papers on someone from black history that they don't be knowin' about, knowhutimsayin'? So I can school 'em on some things. But wassup with you?"

"Man, just comin' from the projects, makin' that money. But dag, gotta get ready for school tomorrow, though. Man, I'm sick of school," he sighed. "But yo, I got my eye on this car, man. I'mma have it soon, too! But yo, you gotta peep this new song that just came out. Listen real close to it!"

He pulled a cassette from his coat and popped it in my box. It was KRS-One's new joint, "Love's Gonna Get You." In the song, KRS is telling a story about a young teenager from a struggling single-parent home who lives in a neighborhood where "if you're soft, you're lost." More so, this teenager's only got three pairs of pants which he has to share with his brother. He gets teased for it in school because "with one and half pair of pants, you ain't cool." But he's too broke to change anything, as "there's no dollars for nothing else, I got beans, rice, and bread on my shelf." And though Deuce and I were both from "good homes," we both had seen periods of struggle where we could relate to certain parts of KRS' lyrics.

Sick of struggling so much while others his age are making such easy money, the teenager decides to sell drugs. He feels good providing for his mother and siblings whom he loves so much. However, he's also slipping deeper into the dangerous drug game.

"C'mon man, keep listenin'!" Deuce all but had his ear right up against my box.

You see, it had always been me and Deuce's plan to go off to neighboring colleges so we could "run things together," as we'd say. But as Deuce was now spending all his time on the corner and no time studying for school, that wasn't looking like a possible reality anymore. Deuce knew he was messing up our plan, too. So he wanted his best friend to know what he was struggling with, and considered this song the perfect fit. It was the first and last time he'd beg me to listen to the words of a song.

"C'mon man, it's almost done! Keep listenin'!"

Deuce was also well on his way to getting that respect on the streets— the respect I so desperately craved myself. Because just like in the other smash-hit urban movie *Juice,* when Tupac's character said he was sick of always running scared from everyone as if he was on "the &$%$$ track team," I too was getting sick and tired of always being scared.

▲ ▼ ▲ ▼ ▲

So time was flying; and I felt fly, myself. I was a "big senior" now, counting down the months until I'd be off to college doing all the crazy stuff those Hollywood college movies portrayed. During the school week, it was work and "all-nighters." But when it came weekends, if my crew and I weren't sneaking into girls' houses as their parents snored away, then we were chasing some of Jersey's grimiest parties. And no matter how ill these parties were, we'd be there.

Like the time we went to this party at Essex Catholic High School over in East Orange right next to Newark. Even though I had spent summers growing up in these parts with both Momma and Mom's two younger sisters, on this night, I was just as much an out-of-towner as the next person. Now getting into this place was stressful enough: droves of knuckleheads (rough-behind girls too) throwing elbows in the freezing darkness as we all squeezed to get through the doors. Fights were breaking out left and right as way too many new sneakers were getting scuffed. And as it was announced that only a few more of us would be allowed inside, because of the fire hazard, it was a relief to muscle through that last layer of Essex County's craziest.

However, inside soon got just as wild. Before I could even score my first phone number from a honey, some of the ones who had been locked outside started breaking the gymnasium windows and climbing inside like ninjas. Then, it was only a matter of time before things followed the usual pattern at our parties. First, the faint sound of arguing (even over the loud music); second, the sound of people trying to beat the eyeballs out of each other; and lastly, as the DJ officially snatched his needle from the record to end the night, some adult chaperone screaming for us all to get out like we were a pack of rats. And at this point, the only thing that mattered was gauging from which dark direction the stampede might be coming, so you could run your tail off and not get trampled. People would get hospitalized from these stampedes alone.

And as this particular stampede was underway, a Catholic priest tried to stand his ground and stop the whole thing, but got sucker-punched and knocked out cold. It was pure chaos, with the utter absence of anything good. So with the coatroom ravaged and all the best jackets stolen—especially leather "eight ball jackets" or NFL football parkas—it was back outside to the freezing darkness, where every person with legs, fists, and teeth was fighting the night away. The most angry and mentally troubled ones were doing the most damage, and the cops were in no hurry to get there, as they even despised dealing with our nutty generation.

The seed-plot of black-on-black crime: this was our weekend social life.

However, because such places were still the "cool" places to be, our minds had been conditioned to call this stressful chaos "fun." Because even our favorite rappers hailed such situations as the place where true manhood was developed and showcased. So we'd just continue searching out such nights as if our life depended on it. And if someone got body-slammed, gang-jumped, or even gang-chased for blocks away, you just callously chuckled about how you were glad it wasn't you.

But while I loved the whole party scene as much as the next person—and even enjoyed watching two dudes with boxing game fight a nice "fair one"—I never really liked the random ruthlessness of it all: the pitbull-eat-pitbull. So then, was there something wrong with me for not loving this type of blind drama (that could very well suck me in next)? I sure felt there was. Why couldn't I just love it the same way the nuttier ones seemed to? And did the fact that they seemed to love it more then me, make them more manly? Well on the streets it did.

And what about that night when my crew went to this other out-of-town party without me and ended up getting jumped by some locals? Even though Keell ended up cracking one of the dudes with a baseball bat, it was still a loss for our side—proven by the dried blood on the hood of Keell's car. That blood belonged to Keell's cousin Smurf who worked at Dairy Queen with me. And as we rolled back to the very same place the next night—only this time, "two cars deep"—I watched the way Smurf pointed at his blood on the hood like he was so proud of it and ready for more. At that moment, I so wished to be more like Smurf.

Then, there was the time at yet another party—this time in the wild section of Newark's neighboring city Irvington—when this crew of Newark cats had us cornered and crazy outnumbered. Starski fearlessly hurled the first chair in their direction to set it all off, and before I knew it, I had jumped a table and jetted off to safety. Now of course we all ended up jetting for safety for sure, but why did I have to be one of the first ones to go in "flight" mode? I mean, was that "being wise? Or was it just weakness? Well to me, it was pure weakness, in capital letters. And doggone Big-fat-Ron the babysitting pedophile, because it really felt like when he broke me down that one night that he somehow "broke" me permanently!

I stood watching from a nearby table, where I could see one or two from my crew fighting to stay on their feet amidst the "jump." I was too paralyzed to even search for a weapon—a chair, the broken leg of a table, even the fire extinguisher off the wall. Anything to run to their rescue like the true homeboy-hero that I always dreamed of being.

"Yo, some Plainfield n*gg*hs shut down the party! Man, don't lemme catch 'dem n*gg*hs in our hood!" The outside mob yelled as we ended up needing a K-9 police escort to our cars. And in one respect, the whole thing actually felt cool, as we had just put Plainfield on the map as the official "bad boys" of the night. Not to mention that anytime you survived a major "jump" without any injuries, it somehow made you more of a man. However, in another respect, I was more than a bit concerned, because this yelling mob was the very mob that had just finished surrounding Deuce as he fled to the top of a car with his fists up (Deuce having fled outside the party without the rest of us), where they were actually plotting on throwing him over the rail and onto highway 280 down below.

Then, believe it or not, even after one of the cops had strictly commanded us to get right on 280 and get out of town for our own safety, we foolishly turned around and went to the same White Castle burger spot that everyone else would be going to—that same yelling mob included. After all, wasn't making fearless statements like this what it was all about anyway? But as we sat there in the parking lot (ironically, only a few blocks up from Momma's house), I was too uneasy to enjoy my burgers and onion rings—knowing full well that at any moment that mob might've rolled up with their killer 8-to-1 ratio.

However, in complete contrast to me, Starski just ate his burger and burped and laughed like we were at the beach. He just kept saying over and over how he so regretted leaving his long blade in Chico's mini van while we were at that party, promising us that if he had it during the jump, there would've been more dudes doubled over on the dance floor than you could count. And at that moment, I wished I could be more like Starski, too.

So it was this sense of inadequacy in the rugged face of black-on-black crime that brought on a self-hatred that I couldn't put into words; though I'd grapple with it pretty often while looking at myself in the mirror. However, since Hip Hop was still all about gallivanting around like you were the best thing since sliced bread, that's exactly what I'd keep doing. And with my sneakers and steady flow of girlfriends looking better than ever, I was quite good at it. But my heart always knew the "real deal," though, which is why sometimes, as I'd hear that TV commercial for those "oldies" records playing the Platters' "Great Pretender," I'd shamefully think, *"Yup, that's me!"*

But I had to succeed on the streets eventually. Couldn't imagine feeling this way forever. And this need was so powerful that even my 3.8 GPA couldn't quench it, or even becoming Wardlaw's first black student to go to an Ivy League university. Now don't get me wrong, getting into all my "dream" colleges had me on cloud nine hundred ninety-nine, for sure. It just felt like my dream cloud was also stuck beneath this ubiquitous gray cloud that would rain on my glory.

▲▼▲▼▲

Getting into some of "America's Top Twenty Universities" from *U.S. News & World Report* definitely sent shock-waves through Wardlaw. I mean, while some of my classmates were elated from being accepted into just one, I had been accepted by three. And while most of my teachers were elated for me—especially the few who knew how hard I had worked as we had taken many lunch periods to work on extra physics and chemistry problems together—others couldn't help but show their contempt, and perhaps their racism as well.

However, I became good at handling such stupidity over the years. Having a dad who had once scaled the uglier mountains of Jim Crow, helped me to see these as mere anthills in comparison. Once, in the middle of English class, I snatched the glasses off a classmate's face for praising Jimmy the Greek who said "blacks are bred like horses." However, once I perceived how the Wardlaw administration focused more on the "angry black student's" reaction than on the racist comment that started the whole thing, I realized that I had to learn to chill.

Therefore, when the headmaster called an emergency school assembly because someone had written "N*gg*r" on the bathroom stall—I chilled. And when the same headmaster, concerned that the black students were segregating themselves (even though we thought it was just a thing called "hanging out"), and recommended that we visit the school's psychologist for some counseling—I chilled. However, our dads decided to pop up at that psychologist's meeting that day, and Wardlaw sure wished they had chilled, instead of attempting such a thing without our parents' consent.

Then, you had my college guidance counsellor telling me that my college choices were "reaches," and that it would be a waste of time for me to even bother applying (after which she persisted in selling me on colleges of a much lower ranking). I mean, even with my recent 3.8 GPA; even with all my honors and advanced placement classes; even with my great teacher recommendations; and even with my job as a part-time manager of a family-owned business, showing both my maturity and my ability to manage my time and responsibilities. Then to top it off, once I was accepted at The University of Pennsylvania, The University of North Carolina at Chapel Hill, The University of Virginia, and a full academic scholarship to Rutgers University—my guidance counsellor retreated from any warm form of congratulations. More so, some of my classmates said the only reason I was accepted was because of affirmative action.

Well, by this point, I had enough—so I refused to chill. Rather than get all loud and argumentative, and play into the angry black student stereotype, I simply marched into the school library, made hundreds of photocopies of my college acceptance letters, and passed them out in the hallways between classes—all of them with "REACHABLE" written across the top in black marker.

After that, I was back in the headmaster's office, listening to him and the guidance counsellor tell me that the distribution of my acceptance letters could be hurtful to others who hadn't gotten into those same schools. And guess what? They were absolutely right; I did need to think of how others were being affected by my behavior. However, I didn't bother mentioning in that meeting the way my guidance counsellor would leap for joy whenever my classmates ran to tell her their latest college acceptance news, but when I did, she just sat expressionless at her desk with her pen limp in her hand.

And no, I didn't get any special awards at my high school graduation—the way I did back in seventh grade with Mr. Newcomb and Mr. Wuest—nor was I looking for any. Wardlaw was officially past tense now, and I had checked out mentally. And I wasn't even mad anymore. Just excited for my next big chapter of success.

Veni!

Vidi!

Vici!

So out of all my colleges, I picked the University of Pennsylvania, for along with Harvard, Princeton, Yale, Dartmouth, Columbia, Brown, and Cornell, it was part of the renowned "Ivy League" and one of the top universities on the planet. Hence, at least one part of my life's "master plan" was set. My fantasy of having my "phat" house on a hill, with a "phat" Porsche to drive to my own private medical practice was closer to being mine than ever.

But, man! As I mentioned before, there was that ubiquitous gray cloud raining on my glory again. Because even with this bright and successful future, without that respect from the streets I still somehow felt like that same "soft punk" all over again—only a more dignified and educated one. I mean, being like *The Cosby Show's* Cliff Huxtable wasn't enough. I needed to be Cliff Huxtable with a Miles Davis swagger.

And then finally, *"Eureka!"* For just like when the self-centered Captain Ahab spotted the mighty Moby Dick with the cry "there she blows," so it was for me as I finally spotted the other part to my life's "master plan:" how to get that respect on the streets. For after endless hours of pondering, my logic was simple. If one of the best universities on the planet meant the best in academic education, then some of the worst streets on the planet would mean the best in street education.

Therefore, at around the same time that I was mailing my response notifying "UPenn" to consider me one of their own, I also made the shocking decision to take a summer job at the infamous Port Authority Bus Terminal on West 42nd Street in New York City. And not as some white-collared intern in their corporate offices, either. Nope, I'd be an official, Newport-smokin', slick-talkin', alley-dippin', scum-scrubbin' street janitor. And this was 1992, back when the Port Authority Bus Terminal ("the Port," for short) was said to be the most dangerous public facility in all five boroughs: the Bronx, Brooklyn, Queens, Staten Island, and the island of Manhattan.

And speaking of islands, just as in *Lord of the Flies*—the book we had read back in Mr. Vozar's English class—this private school boy would now be crashing into his own "jungle"—the concrete jungles of New York's notorious "Hell's Kitchen." And there were all types of animals waiting for me there, too, maybe even that same dude who had tried flipping my mother down those escalator steps that one night. But I was purposely crashing into this jungle to locate my wild side; so that years down the road, once everything went according to my master plan, words like "soft" and "punk" wouldn't stick to me even if someone tried branding them on my chest.

The Ivy League plus The Port: to some it was a pretty insane undertaking. But to me, it was my silver bullet for absolute happiness and peace.

Ready . . .

Aim . . .

Fire!

XI

HELL'S KITCHEN, NYC

"So Aaron, you're really gonna work as a janitor at the Port Authority in New York?"

I loved it when Brian would ask me that question during our final days in English IV honors. In fact, it almost became an everyday thing. First, he'd check his stocks in *The Wall Street Journal* (probably the same stocks he'd been given back at his unforgettable Bar Mitzvah); next, he'd peek out the second-story classroom window to check on his convertible BMW; and lastly, he'd look my way and ask yet one more time. And as I'd give him that same confident nod, the amazement in his eyes had me feeling more like a man already.

Even Jersey's most sheltered kids knew the streets of New York City were no joke. And again, this was way before West Forty-second Street was transformed into the kid-friendly "Disney World" that it is today. I'm talking back when it was nothing but a dark underworld dubbed "Forty-deuce"—a wasteland of 25¢ "peep shows," pimps, hookers, homeless, and drug addicts; where "John Does" died so regularly that it never made the papers. And although I still had my own fears about this whole thing, wasn't that why I was injecting myself into this rat's nest to begin with? For I knew that if it didn't kill me, it would only make me stronger.

So, I quit my job at Dairy Queen. And though leaving this sweet, Italian family of owners was harder than I thought, I gave them plenty of notice so they could adequately fill my absence. As I went to get my last paycheck, Mr. A., the owner, invited me outside so we could talk in private, which he always loved to do. Once we were outside, he lit up one of his trusty cigarettes and began.

"Now, Aaron, you've been with me for four years now, and you've done very well for yourself. Your parents have worked hard to give you the best, and now you're going to an Ivy League school. But I'm not surprised, Aaron. I always knew you'd do that from the very beginning, and I'm so proud of you!"

His eyes grew teary.

"And now, Aaron, you're going to New York City. And I know this janitor job is gonna pay way more than I could ever afford to pay you, to help with college. But you listen to me now!"

And while Mr. A. was already serious, he suddenly got so stern that to an onlooker it might've looked like he was about to punch me in the mouth.

"Aaron, when you're out there on them streets of New York, you'd better watch your #&&! You hear me? Because they'll stick ya' out there! They'll stick you in your freakin' rear! You understand what I'm saying to you?"

"Yes, Mr. A."

"Okay. Now c'mere and gimme a hug." Calming back down just as quickly, he kissed my cheek as he always did. Mr. A was like the grandfather I never had, and I often told him so.

"They'll stick you in your freakin' rear!" I'd replay those words for months to come.

▲ ▼ ▲ ▼ ▲

3:45 a.m.

Wow, the time had really come, and I was actually going through with this!

No shower needed for this one, I just got up, grabbed my janitor uniform, ID badge, baseball cap, and the Timberlands I cared least about. This was the fastest I had ever gotten ready for something.

3:48 a.m.

Mom dragged her feet behind me as I reached our front door, where Dad would be arriving at any second to take me to the only train that left this part of Jersey for New York at such an hour. Rubbing my back, she muttered, "Aaron, I'm begging you, baby— be safe, okay?"

"I will Mom; don't worry."

But of course she'd worry all day! She had become used to watching me balance my two different worlds all my life, but this was taking things to a whole new level. And of course she hadn't forgotten about the mugger on those escalator steps. The very escalator I'd now be using to catch the bus back home, myself.

"Really Mom, I'mma be okay. I'll see you later on today."

And with that, she nodded like she had no other choice and shut the door. She would've loved to choose a different chapter for me at this point. However, while I hadn't shared a thing with her about my great master-plan for manhood and happiness (of course), she at least knew that I needed to make this kind of money to pay for my books and meal plan in the fall. It was basic arithmetic: Dairy Queen paid me $7.50 an hour, while the Port paid almost $14, which was serious loot for an 18-year-old back then.

As I took a moment to sit on my cold, slate porch—ducking to avoid the large beetles that dipped under our porch light—I could already hear Dad's van cruising up our sleeping street. I got up and headed down our walkway as his van climbed in our driveway like a slug on wheels. Dad always drove extra slow, ticking off tailgaters and not caring one bit. I climbed into his van and plopped onto its cozy seat.

"Hey son." His hair was all over the place like an Indian-black Einstein.

"Hey, Pops."

"So what time is this train, 4:15? Okay, we got twenty minutes then." And with that, I zonked right out, not opening my eyes again until we pulled into the Menlo Park Station two cities over. The station was still so dark that if it weren't for the schedule promising a train, we might've sworn it was closed.

4:10 a.m.

Two minutes left.

Pops and I locked hands.

"Be safe, my man."

"Alright."

He wasn't nearly as worried as Mom. For one, he was a "man's man," and for two, he didn't know enough about the Port to be that worried anyway. Shutting the van door, I jogged up the concrete steps to the train platform where the "iron horse" was now due. Apart from two white men in suits, there was nobody in sight. Then the piercing light of the train appeared.

Business as usual, the train screeched to a halt and the conductors jumped onto the platform, full of energy. I boarded the dreamy express and quickly picked which pleather seat I'd pass out on. Then off we were, so fast that someone arriving at the station just a minute late would've sworn the train still hadn't come.

"Where to?" The conductor clicked his hole-puncher out of habit.

"New York." Penn Station on West Thirty-fourth Street, to be exact. Eight blocks away from the Port, Penn Station was the only place I could go this early to make my punch-in by 6 a.m. So the conductor took my money, gave me my first of many tickets, and that was that. With an hour-long ride ahead of me—into the unknown—all I could do was lay back with my Walkman and rehearse the few things I did know, like my trip to the Port the day before.

"Orientation" is what they had the nerve to call it. I mean, here I had ridden the cramped bus for over an hour, just to meet the screwface of a stressed-out Jamaican man sitting at a messy desk. Mr. Barrett was his name, and I knew this would be nothing like Dairy Queen when I saw how his dress shirt was chucked over a nearby chair while the stretch-marks on his chubby shoulders forked from his tank-top like cracks in a store-front window. He wore a thin but strong-looking gold chain and only took breaks from shuffling papers to slurp his 16 oz. pineapple soda through a straw or answer the ringing phone with a wearied Brooklyn accent. And while the rest of his muggy office was packed wall-to-wall with sweaty men looking for work, Mr. Barrett had this huge fan aimed only at him.

With no time for small talk, he asked my name, shuffled his paperwork until he found what he needed, reached over and tossed me a bright-red company jumpsuit, and then printed out my schedule: Monday through Friday, 6:00 a.m. to 2:30 p.m. And when he saw that I didn't have a passport photo for my ID badge (which nobody told me I'd need, by the way), he sucked his teeth like I was giving him a headache and dismissed me into the streets to find one. Then, when I returned forty-five minutes later—sweaty and a bit surprised at how he couldn't have cared less—he summed up my "orientation" with a warning.

"You show up for work just ONE MINUTE LATE tomorrow, you go back home! Got that? I got lots of people here that want your job!"

And as he said that, I could feel some of the grown men along the walls looking me up and down, like I was now on some "bad list" for not having my passport photo and they were more than ready to take my place. And when I finally confessed to Mr. Barrett that I had no idea where I was even supposed to show up the next morning, he sighed like I was the bane of his existence. Then, to show off his power, he commanded one of the grown men along the walls to show me to the Port's basement. Without one word to me, the man got up, stepped onto Ninth Avenue, walked across the street to the Port's colossal building, took the steps down to the third basement, and walked the dimly lit corridors into this big supply room full of supervisors and cleaning equipment. (Good thing I kept up with the guy.)

"Orientation" over.

So with all these grown men in Mr. Barrett's office who were bigger, stronger, and much more street than me, how did I even score this big-paying gig to begin with? Well, the owner of the Port's cleaning company actually lived in Plainfield, and rubbed political shoulders with my dad. He was also Deuce's uncle, which was why Deuce had worked there the summer before. And now, all Mr. Barrett knew was that "the boss-man" had called, and said an "Aaron Campbell" was to be put on the schedule for the whole summer, period. Sounds pretty official, right? But I was a little concerned about this whole arrangement, because the last thing I needed was for people out there to think that I was some rich Plainfield kid expecting special treatment.

Besides Deuce, some of my older friends from Plainfield had already worked there as well. Like my man Big Mike, who would return from the Port every evening like a man returning from war. He'd look exhausted, perplexed, and pissed off all at the same time. And whenever he'd attempt to tell us about the sick things he had witnessed (in empty stairwells and subway corridors), he almost wouldn't be able to finish. Then there was Big Dave, who had worked on the Port's infamous "graveyard shift." Well one night, while sweeping down an empty corridor, someone crept up behind him, rammed a "gun" into the base of his skull, and robbed him. Once the robber slid away, Big Dave realized that the guy might've been using his two fingers (in place of a gun) the whole time.

So such were the stories I'd heard, and for all I knew, the next psycho story might involve me. For after dark especially, the Port was a place where you could vanish, just like that. Or maybe you'd just end up losing your mind instead, like some of the homeless people there who had once been functional, until they were victimized and psychologically stranded there, stinking and gangrening away. It was sad, but true.

So here I was, just turning eighteen years old with not a lick of facial hair, let alone much hair under my arms, late-bloomer that I was. A baby with a babyface, entering a place that would have even the roughest dudes from the roughest prisons on high alert. Even the majority of New Yorkers knew nothing about the Port, other than to stay far away.

I was far away from home, too.

"Penn Station, New York!" The conductor's bellow jerked me out of my sleep, and to my surprise the train was now packed with commuters. Screeching to our final stop, the silver doors slid open and we all poured onto the platform. It was like a mass migration, and my mission was simple: blend in perfectly until finding my way outside to the streets so I could walk eight blocks to the Port.

Hustling up the corridor with its monochromatic white tiles, a few sets of jaundiced, homeless eyes were already checking me out. Maybe it was just my mind playing tricks on me, but it felt like people could see "new jack" spray-painted all over me. Corridor after corridor, there were more signs than I could possibly read—subway trains designated by all these different numbers and letters inside of different color shapes. I felt like a tourist. Plus, the herd of commuters I had been camouflaging myself with was just about thinned out.

Frustrated now, I grew angry with myself for not being better at this. And so what if I was only eighteen and a first-timer? All I knew was that here I was, in big-time New York City, but still feeling like that same sucker from a small town in Jersey. Maybe this whole thing was just gonna backfire? But I wouldn't let it. I couldn't.

Finally arriving upstairs from the labyrinth below, I walked across Penn Station's immense concourse with its giant illuminated Gap billboard featuring some pretty white girl's face. I knew that I was now directly beneath the famed Madison Square Garden—home of the New York Knickerbockers. In fact, the last time I had been to this place was ten years ago, back when one of the Knicks had a crush on Mom and would drive out to our house, always bringing another player from the team (like Trent Tucker) along with him. I remembered Vince as being surprisingly shy and very polite; and he'd always leave tickets for me, Brett, Mom, and one of Mom's girlfriends to come to "the Garden" and watch him play. But back to my mission of finding this colossal Port, which in this big city was still like searching for a hypodermic needle in a haystack.

5:10 a.m.

I finally made it outside to the streets, and there was nobody in sight. The sun hadn't risen yet, so along with this eerie gray, pervasive hue, there were shadows everywhere. I could see why no commuters ventured out here.

A dirty, "off duty" cab broke through the steam of a manhole in the middle of the street. If that cab had been "on duty," I might've hollered after it like a damsel in distress. I mean, I didn't even know which corner of Penn Station I was even on, let alone which direction the Port was in! But it was time to be a man now, the very reason I sent myself here. So the damsel in me would have to become the Rambo in me.

My eyes adjusted to the darkness, and I could see other life forms. In fact, there were people lying all over the place. They were stretched across sidewalks, buried under mounds of blankets or cardboard, or balled up in the fetal position over warm manholes. Crack addicts were huddled in little nooks, rocking on their haunches from their highs. I had just learned my first lesson out here: even when you thought you were alone, you weren't.

Trash was piled on both sides of the street like sandbags before a flood. Only these bags were filled with nothing but paper, twice-picked-over food, empty liquor bottles, and squirts of deadly venom; just one brush against the wrong bag with an infected needle sticking out could leave you with AIDS quicker than the quickest one-night stand. (What a relief it was to see the first street sign indicating that I was headed in the right direction, after all.)

A gang of transvestites strutted by and glared at me like they ran those streets. Outside of a "XXX" joint on the next block, a group of men blew cigarette smoke and paused to check me out as well. Clearly, I was the new kid on the block. Finally, there was the Port's colossal silhouette in the distance. Two buildings wide and multiple stories tall, the Port was the largest bus station in the country.

Crossing Fortieth Street onto the Port's red brick sidewalk, I was blown away by the many homeless and druggies already hanging around the Port's doors like a crowd before a concert. Many of them looked like zombies, and many of these zombies were now looking at me. And mind you, I wasn't so worried about somebody doing something to me right on the spot. My concern was more with someone plotting for one of my next eight-block, witness-less journeys through this area notoriously dubbed "Hell's Kitchen."

Eager to get inside now, I headed for the first set of doors. But to my shock, they were locked. The next set of doors were locked, too. Even the next. Man, the whole building was locked! And of course nobody had told me this in "orientation." I felt like one of the three blind mice, and as much as I was trying to play it cool in front of all these watching eyes, my cover was now officially blown.

So I stepped across Forty-first Street to try the doors of the Port's second building. And what would I do if those were locked as well? Ask for help? Call the police? But what a phenomenal feeling it was when that first door opened! So I was inside now; however, I still had no clue where to go, since on the previous day I had been lead through a totally different entrance—of which the Port had too many to count. Spotting a group of janitors who were finishing up their graveyard shift, I approached the friendliest-looking one. "Yo wassup, man? How do I get downstairs to punch-in?" He smiled and gave me the easiest directions, and I appreciated him much more than he knew.

5:30 a.m.

I was back in the same basement as the day before. The big supply room was already full of Newport smoke as if it were midday, and the supervisors stood behind a long counter with ashtrays that needed dumping. I approached the supervisor who looked the least busy and handed him my schedule from Mr. Barrett. With no words, the supervisor simply filed away my paper, handed me a time card, and motioned me over to the time clock on the wall behind me. So shortly after 5:30 a.m., I officially began as a New York City janitor.

"Now go stand over there until your name's called!"

And that's exactly what I did—for ten, twenty, maybe even thirty minutes. But with all there was for me to take in, I appreciated the time. On the supervisors' counter was a little radio playing the hot new single, "Jump Around," by rugged Irish rap group House of Pain. I wasn't surprised though, because most of my supervisors looked just as rugged. The song's fast tempo matched the adrenaline in my body.

Standing against the wall next to me were two dudes who were slightly older than me. Every morning, "stand-bys" would show up at this early hour, put their names on a list, and then just wait and wait, in hopes of getting on for the day. The one standing closest to me was a loose cannon for sure—the type you knew had been all over NYC, from party to party, projects to projects. And just as loudly as someone might talk about shopping for a car, this dude was talking about stealing cars.

"So anyway, I'm tryin' to tell you, man! My cousin be stealin' so many cars that he don't even do it for the money, no more! I mean, you know how people be hangin' up deer heads on they walls? Man, my cousin be hanging steering wheels on his walls! Man, he even had this one joint hangin' up with two Clubs still attached to it! So I said to him, 'Yo cuz, why you had to take this one with the Clubs?' And he said, 'Because man, I just had to! All them Clubs on it, man, it was daring me to!'

The other dude chuckled. I couldn't help but chuckle, too. Only in NYC.

Meanwhile, the corridor was getting crowded now as the graveyard shift was coming down to turn in their equipment. Watching my new colleagues closely, this was the motliest crew I had ever seen: black, Caribbean, and Latino, male and female, young and old, gold teeth by fashion and gold caps by dentist. I mean, you had your quiet-but-observant Brooklyn dudes, your crazy-cool Queens cats, your flamboyant Harlem and Bronx boys, and everyone in between, along with a handful of whites. I loved it all.

And I couldn't help but notice this one dude who was about 6'3" and as muscular as the Hulk, with a Latino-curly ponytail. Making noises almost like Chewbacca, while communicating a ton with his hands and facial expressions, he was obviously deaf. It was clear that everyone adored this guy. It was also clear that this guy would break someone in half if they touched any of his people. Man, I looked forward to when I'd share that bond with him, too.

There were four different janitor shifts: the morning shift (6 a.m.—2:30 p.m.), the day shift (8 a.m.—4:30 p.m.), the evening shift (2 p.m.—10:30 p.m.), and lastly, the night shift, or "graveyard" (10:30 p.m.—6 a.m.). Each shift had 50 or so workers. And though that might've seemed like a lot, then again, there was a lot of the Port to be safeguarded and heavily disinfected every second. And now, as I looked at this gang in red jumpsuits barreling down the corridor for punch-out, they were ready for whatever Hell's Kitchen would try to defecate on them.

I mean, imagine if Ali Baba had hundreds of thieves instead of just his forty. Then, imagine each of those hundreds of thieves thinking they were indeed the true Ali Baba; and that's exactly what this crew was. So if Eighth Ave and "Forty-deuce" were the "seven seas" and the Port was the pirate ship, then these were the pirates. And just like some pirates, the aim of every eight-hour shift was to make it back to this basement with whatever you could find. And they'd find it all, too: lost jewelry and diamonds, "hot" stuff sold for pennies by crack addicts, even stumbled-upon sacks of money that drug dealers would stash around the building, thinking it would never be found. The pirates of these seven seas knew everything and found everything; yup, I was definitely in the right place for my manhood.

"Campbell! Campbell!!"

Hustling back to the counter so my name wouldn't have to be yelled a third time, the supervisors were now assigning everyone to their daily stations, and my turn was up.

"Hey, you're new here, right?" The supervisor blew his Newport right into my face.

"Yeah."

He continued directing me. "Well okay, just step right over here and . . . HEY MAN, WHAT ARE YOU DOING DOWN HERE? MAN, I DON'T WANNA HEAR IT! YOU PUNCHED IN AND GOT YOUR STUFF ALREADY, SO YOU BETTER GET OUTTA HERE! HEY, IF YOU GOT A PERSONAL PROBLEM, I PUNCH OUT IN AN HOUR, OKAY?"

The supervisor got so enraged that he seemed to forget I was even standing there, yelling at that other janitor like a corrections officer in a prison yard. In fact, that's pretty much how this whole thing felt. A good number here were on work-release, anyway. So after steaming a little more, the supervisor turned back to me, but with much less patience now.

"Now, you're gonna be working the second floor bathroom in the south-wing. Do you know where that's at?"

"South wing? Uh, no."

He sighed like it was my fault. (And by this point, I was getting sick of people here expecting me to know everything.) "Okay, someone will show you then . . . HEY, SOMEONE GET THIS YOUNG MAN SOME SUPPLIES!"

In assembly-line fashion, the old men from the supply room began handing me more stuff than I could keep up with. One handed me a big blue pushcart, another handed me a mop and bucket with ringer, another handed me a broom and metal pick-up pan, and the last one handed me everything else: two armfuls of toilet paper, garbage bags, spray bottles, sponges, rags, pink soap, and even a paint scraper.

Once I was loaded up, the supervisor gave me my final commands.

"Okay, listen close. This here is your cleaning cart. You gotta watch this cart at ALL times, you got that? Because you see them homeless people outside on the corner, cleaning car windows at them red lights? Well, that's our spray bottles and soap they be stealing from our carts! So don't you let them have none of your stuff! Also, you are to stay in your bathroom for the ENTIRE eight-hour shift, except for your fifteen-minute coffee break and forty-five-minute lunch break. Other than that, you are NOT to be found away from your bathroom, you got that? You leave your bathroom outside of lunch, you get written up! You get written up, you get fired. Do you understand?"

"Yeah."

"Good." And with that, I no longer existed to him as he was already barking the next person's name. So I turned and pushed my loaded cart to the freight elevators just as I saw everyone else doing. No training sessions here; it was all monkey see, monkey do. And I still had no clue where the second floor, south wing bathroom even was.

As I waited my turn at the freight elevator, this older Latino man came over to me. He had a pleasant face, but still looked shrewd enough for any scenario.

"Hey Poppy, where they got you today?" And of course he had first tried talking to me in Spanish, swearing I was Puerto Rican.

"I'm in the second floor bathroom, south wing."

"What?" His eyes got big as police badges. "Aw man, they gave you 'da Meat Rack? Ain't you new here? Yo everybody, check it out, they gave my man right here 'da Meat Rack on his first day!"

And if "Meat Rack" didn't sound bad enough, it was worse having all these people now shaking their heads and giving commentary about it. One Caribbean woman even hissed in disdain. The Latino man continued:

"Man, I can't believe they did that to you! Woo-hoo, you gonna get a welcome to the Port, all right! But hey, just stick with me, Poppy. I'll show you the way there, okay?"

So we took the freight elevator to the second floor, and I followed close behind as he pushed his own cart. First we walked by this wall of loitering men, where a couple of them even made loud kissing noises at me. So raw and predatory were these streets, and so innocent and scarless was my babyface. At last, he lead me to this bathroom right in the middle of the second floor, and I quickly saw why that Caribbean woman had hissed in such a way. If this part of New York City was Hell's Kitchen, then the Port should've been called Hell's Zoo!

For starters, when I stepped inside the bathroom, the smell assaulted me like a pack of muggers. I could smell everything from mildewed clothing to wino-urine to diseased bowels, right down to the deranged, naked man standing there at the sink— scrubbing the crack of his gigantic butt with a fist full of soggy toilet paper turned brown. And making it clear that he wasn't moving any time soon, he paused for a moment, slowly looked me up and down like my cleaning equipment meant nothing, and then went right back to his butt-scrubbing.

To make things worse, he even had one of his blackened socks stretched over the mouth of the activated hand dryer. The funky, hot air mix almost made my eyes water. It was humid, sticky, smelly, and even hazy from the addicts smoking crack in the stalls. Basically, it was a tuberculosis incubator (which is exactly why there were all these warning signs about "TB" in our basement).

Well, my Latino coworker wasn't trying to spend any more time here than he had to, so he quickly showed me where to put my cart, where to get water for my mop bucket, and then jetted. So no more monkey-see, monkey-do, I figured. It would now just be monkey-survive.

The bathroom was mid-sized and had eight stalls and six urinals. And it was already packed with people, as 6 a.m. was also the time when the Port would reopen its doors for the day (which explained why I had seen that mob of zombies waiting outside). So now, every stall was taken, and every urinal occupied. And to top it off, nobody could even wash their nastiness off their hands because the naked guy had claimed the whole sink area as his own.

At a total loss for where to begin, I pushed my cart to the rear of the bathroom and stood there for a minute. Men grunted shamelessly behind the stall doors as their number twos echoed like mad in the stainless steel. Worst of all, the whole rear of the bathroom was covered with overflowed toilet water. The squirmy bits of toilet paper made it somewhat like a slush—a slush that I was standing in. I vowed to never wear these boots in my house again.

Now as I continue, please bear in mind that even the best adjectives will fail to convey what this was like. Also bear in mind that I'm writing about a Manhattan that simply doesn't exist anymore. For as I previously mentioned, 1992 marked the height of New York City's homelessness, AIDS, crack, and crime epidemics. It was a time ruled by the tooth and the claw. A time of bloody gashes and ejaculations, when you could innocently rest your hand on a flat surface and have no idea what wetness you had happened upon. And as Hell's Kitchen was first coined for this neighborhood back in the 1950's when it was a haven for prowling gangs, now it was a haven for every indescribable evil.

Anyway, as I stood at the back of the bathroom by the stalls—still trying to figure out what to do next—this Puerto Rican woman had the nerve to come strutting into the bathroom. She was my height and had the tightest clothes sculpted to her taut body.

"Yo, you can't be in here!" I barked at her.

But before I could say it twice, she walked over to the first empty urinal, pulled up her miniskirt, and joined the rest of the fellas. Man, I would've never guessed, and I couldn't help but watch "her" for a second. But that's when I noticed something else: The people standing at the urinals weren't even "going;" they were all just standing there, taking their sweet time examining each other's stuff.

Clearly, I was the only one bothered by any of this. I mean, as if I was the crazy one (and not the naked man at the sink with his fist in his behind)! So when another "her" paraded in, opening her shirt and presenting her poorly pieced-together implants to the whole bathroom, I was through for sure (though one geeky-looking white man jumped at the chance to handle her free display). Snatching my broom off the cart, I stormed outside and stood at the bathroom's entrance. That place could've detonated for all I cared.

At this point, another Latino coworker came whistling by with his morning coffee, and upon seeing my frazzled face came right over. With no introduction, he went straight into schooling me like he knew I so needed it.

"Okay, you see all them over here along this glass wall that wraps all the way around to the escalators on the other side? Well this is called the Meat Rack. Don't ever lean against them walls! Because that's the pick-up spot for all the ones in the Port that go 'that way,' ya know?"

And sure enough, the glass walls were lined with nothing but men and "hers," grabbing on other men and "hers," all of whom were masquerading in the most bizarre fashions—from African dashikis with fishnet stockings, to sailor suits, even to tight leather with buckles and chains. And although many were doused with enough perfume to drown even the bathroom's stench, you'd best believe they still had all the makings of a street gang. Some were skinny enough to "vogue" dance into a pretzel; others were muscular enough to knock someone out cold. And I was too embarrassed to tell my coworker how a few of them had puckered and whistled at me.

My coworker schooled me some more:

"See man, they be picking each other up here. Even some of those big, rich execs from Wall Street and whatnot be in on this. They be coming through and taking these young black and Latino boys shopping and buying them nice things in exchange for you-know-what. See, these young ones are like male hookers, ya know?

"But here's where you gotta watch, my man! Because when they be picking each other up like that, they be going right into YOUR bathroom so they can have sex in YOUR stalls. But see, they be going to the urinals and whatnot first, so they can check each other out first. So you gotta be kicking all them outta there, man! You gotta kick EVERYBODY out!

"And look, you can't even call the cops, man, 'cause see, they won't even come to this jacked-up bathroom you got! So it's all up to you, my man. Because if you just let people push you around and do whatever they want in your bathroom, then what ends up happenin' is that all the homeless and freaks are gonna start flocking here. See, everybody be talking with each other in this place, my man. Everyone on these streets knows everything about everyone, so don't be letting nobody disrespect you. You gotta watch!"

Needless to say, I had tons to think about. Tons of toughness to drum up, too.

And just as my coworker finished schooling me, the naked man from the sink was now dressed and dragging his feet out of my bathroom. But as I looked back inside, of course he left this pile of nasty-brown toilet paper in a big puddle, just for me.

My coworker just smiled, as if to say, *"See why you gotta be kickin' people out?"*

A mere fraction of my first day there.

2:30 p.m.

I punched out and boarded the bus for home, riding Mom's old escalator and all. And when I got home, I scrubbed my skin in the shower until it hurt and went straight to sleep.

And to think, I actually chose this to be my summer before college.

XII

Hell's Zoo: Take Two

"*DAG!*"

Could you believe it? My second day on the job and I overslept! And I couldn't even call my supervisors to tell them because nobody ever gave me the number to the Port's basement.

Well, I made it back to Penn Station; only this time, I sprinted up Eighth Avenue like my life was on the line. Man, I hated how this job had me so stressed already. I mean, wasn't I going to an Ivy League university in the fall, anyway? I didn't need this mess.

But then again, I actually did need "this mess." Because once again, it was all about achieving my master plan.

Sweaty and disheveled, I finally made it to the Port's basement. And to my surprise, instead of seeing the same hot-headed supervisor from the day before, it was a different one, a chill one. However, she still looked like she wouldn't hesitate to bark at a fool trying to play her meekness for weakness. Well since it was only my second day, not only did she forego writing me up, but she even let me get on the 8 to 4:30 shift for the day. Man, I liked her already.

"You'll be sweeping outside the south wing perimeter with Akwei. Stick with him all day except your lunch break, okay?"

And almost on cue with his name being said, into the supply room walked this short African man. Without a word to anyone, he walked over to the outdoor brooms and began examining them.

"Akwei, this is the guy that's gonna work with you today!"

Still saying nothing, he simply nodded that he heard her while finishing his search for the best broom. When he finally made his choice, he headed for the elevators, and I just took that as my cue to grab the first broom I could reach and follow. Reaching the ground

131

floor, we walked out of the south wing building, across the street, and into the north wing, but not before first going into Zaro's Bread Basket so he could buy two coffees.

Following Akwei into the north wing compactor room—housing the largest dumpster I had ever seen—he then grabbed a seat and motioned for me to do the same, so I did. And to my surprise, he generously handed me one of those coffees, then began in his heavy but pleasant accent.

"We're gonna sweep all of Eighth Avenue, down Forty-first, across Ninth Avenue, and back up Fortieth Street, all day long. We gotta pick up everything we see, okay? That means everything."

He got up and walked over to the wall where there were two debris carts, both four times the size of a regular wheelbarrow. He steered one of them towards me, and I couldn't help but notice the way he treated every tool with such respect.

"We are going to fill these up. Every time they get full, we come in here and dump them in the dumpster. Cardboard boxes, crates, trash, everything you see, pick it up and put it in your cart."

Then he stood in front of me and got a tad more serious.

"Now, the supervisors and building staff never ever check up on me. I've been here a long time, and I've always done a good job. In the past, when young guys don't want to work hard with me, I just say 'okay,' and then I call down to the basement and tell the supervisors. So for us not to have any problems, let's just work hard and finish it all out, okay?"

I got his point: he'd report me in a heartbeat before letting me tarnish his spotless record, and I couldn't blame him for that. Besides, I had no problems with hard work anyway, thanks to all the times I helped Dad in renovating the run-down houses he was prepping to re-sell. And whenever Dad wanted a job done perfectly, he'd just say, "give me an Indian man's job!"

Anyway, Akwei and I finished our coffees and hustled out to hectic Eighth Avenue where the streets were dirty already. And quickly seeing how hard it was to sweep amidst all the foot traffic, I just imitated Akwei and "spot-swept," knocking what felt like hundreds of cigarette butts into my metal pick-up pan.

We then turned the corner and started sweeping down the much quieter Forty-first Street. Now Forty-first is what bisected the Port's two buildings: the five-story north wing and the seven-story south wing. And as the two buildings were connected at the second floor, this block looked more like a long, dark tunnel.

While sweeping down this dark, hundred-yard stretch, there were homeless sleeping everywhere—street-scarred legs and limbs protruding from cardboard boxes, soiled blankets, and piles of newspaper. Some legs wore tattered miniskirts, some wore soiled jeans, and some wore absolutely nothing—butt cheeks exposed like the day they were born and cried their first cry. There were even husband-and-wife sets of legs.

Then lining the long, dark curb like a bunch of parked cars (and with even more legs protruding from them) were those canvas laundry carts, most likely taken from a nearby hospital or hotel. And as the hot vent from Zaro's Bread Basket blew right into this whole area, it broke my heart that these people had to smell fresh-baked bread all morning, while their only hope of getting some was after some commuter had chewed all over it and chucked it in the trash.

A man stood against the wall taking a piss, while his rank, homemade river ran across the sidewalk and into the street. Sweeping right past him, I just lifted my broom and stepped over his river like nothing. The smell of wino-urine was already thick in the air, anyway. However, some fifty yards later, as I swept past some loose feces running down the wall and growing in nastiness at the bottom, I stepped clear aside and held my breath, for sure. It was obviously fresh; and with no toilet paper in sight, it was obvious that nobody had wiped. But then again, there was a lot of brown on some of the newspaper blowing around and trying to wrap around my broom.

These were the pre-Giuliani days—a very different New York City.

Well I quickly realized that being outside was just as wild as the bathrooms inside, with the exception of more elbow room and the sunshine. So as the sun kept rising, horns from the perpetual traffic kept honking while tempers kept flaring, trash kept reappearing, and I kept sweeping. And since no walkmans were allowed on the job, to combat the onset of boredom, I just started counting the different color crack viles on the sidewalk. Then, I stumbled upon some crack nuggets that had obviously been dropped. However, the quick smear under my boot confirmed that it was only chunks of white soap that someone got suckered with.

"Hey, you! Yeah, you! Come 'ere!"

A cop called me over to him as he stood by one of the cardboard boxes with a set of legs sticking out. Not only did the Port have its own police force, but they even had their own K-9 unit on the seventh floor. And speaking of K-9's, this cop had a perfectly built German Shepherd with him, baring its fangs and pulling towards the homeless man who was now awake and scurrying from his "home." Clearly those dogs were trained for this; you could tell by the way they went berserk whenever they got near someone on the ground. And clearly this cop was trained for this, as well. He looked like the type who pumped weights for hours while replaying violent scenarios.

Well, he could tell I was new; which is probably why he felt he could boss me around, even though he was hardly my boss.

"Hey, you gotta get all these homeless people out of these boxes! Then you gotta pick up all these boxes. Every one of them on this whole block. You got that?"

"Alright," I mumbled while pulling my work gloves from my back pocket. And as the cop stood and watched, I first used my boot to sift through the nasty newspaper "blankets" inside the box (making sure there were no needles to poke me), then I held my breath and hoisted the urine-soiled box into my debris cart. The muscles in my arms screamed as I strained to keep every part of it from touching my body (but of course it touched me).

"Good. Now you're gonna do that with all these boxes." And with that, the cocky cop yanked his K-9 and strutted away, looking so impressed with himself for making this rookie janitor do the unimaginable.

However, as power-trippy as some of them could be, many of these very cops would one day be national heroes—crushed under the 'sky-high' weight of the Twin Towers—as they raced downtown and inside the buildings just after the airplanes first hit on 9/11. Perhaps even this very officer who I was now ignoring and cursing in my mind.

▲ ▼ ▲ ▼ ▲

It was midday now, and the streets were wide-awake. Electronics and porn shops sizzled with business, while street vendors sizzled their "street meat." Some street vendors looked legit, but with others, you didn't even know what kind of meat it was—let alone how many days reheated it might've been. Plus, it was nothing to see some scrappy homeless guy helping these types of vendors out by handing out their can sodas for just a few bucks a day.

But guess what? These streets now had me so hungry—with their grittiness making me feel so gritty—that I didn't even think twice about gobbling down that mysterious meat. Nor did I care about the homeless man's dirty hands, let alone my own contagious fingers. For just as in *Lord of the Flies*, it wasn't taking long at all for some inner-savage to emerge from this private school boy.

Well, just like wasps in response to the heat, droves of homeless were now everywhere and doing everything. Drunken laughter, drunken yelling, and even drunken sexing in the darkest corners, all blending into one chaotic undercurrent of society. Then there were the fights: fights over liquor and crack, fights over some homeless girl, fights over sidewalk real estate, or simply fighting because they were insane or de-mon-possessed.

And whatever drugs you didn't see directly, you could see it in people's behavior. This one bony, dark-skinned woman parted the crowds of commuters like the Red Sea as she walked down Eighth Avenue, but not because she was bleeding or wielding some weapon. People were jumping out of her way because she was high on crack and topless with her saggy breasts exposed, breathing lustfully while scanning passing faces for some male eye contact.

Then lastly, there were the "leaners." Leaners were those who'd be so high on morphine that they'd lean over motionless for minutes at a time, in the most gravity-defying positions. See, the local drug clinics gave addicts free morphine to help their brutal "withdrawal" from heroin, but honestly, it was hard to tell which drug did them worse, as these leaners looked something like the living dead.

One leaner was leaned over on the very edge of the curb on busy Eighth Avenue, as cab after cab whizzed by within just feet of his head. Wondering if he was gonna end up getting smashed or even decapitated, I had to stop and watch for a while. Then some wino dude with no teeth came and stood right beside me.

"Hey young blood, how much you wanna bet he don't fall over in traffic?" He laughed. "Man, I'm telling you, he'll be there all day without fallin'! So how much you wanna bet?"

And to be savagely honest, a side of me actually wanted to see him get hit, just to see what would happen. And on these streets, it was crazy how sick and evil thoughts didn't even feel all that sick and evil anymore. For just like a needle addict locates a vein, I was starting to locate the "vein" of these streets' rhythm.

XIII

The "Zoo" In You

B y the end of summer, I enjoyed this routine of being in Hell's Kitch-
en before dawn. In fact, on many mornings I loved nothing more
than punching in before 6, grabbing a quick coffee, and stepping outside
for those last moments of calm as the sun was rising between the buildings: the distant sound of metal door grates rolling as a few storeowners
unlocked their businesses, a garbage truck squeaking to its few last stops
before rush-hour, the homeless still asleep in the retreating shadows, and
the smell of Zaro's fresh bread mixed with all the stenches rising from
the sidewalks. Yup, I was tapped in, and it was all in my capillaries now.
And it's not like it hit my bloodstream in some big, mystical way like I
might've imagined. It's just that after almost three months of being there
five days a week and for over eight hours a day, I just found myself feeling
quite at home.

I knew just about every secret stairway in the Port and almost every
alleyway outside the Port. I also knew many of the homeless, hustlers,
and addicts as well, as together we formed this spiny subculture of midtown society. And yes, "together" was the right word, because I could tell
by the way commuters shrank away from me and my smelly uniform that
they had also grouped me with the lowest of the low. And believe it or
not, I actually liked it that way. So while the upper-, middle-, and even
lower-class stayed commuting in their herds, I was content to be amongst
my own in the "gutter class." It felt good not having to worry about my
reputation or social responsibility—even being able to scratch my behind
or crotch right on the corner while having a crack addict run and buy me
a burger. I was a "first-class" New York City janitor—unpure and proud.

But don't get me wrong, I wasn't a true-blue veteran just yet. Because there were still plenty of things that tripped me out, like the day

that stressed-out businessman plunged from the top of a high-rise on Eighth Avenue as I watched while sweeping below. And what shocked me the most was that, as the man was still pacing the ledge above, some of the homeless around me started yelling up to him to just do it. And then after he jumped to his fatal gore, they even applauded and whistled.

Then there was the time I was deep in the Port, sweeping down a remote flight of steps, and stumbled upon this group of older men who were having their way with a small teenage boy. And what made it worse was that when I barked and caused them to scurry, the teenage boy willingly scurried right after them for more sexual abuse—as if that was all he was worth.

Lastly, there was the crack addict with the cute son, Eddie. And while it was nothing to see crack addicts shuffling through these streets with their little ones in tow, Eddie stood out to me because he looked just like me back when I was eight years old: light-skinned and obviously "mixed," with big curly hair. His mom even dressed him the way Mom once dressed me, right down to the brown leather sandals with white tube socks. So as Eddie's mom continued getting high in the women's bathroom next to mine, I just adopted Eddie as my "little man."

In a week's time, I really had love for this kid. And his hyperactively defiant little mind knew we had something special, too. Until one day, his mother stormed out the bathroom with a major attitude, like she suddenly needed a new place to get high. She summoned her son to start his usual jog behind her, and as Eddie sorrowfully turned back and waved goodbye to me, we both knew it was goodbye for good. Watching him disappear into the crowd, there was nothing I could do but hurt. And the things I would've told Eddie if I knew I had only five minutes left.

So day in and day out, I smoked my Newports (even though I once vowed to never become a smoker), weaseled the streets on lunch breaks, collected fly girls' phone numbers like a hobby, and slammed five-inch roaches into the walls until they became unconscious "hockey pucks" for me and the other younger janitors to play broom-hockey with. Yup, my master plan was coming along indeed. I was feeling way more manly already, and thus more happy. And as for the University of Pennsylvania in the fall, I hadn't forgotten about it, one bit. In fact, I even kept UPenn's newest brochure in the back pocket of my smelly uniform—rolled up inside a porno mag.

▲ ▼ ▲ ▼ ▲

There were plenty of codes I had to learn in this place, as well. Some the easy way and many the hard way.

Rule One: If there was a crime, you ain't seen a thing!

Like the time some suit-and-tie commuter walked into my empty bathroom while I stood at the entrance, staring off into space as usual. Unbeknownst to him, this grim-faced hustler was following him in, and just before going inside as well, he looked at me as if to ask if it was okay for him to do what he was about to do to the commuter. Shrugging my shoulders with a roll of my eyes, I gave him all the "I don't care" he needed, because I wasn't gonna be no snitch.

Hardhearted, I know, but it was easy to be this way. Just like it was so easy for all those corporate folk to step right over the convulsing body of their fellow businessperson, who might've been dying as he was purple and gagging right in the middle of Eight Avenue. Then, throw in the Wall Street execs who picked up male hookers at the Meat Rack, and it was quite obvious that there was a "Hell's Zoo" inside us all!

Rule Two: You were always being watched, whether you realized it or not.

Like the time some "detective" called one of my supervisors, described me to a "T," and said I had witnessed a serious crime and needed to be interrogated immediately. Well, I was rushed downstairs to the company phone where the "detective" quickly called right back. However, after making sure that I was the only person on the phone, he finally confessed that he really wasn't a cop after all, but just wanted to make me a sex proposal for money. The Meat Rack! I could hear his gang of marauders in the background now giggling along with him; and there was nothing worse than knowing that people I couldn't even see were plotting on me. People did whatever they wanted in Hell's Zoo, and with zero fear.

By the way, I still wanted that "zero fear."

Rule Three: If a fellow janitor got into some beef, whether it was their fault or not, you'd better step in and help. If you didn't, you'd either be "visited" later on in the locker room, or simply written off as "on your own." So one day, as I was sweeping Eighth Ave with Cowboy, and he suddenly felt the urge to live up to his name and challenge a whole group of homeless dudes, I had no choice but to lay my broom against the wall and let him know I was right there. Even though I was hoping that it wouldn't happen. I mean, I hadn't even known Cowboy for three full hours yet!

Rule Four: Getting drunk on the job was manageable.

I remember the first time I drank with some of the older janitors on one of the Port's rooftops. These were some real street veterans, for sure. Not only had they been working at the Port for years, but it was clear they'd been drinking long before that.

Anyway, paranoid as I was about getting caught by a supervisor, I thought I was still being cool by at least having a quart of Pink Champale malt liquor from the Korean grocery store that never checked ID. That is, until the veterans spotted what I was sipping and exploded with laughter.

"Man, young blood, what's the point of that? Man, you gonna have liquor on your breath and not even be buzzed! But hey, if fruity juice is what you want then that's fine with us!"

But that's another thing I was learning: there was a difference between laughing "at" somebody and merely laughing "with" somebody, the way family did. Because these big red uniforms made us family for sure, and we all stuck together no matter who was suddenly the butt of a family joke. For it was these same veterans who always took the time to school me on everything, like how to sharpen a paint scraper against brick until it was sharp as a blade, how to bluff in a heated confrontation to back down a crazy crack addict, which druggies sold the best "hot" merchandise, from Gucci watches to Amtrak tickets, and finally, how to detect fake gold when buying it from a hustler—even watching out for their trick of showing you a real gold chain first, and then after you tested it and wanted it, they'd quickly switch it with a fake one balled-up in their other hand.

If the Port didn't have the hustle, then the hustle didn't exist.

▲ ▼ ▲ ▼ ▲

There was one last thing every janitor had to learn: how to establish your own routine amidst such grueling monotony. So if I wasn't reading the crime section of *The New York Daily News*, watching my back, or just thinking real hard, then I was killing time with the homeless, crack addicts, hustlers, and pimps. (This was when "Forty-deuce" still had plenty of pimps; some still wearing crazy stuff like big yellow hats and platform shoes.)

ANGEL

Angel was one of the first bathroom regulars I ever befriended. Born in Puerto Rico, he must have been in his early forties. Angel was homeless, but you would have never guessed it. Aside from missing a few teeth, his clothes were always clean, his mustache always groomed, and he never smelled because he took daily showers at one of the shelters. Angel's right eye was permanently crossed, but he was still sharp as a tack. Besides, if he did miss something, his wife was always right there, not saying much but studying everything with the sweetest smile.

Angel would always find out which bathroom I had been assigned to for the day so he could come see me. And if I hadn't gotten my breakfast sandwich yet, Angel was more than happy to get it for me, along with my coffee and newspaper. And of course I'd give him enough for he and his wife to get whatever they wanted as well.

While many homeless spent their days guzzling liquor, chasing crack, and facing-off with each other, Angel never smelled like liquor and was always looking for work with a copy of the want ads in his back packet. And while many homeless would just bumrush your bathroom and drop their filthy drawers at your sink, Angel would politely ask before even shaving his tiny bit of scruff.

"Hey man, is it okay with you if I just shave real quick? I got a job interview today, and I want to look real clean, ya know?"

Angel represented that segment of homeless society who still had their self-respect and loved an honest wage. I never once heard him bad-mouthing the other homeless in some self-righteous attempt to distance himself. Besides, Angel's character was so strong that he didn't need to. So as demonic as it was, Hell's Zoo still had its "Angels."

SHORTY

Shorty was well under five feet, hence his nickname. No older than thirty, he was still in fit shape and had this boyishly-shy smile. Shorty and I liked each other a lot, and whenever he'd see me—whether in the Port or on the streets—he'd make sure to holler "wassup" with that same big smile.

Shorty's girlfriend was over a foot taller than Shorty, and though she looked like she had been homeless for over a decade, sadly enough, Crystal was only nineteen—just a year older than me. Sometimes, I'd be cutting through one of the dark tunnels beneath the Port and stumble on Shorty and Crystal in the middle of sexing under a raggedy blanket. I'd tiptoe away, but they wouldn't even notice me. Just like homeless learned to sleep soundly on the busy sidewalk, they had also learned to tune out passersby when being intimate on the concrete.

However, my heart broke for Shorty. Because as much as he loved Crystal, she loved that crack. Sometimes she'd get high and start flipping out on him for no reason, punching him in his face and everywhere else. All the while, you could see in his eyes just how much he loved her, which is why he'd never hit her back and never left her side.

One time, when Shorty wasn't around, Crystal came out of the women's bathroom and began smiling and whispering to me about us going off somewhere for a quick one.

"Yo girl, you better get outta here, man! Go find Shorty!"

And with that, she just shrugged her shoulders like it was all my loss, and then switched her hindquarters away. Crystal knew how close I was with her man, but that's what crack did. And of course, I never told Shorty.

Well Crystal soon became pregnant, and Shorty sure was excited. Only a couple of months later, she miscarried right on the sidewalk on Fortieth Street—Akwei's station, so I guess he cleaned the dead baby up.

Over time, Shorty didn't smile as much as when we had first met. And I sure missed that smile because nobody could smile like Shorty.

REAL ESTATE MAN

Real Estate Man lived, breathed, and even yawned real estate. A black man in his mid-forties or fifties, he was more than likely a professional who at some point had lost his mind and lost everything—or vice versa. You'd be hard-pressed convincing Real Estate Man that he wasn't still that same savvy guy.

He could always be found in the second floor bathroom in the north wing. Donned in a tan three-piece, corduroy suit and a black skully-hat over his wild fro, he always carried two briefcases, busting at the clasps with paperwork, and a Polaroid camera around his neck. The camera was busted, of course.

Walking into the bathroom every day like it was his office, he'd only use the extra-large handicap stall in the way back, where once he got in, he'd stay for hours, though he never really used the toilet. He would only sit on the toilet like it was his chair, while spreading the real estate sections from old newspapers across the unspeakable floor. Real Estate Man pretty much kept to himself. That is, until you stepped to him about buying some property, then he'd really come alive. And as bored as we janitors got at times, let's just say we "purchased" tons of property from him.

"Yo, Real Estate Man, I wanna house, man!"

Using his hand to raise his half-broken and twice-taped glasses on his nose, he'd take charge of the whole convo. And he was so articulate and serious, that if we weren't such hyenas the whole thing would've broken our hearts.

"Well let's see, what neighborhoods do you have in mind, sir? And are you married with a family, or will this just be for yourself?" And while we could never hold back our goofy smiles, the only time Real Estate Man smiled was when trying to be the best possible salesperson.

So in the smelliest and freakiest of places, there we were—working for a business but acting insane while talking real estate with an insane man who was nothing but business.

SUGA' BEAR

Suga' Bear could be found literally anywhere—from the bathrooms to the streets to the subways below. A short, dark-skinned woman who was maybe in her forties, she always wore a light blue sweatshirt with the cereal box superhero Sugar Bear on the front. She had this roughed-up wig that sat on her head more like a cool hat, since she made no attempts to wear it properly.

Now Suga' Bear moved like lightning. I mean, it was like one minute you'd see her outside the Port, then as you walked eight blocks downtown, she'd suddenly dart across your path again—almost as if she had an identical twin with the same crooked wig. But it was the crack that kept her moving that fast, running her mouth non-stop while talking to nobody in particular.

Whenever I saw her, I made sure to yell her name.

"Yo, Suga' Bear! Wassup, momma?"

And without fail, she'd quickly stop to flex her muscles and smile as if she really was Sugar Bear. She definitely dug the nickname I gave her. Matter of fact, I had coined quite a few of these nicknames, from Real Estate Man to Loco.

LOCO

Now as the bathroom janitor, you were the cleaner (coming across the unimaginable), the paramedic (as you sometimes had to poke people in the stalls to make sure they hadn't overdosed and died), the social worker (even when it meant convincing a man that his babydoll stroller with the raccoon's tail in place of a baby would be safe while he did diarrhea in the stall), and lastly, the police officer (kicking everyone out of your bathroom who wasn't really using the bathroom).

And although some of my coworkers scared addicts from getting high in their bathrooms by doing stuff like kicking in the stall door and breaking their glass pipes just as they were holding them up to their faces for a hit, that wasn't my thing. Besides, even if it were my thing, Loco was one dude whose pipe nobody could break. Simply because nobody could ever catch him.

Sort of like a Puerto Rican male version of Suga' Bear (and just as little, too), Loco always ended up in my stalls undetected. I mean, it was like I'd just finish kicking all the addicts out of my bathroom, when suddenly, one of the stall doors would fly open; and as the light cloud of crack smoke came floating out, so would Loco. He always wore the same denim jacket with the collar up, and always had a giant garbage bag slung over his shoulder like an elf from the North Pole.

Now, the word on the streets was that Loco was "the man" when it came to nabbing hot electronics. And once I found that out, Loco was welcome in my bathroom anytime.

"Yo Loco, c'mere!"

If he was super high, he'd always stare at me for a while first while turning his head sideways, just to make sure it was really me. Then once he deemed it safe, he'd scramble over while nervously looking over whichever shoulder wasn't blocked by the garbage bag.

"Yo Loco, I want a palmcorder man! A palmcorder!" I even took the time to act out holding a palmcorder in my hands. He quickly nodded like he got my point a long time ago.

"Okgimmeagarbagebag! Gimmeagarbagebag!"

One garbage bag? I gave him two garbage bags instead, thinking it might somehow motivate him to come back with two hot items.

"Ok, latertodaybythe . . . Luego!" He finished his sentence in quick Spanish and vanished, and I had no clue what in the world he had just said. Oh well. But this was all part of the daily gamble in this place—waiting for that next dude to whisper you over to his bathroom stall so he could show you what hot items he had in his own bag.

▲ ▼ ▲ ▼ ▲

Well, just like the cliche' "faster than a New York minute," my first summer at the Port was over. On one of my last days there, I stood on the Port's roof finishing my "forty" of Crazy Horse while staring at the crazy traffic below. "The Big Apple," the legendary place where dreams came true, now felt like my apple—my forbidden fruit, even. And I had just taken such a big, summer-long bite, that its juices were still running down my chin and neck!

Things felt great. I had a pocket full of money; I had girls; I had my "book smarts"; and now even "street smarts" galore. And to think of how far I had come in such a short amount of time! I remembered how I had scurried down Eighth Avenue like a scaredy-cat back on my first day. But not anymore, as this was the very type of change I had in mind from the beginning! So no wonder that I now felt fly enough to just fly right off the Port's roof and touch the sun. However, it was time for college now.

Still, I was gonna miss all this. I'd miss Loco, Shorty, and Angel. I'd miss the lights, the cameras, and the action. And of course I'd miss my janitor family, from Akwei, the hardworking African, to Brady, one of the veterans who stayed drunk and always bragged about how he could smell supervisors coming before they'd even pop up. And by the way, remember that muscular, deaf janitor who made noises like Chewbacca and looked like he'd break someone who touched one of his own? Well his name was Shawn, and we were gonna miss each other, too. Lastly, I was gonna miss Van' Puddin'.

Funny thing is, I knew about Van' Puddin' before I even knew his name. He was a Brooklyn boy, about twenty years older than me, well over six feet tall and with arms and fists that you couldn't forget. But what first caused me to notice him wasn't so much his size, as it was the way so many grown men followed after him—laughing at whatever Van' Puddin' laughed at, and dissing whatever he sucked his teeth at. I mean, you'd think the guy was a big-time loanshark or something. And that's exactly what he was.

The main reason he even worked at the Port was that, apart from making such easy janitor money, Hell's Kitchen was the base of his entire operation. And nobody dared cross Van' Puddin' (just like nobody dared cross him back in his Brooklyn domain). I mean, we'd all heard about the time he made this dude Shylock strip to his underwear right on the crowded subway. Then, bending naked Shylock back over his knee, Van' Puddin' warned him that the next time he didn't pay up, he'd crack his back.

Well by midsummer, Van' Puddin' and I started getting close. By summer's end, he even began referring to me as his son, giving me the nickname, "Fam"—short for "family." And not only did that make a difference in how people started treating me, but it also made a big difference in how I felt personally. The desire of that scared little Plainfield boy for a big brother was more than fulfilled.

But again, it was Ivy League time, the very thing Wardlaw and my family had been preparing me for all my life. Thus, the next part of my master plan was set to begin.

XIV

Ivy League: The Secret of My Success

Thick or thin? That's really all it boiled down to when getting back those letters from the colleges you applied to. I mean, first were those January application deadlines, where you procrastinated because of Christmas and all, and then raced like a madman to get everything off in time. Second, was when you counted down the months and tried not to worry. Then, at last came that precious first week of May, when you memorized exactly what time your mail carrier arrived, along with his or her first name.

And once that coveted letter hit your mailbox, you pretty much knew the answer already. Because while a paper-thin letter basically meant, "thanks, but no thanks" (since it only took a single page to say "no"), a thick one, on the other hand, meant "congratulations," as it also included stuff like financial aid, meal plan, and dorm info. And on that sunny day in May when I got home from Wardlaw and saw UPenn's "thick" letter waiting for me, I could've moonwalked for joy.

I couldn't wait to show Mom. By this point, Mom had been teaching adult education over in Newark's neighboring city of East Orange. Since we didn't have a car at the time, Mom would either get rides from a colleague who lived nearby or ride the six long buses to and from work. (She never liked being a burden on anyone.) So on this special day, I sat at the window until her ride stopped in front of our house and then quickly ran out to meet her as she was climbing out the car.

"Hey, baby," she greeted me as she hoisted her bag from the car like it weighed a ton.

"Hey Mom, read this," handing it to her face-down with my best poker-face. Perhaps assuming it was some last-minute bill from Wardlaw, Mom took the letter, gave a gentle sigh, and then proceeded to read what unbeknownst to her was her fondest dream come true.

"Ahhhhhhhhhhhhhhh!"

Struck by the lightning of single-parent victory, Mom screamed at the top of her lungs and even leaped into my arms like a little girl.

"Ahhhhhhhhhhhhhh!"

Like a hot kettle contained for too long, she was releasing way more than I could understand. Way more than her colleague watching from her car could understand, too. In fact, nobody could really understand, except for another single parent who had sacrificed everything for their kids.

For just as they say, "the darker the night, the brighter the dawn," we had definitely endured our share of dark nights to make this "dawn" especially bright. I mean, there were the cold nights, where she'd hold us extra close to keep us warm. There were the stranded nights, as our unfaithful Audi had broken down in no-man's land once again. There were the scary nights, where we whimpered and counted the minutes until daylight. There were the sleepless nights—me waking up in the wee-hours just to hear Mom sipping hot tea while trying to divine with "I-Ching" coins: a lonely, young woman's meanderings. Then lastly, there were those night rides in neighbor's cars to far away colleges, as Mom would ask if she and her two boys could tag along, just so we could get as much college exposure as possible at a young age.

Therefore, all of the above is why this caged bird now sang in the middle of our street.

"Can't nobody tell me @#$#! You hear me?"

And who exactly was Mom yelling this to? Well, I guess it was to anyone and everyone. See, Mom always felt like people were watching her, especially people who knew my dad, since he was so well-known in our city for his business and politics. And even though they had been divorced since I was little, people still recognized Mom. I mean, she'd be walking home in the rain with armfuls of groceries, and they'd recognize her, honk and wave, and keep right on driving. Or she'd be waiting for her bus in the blustery winds, and again they'd recognize her, honk and wave, and keep right on driving. And like most single moms, Mom worried about what people might be saying about the job she was doing in raising us—even convinced that some had predicted she would fail. Well, she definitely hadn't failed.

"Can't nobody tell me nothing, I said!"

Completely spent now, she reached for me one last time with the happiest tears.

"Awww, my baby boy, you did it! My firstborn, you did it! Can you believe it? Awww, I love you, baby."

"Love you too, Mom." She and I could've danced right on the spot.

"C'mon, let's go inside and call Momma now!"

And as for my grandmother—a widow of over two decades, who back when my grandfather first died, sat at her kitchen table crying, "I can't go on"—this was a dream come true for her as well. For not only did she "go on," but her firstborn daughter "went on," too—even giving her a firstborn grandchild who would now "go on" to an Ivy League university.

▲ ▼ ▲ ▼ ▲

September finally arrived, and my army duffles and college trunk were already waiting in the front yard. It felt strange leaving Brett and Mom for the first time, especially since Raymond, Mom's longtime boyfriend and our unofficial stepfather, had just moved out. In a way, it even felt like I was bailing on them. But I knew I had to go.

Before my final exit, I stepped to Brett's bedside for an official goodbye. There he was, my "little bro," snoring away under a mound of blankets just the way he loved it. And sure enough, that baseball bat was still between his bed and the wall, even ten years after that horrific night with the Evil at our back door.

"Yo man, I'm out now. Take care of Mom."

Without a word, he stuck out his arm from under the blankets so we could lock hands. And as we took our time letting go, the sudden flood of memories turned this cool grip into some sentimental hand-holding: playing Star Wars figures for hours, teaching him to cook Taylor ham and eggs, cleaning his vomit off the walls the time he got sick while Mom was at work, all the way up to us having girls over after high school and competing over whose were prettier. Man, we loved each other. And what I didn't realize then, was that part of the reason he stayed under his blankets that morning was because it was that hard for him to let his "big bro" go.

I took a last look at our living room: same artwork, same books, and same plants in the window. I was going to miss it all. I'd even miss our used carpet that one of our neighbor's handed down to us, with it's permanent doo-doo stains we always did our best to scrub out. Because after our Bullmastiff died, we got Isis, an adult Rottweiler from a dog rescue. And while Isis continued to keep the Evil away, she had never been housebroken. So sometimes home smelled more like a zoo. However, it was still the best place on the planet.

So after one last look, it was out to my front yard where Dad's van was crawling into our driveway. Only this time, there was no New York train to catch, and this time, he was wide awake and well-dressed. And of course he had every reason to be—for this Jim Crow country boy was taking his son to the Ivy League!

There was one other thing different about this ride: it was the first time since I was a toddler that me, Mom, and Dad would be in the same vehicle. So surreal as it was, Mom hopped in the front with him, I hopped in the back, and off we were. For the most part, it was a quiet ride down the New Jersey Turnpike to Philly. And whenever there was some convo between Mom and Dad, it was all smooth, just like Dad's "Down Home Blues" cassette that he loved playing on auto-reverse. Besides, I wasn't worried about any dumb arguments, anyway. That stuff had stopped years ago.

Arriving in Philly at last, we pulled in front of The W.E.B. DuBois College House, UPenn's African-American dorm. I still couldn't believe an Ivy League university would even have something like that, but best believe I was more than elated to experience it.

So joining the row of double-parked cars with blinking lights, we wasted no time unloading my stuff from the van. Dad and I carried everything while Mom inspected everything the way moms do. I couldn't believe I was actually at college.

My dorm apartment was way nicer than I thought. It had a small kitchen, bathroom, double-sink in the hallway, and three bedrooms with the largest one meant to be shared by two people. But since all three of my roommates had already moved in, and since I was so set on having my own bedroom for the first time in my life, I took the living room instead, making plans to hang a thick shower curtain at the entrance in place of a door.

So officially in my new home, I walked my parents back to the van for a final goodbye, where Dad hugged me and said "kick #%%, son" (like he always did), and Mom squeezed my neck until she got watery-eyed.

"It's gonna be cool, Mom. I'mma do my thing down here so I can get you that Benz you always wanted, remember?"

"Okay." She laughed as if deciding not to shed tears after all. "Boy, we sure did pay dues to get here though, didn't we?"

"Yup. And I'mma do my thing down here so I can give you the world."

"I know you will, baby."

And with that, Mom and Dad headed back to Plainfield and I headed back upstairs to start this next segment of my master plan.

Speaking of such, I had long since decided on pre-med studies. However, since UPenn didn't have a pre-med major, it would be biological basis of behavior, with a concentration in neural systems. And why was I so bent on being a doctor? Well, it was quite simple. You see, at a young age, while visiting my classmates' houses and enjoying the lavish lifestyles of those who had doctors for parents, I quickly decided on the same future career for myself, so that my kids could one day enjoy the same. Then by middle school, when Momma was diagnosed with breast cancer, I decided to specialize in oncology—eager to join the fight against this disease that made her lose those two Cherokee braids that once fell so regally over her shoulders. Thus, pre-med it was, and I had been stretching my mind with extra science and math classes since ninth grade.

Well, the very first thing I unpacked from my college trunk was my box, plugging it right in and blasting the latest in mixtape flavor. Mixtapes were recordings put together by NYC's underground DJ's, where they'd even invent their own "blends" by picking R&B acapellas to go over the zaniest Hip Hop instrumentals. You could only buy mixtapes on the streets, preferably from "Flavor Man Jamal," the cat who wore army pants and fur coats on the corner of Harlem's 125th Street and Malcolm X Boulevard. Mixtapes were still so new and unheard of that when two freshman females were already knocking at my door to introduce themselves and ask about my music, I wasn't the least bit surprised.

I was loving this college thing already.

Welcoming them into my room, their names were Gayle and Deborah. Gayle, a Jamaican girl, had the thickest and cutest Bronx accent, while Deborah, an Afrocentric West Philly girl, was part of the urban sect, "Five Percenters"—formally known as The Nation of Gods and Earths. Started by a Harlem man in the 1940's, Five Percenters were a spin-off from The Nation of Islam. They believed that while 85% of the world was "deaf, dumb, and blind" to everything around them, and 10% represented the evil blood-suckers who kept the "deaf, dumb, and blind" oppressed, Five Percenters were the remaining 5% of "poor righteous teachers" who's duty it was to "give sight to the blind."

Their teachings were broken down into lessons called "mathematics," which taught that "the black man"—all men of color, from black to brown to red—was actually the true god, while each black woman was of the mother earth. Some Five Percenters even believed that the evil blood-sucking 10% was exclusively "the white man," who was mysteriously created on an island by some mad scientist long ago.

Deborah was the first Five Percenter I'd become crazy cool with, but this belief was hardly new to me. For not only was it heavily propagated on the streets, but most of our favorite rappers growing up were Five Percenters as well: like Rakim, Big Daddy Kane, Sadat X, Poor Righteous Teachers, and others. As a kid, I even remembered this older dude up the street from my house who always wore the Five Percenter symbol (the Islamic crescent moon with a star and the numeral "7") on the back of his leather jacket.

However, in practice, the whole concept of actually being "god" and white people being the devil was impossible for me to swallow. I mean, although I had dealt with my share of racism from some whites over the years, I had also spent too much time with many whites who were no less adorable and sincere than my very own family. My Aunt Carol had even married a Greek med student, who not only became a successful doctor, but also became the generous anchor and backbone of our family. And lastly, while early American history was loaded with "ripped out" pages of whites doing some devilish things, I'd also be a liar if I denied that some of the most devilish things done to me personally were by non-whites. Therefore, it seemed that all races had their own "devil" within.

So as ego-boosting as it was to have Deborah's lion-faced, older cousin show up at my dorm later and greet me with that unifying "peace, god," I simply said the same thing in return and then left it at that. But I sure dug the idea of him going to the liquor store and grabbing some forties of Old English 800 for us all.

So after a full day of unpacking, meeting people, and even seeing everyone's faces at the college house's first big social, my first day at Penn was just about over. As I sat alone in my room, sipping my forty of St. Ides while listening to another mixtape, there was a lot to think about. I even thought about my best friend, Deuce, remembering how our plan had been for me to come to UPenn while he played basketball at Temple over in North Philly. However, I was at UPenn now, but he was back home moving bundles of crack and heroin around the projects.

"Man."

And what did we do in our culture when we missed someone tremendously? I simply leaned over on my bed, stuck my forty out the window, and poured some of my drink onto the sidewalk two stories below—subtracting what Deuce would have gulped down himself had he been there with me.

But I was worried about him, too. For as fly and charismatic as he was—and to be making such quick money as he was—it would only be a matter of time before he'd become the rising envy as well as the dream bust for every undercover narco.

"Love you always, Deuce."

▲ ▼ ▲ ▼ ▲

My first day of classes. Off went my alarm, and up went my head from the pillow. No coffee needed for this one, I was wide awake as ever. But I was nervous too, as this whole thing felt like some big job on Wall Street. Because once I walked out my dorm, I'd be joining 11,000 of the most competitive minds on the planet. And my "job," if you will, was to rise above the mean, while also making a pretty mean name for myself in the process.

Pushing aside my "bedroom's" shower curtain, I saw that my three roommates were already up and dressed: Elvin, a senior, majoring in electrical engineering; Ron, a junior, majoring in African-American studies; and J.J., another freshman, was on the pre-med track just like me. And while all three of them were really nice guys, there was one other thing I couldn't help but notice. While me and all the other nice people I met were still into our sexual R&B and gun-busting Hip Hop, my roommates always had church music playing! I felt unlucky, realizing that my

summer-long dream of having that cool, partying apartment was officially dead. (But little did I realize that God was up to something in my life.)

As far as I was concerned, God wasn't something that any "busy"
person had time for, anyway. I mean, there was always something else to
do, somewhere else to go, or someone else to see. And never mind how
much of my "busy" time I might've wasted with being naughty. That was
my personal business, right? And as I said, anyone with "business" simply
didn't have time for God, Ivy Leaguers especially. So with my White Sox
baseball cap, my Guess sweatshirt, my Sony walkman, my new napsack,
and my truckload of arrogance, I was smelling good and out the door in
no time. My first class, Biology 101, was at 9 a.m.

I found my way to Leidy Laboratory's Room 10, and it was like
nothing I had ever seen—an amphitheater packed with hundreds of students seated and poised for action, their coffees in hand and notebooks
already out. While here I was, perfectly on time, but felt like I was an
hour late. This was the major leagues, all right. At first I didn't think I'd
find a seat amidst my competitors, but I finally located one.

And competitors is exactly what they were. For since our exams
would be graded on a curve—a high and difficult curve at that—it was
student vs. student. This explained the stories I'd already heard of students finding fellow classmates' notebooks lying around, and instead of
turning them in just throwing them away. Anything to keep the class
average as low as possible, so their grades might be as high as possible.

The room was mostly white, Asian, and Indian; and out of the four
hundred or so students, there were only a handful of blacks and maybe
one or two Latinos. But I already knew that science was a field that few
minorities ventured into. And though it was exciting to be one of those
"few," I also knew that because of that, a lot of my classmates might not
take me as seriously when it came to forming those crucial study-groups
and such. Thus, I felt big and little at the same time, if that makes sense.

The biology professor made his entrance at 9 a.m. sharp, unmoved
by the silence of the watchful crowd as he descended the endless steps to
the bottom of the room where a large table awaited him. Four teacher's
assistants followed close behind, each looking destined for scientific success. Wasting no time, the professor jotted his name and office number
on the immense chalkboard, clipped the mini mic to his lapel, tapped it
for a sound check, and began.

"I'd like to welcome you all to Biology 101. Here we will be studying the plant kingdom on a cellular level. Please note my office number on the board. Now, you should've already grabbed a syllabus located on the ledges by the doors when you first came in. Pull out that syllabus and let's begin."

And unlike Wardlaw, where even in our honors classes the first couple of days could be rather fluffy, this class was underway like our first exam was tomorrow. But all this was to be expected. So since most of us were from top college-prep high schools, we already knew how to take copious notes until your hand burned like fire, pause and shake it like silly until the pain subsided, and then jump right back in for more.

Next was calculus, and with only ten minutes to get across campus, my steps looked much more hurried than cool. Finally locating David Rittenhouse Laboratories, I was relieved to see that my calculus class was smaller and less tense than Biology. And as class was soon underway, I was ecstatic to see that we'd be doing the same exact stuff I had just learned in high school. Now just as biology had an additional three-hour weekly lab, calculus had a weekly recitation where we'd be regularly tested on what we learned. So calculus would still be intense in its own right; our expensive graphing calculators alone attested to that.

Speaking of expensive, my jaw all but dropped when I went to the campus bookstore to buy books the day before. Yes, I had made great money at the Port. It's just that after gambling with the other janitors, shopping for my high-end clothes, helping out with bills at home, treating Mom to a few nice things, and paying for my yearly meal plan, I ended up coming down to Philly with only $500. And as I stood at that bookstore register with my monstrous biology text, my calculus and Latin books, study materials, and gadgets, that $500 was good as gone—officially making me another "broke freshman." But I wasn't worried, because my financial aid package included me getting a work-study job right away.

Anyway, calculus was now over, and it blew my mind that every Wednesday I'd actually be done for the day by 11 a.m. So leaving the lecture hall and stepping into the sun again, I threw on my headphones and started the trek back to the top of campus, where DuBois College House and the Commons cafeteria were. Extending from Thirty-third to Fortieth Streets while hedged in by Spruce and Walnut Streets, UPenn's campus was like one giant rectangle, for the most part. Locust Street was between Walnut and Spruce, but as it bisected the campus it became Locust Walk—or "the Walk"—only open to foot traffic. And even though UPenn was surrounded by rugged West Philly, the campus was still insulated by its big historic buildings, meticulous landscaping, and its very own police force. And every time I saw that famed English Ivy creeping up the buildings, I'd get giddy inside all over again.

I mean, this place felt like paradise. The only things missing were the sand and the grass skirts. And speaking of skirts, there were gorgeous girls from all over the globe—Brooklyn to Bangladesh, Manchester to the Middle East—with sun-kissed skin tones in every shade.

A little further up Locust Walk was Van Pelt Library, and next to that was the "College Green." Packed with students tossing frisbees and lying on blankets, College Green was something like UPenn's Central Park. And though it looked like one big mass of people there, you could still make out the different cliques. You had your Grateful Dead hippie section, your yuppie section where gals smoked imported Dunhills, and even your overdressed nerdy section. However, being nerdy was hardly despised at UPenn, since come exam time, that's what we all wanted to be.

Heading up Locust Walk some more (across from the renowned Wharton Business School), there was a row of the most pristine fraternity houses, all connected like a bunch of mini-castles. It was like a separate paradise within UPenn's paradise, and while the rest of us students were stuck in napsack-to-napsack traffic, these fraternity kids stood aloof in the elbow room of their front yards, with leather couches plopped on their grass. Meanwhile, Bob Marley's "Jammin'" blasted through a speaker in one of their large windows.

Almost shrouded in mystery to the rest of us, it was even said that these houses had personal chefs who cooked the frat kids' every meal. And as I now saw a small pig roasting over an open fire in one of the yards, it was easy to believe. Not a care in the world with these guys (so it seemed), and for a minute I couldn't help but covet it all.

After taking in some more sights, I ate my lunch in the cafeteria and headed back to DuBois. DuBois was clearly the least renovated dorm on campus ("the projects" is how we jokingly referred to it), but we were still proud to call it "home." And with each of us students bringing a piece of where we were from—from Nigeria to the Caribbean to Cali—a simple walk down our hallways would have you hearing and smelling it all: reggae, jazz, Egyptian Musk or Coco Mango incense, fried chicken, plantains and curry, and sweet-smelling hair products.

"Yeah Mom, it's great down here!" I'd tell her as she called me almost every evening. The University of Pennsylvania—"Not Penn State" as our T-shirts arrogantly boasted. And as my first batch of mid-terms came back golden, this next segment of my master plan was off to a dynamite start. An amazingly dynamite start, even. Because two months into my first semester, I was also graced with the opportunity of a lifetime: a black doctor, who lived in Dubois as a faculty resident, singled me out during "parent's weekend" and offered to mentor me.

"If you're serious about wanting to become a doctor, Aaron, you can start accompanying me on my rounds in the hospital."

And without even looking at Mom, who had taken the train down for the weekend, I knew her mouth was dropped. I mean, this was an opportunity that pre-meds went their entire college career without experiencing.

"All we'll have to do is look at your schedule, find your biggest window during the day, and then see where that fits in with my daily rounds. You'll just need to go to the medical bookstore and get yourself a resident whitecoat and stethoscope."

"Sure. Thank you." I didn't really know what to say. But inside I was like the 4th of July.

So before Mom boarded her train back to Jersey, she insisted on giving me money for khakis, shoes, and that special whitecoat. And within a week's time, there I was, looking like a full-fledged med student as I strutted across campus to join Dr. Green in the hospital's geriatric unit. And along the way, I could just about tell who else was pre-med by the way they'd stare at me, as if saying to themselves, *"Where in the world is he going, and how can I get something like that on my résumé?"*

Success in the palm of my hands, UPenn was my cake.

And if the streets of New York was my icing, then could it be said that I was having my cake and eating it, too?

XV

IVY GROWS WILD, TOO!

___

There I was, in bio lab on another Friday afternoon, and I couldn't stop stealing looks at her. And I'm not talking about a "sista" from DuBois, or even some "mommy" from the Latina sorority. Nope, it was my lab partner, a blonde-haired, blue-eyed white gal from Connecticut named Courtney. And as our eyes sometimes met, I could tell she was digging me back.

"*But never that,*" coaching myself away from those ocean-blue eyes one more time. See, Spike Lee had just come out with his controversial film, "Jungle Fever," which now left most black dudes scared about dating "the other side" and getting black-balled as a "sell-out." And how real was this? Why I'd already overheard a few sistas in DuBois making those very types of comments about someone else! So I wasn't gonna mess around on this one, as even a cultured and intellectual place like UPenn wasn't exempt.

But man, Courtney was pretty. I would've loved to just ditch lab and drive her off for a picnic, where we could play my Hip Hop as well as her Grateful Dead or Pearl Jam—even do something goofy like throw dandelions at each other. But like I said, "*never that.*" My dire need for identity and acceptance was already too wrapped up in UPenn's black community to risk it.

Now UPenn's black community was considerably big. Along with Harvard, it was said to be the largest in the Ivy League. More so, with most of us minorities having grown up in predominantly white prep schools all our lives, our community at UPenn became all the more sacred to us; something we had spent much of our lives dreaming about. This also explains why some black gals came to UPenn and so quickly "flipped the script" into Afrocentrism, chopping a lifetime's worth of permed hair

159

into "naturals," rocking kente cloth in place of name brands, and quoting militant poetry full of words like *"Sankofa"*—an African word meaning "to take back that which had been forgotten."

Then, as many of our late-night discussions in DuBois centered around our respective bouts with racism back in our high schools, some black students ended up not wanting anything to do with UPenn's white community all, even going as far as giving dirty looks to a white student sitting next to them in an African-American studies class. All of this in the name of giving "them" a taste of how "we" were often made to feel. Thus, there were black students who became somewhat racist themselves, though they never would've admitted it.

Now whether your "all-nighters" were spent in Van Pelt Library or simply in your room with a 2-liter of Mountain Dew, what every race would always have in common was that we all knew how to study hard. Then, once those big exams were over and the weekend came back around, we also knew how to get so drunk that it sometimes took two full days to feel normal again. The way we'd party was dangerous to say the least, but to us it was just a normal form of stress relief.

So on a Friday night, you could plant yourself almost anywhere on campus and see all the drunken action, from rich gals puking all over their Tiffany jewelry, to poor, foreign students drinking cans of the cheapest beer. And as for me, I didn't know which was more intoxicating: the tequila and "Jello-shots" combined, or the fact that at eighteen years old, I had more older women inviting me to their fancy off-campus apartments than I could remember.

Now, as far as marijuana went, even though my homies from home had started smoking years ago, it was still something I had never tried. Because while I didn't mind stumbling into my house with wino-liquor on my breath, I just couldn't imagine walking under Mom's nose reeking of weed. However, all that was about to change now that I wasn't home anymore. And while there were many in DuBois who would've been honored to hand me my first blunt, my first time getting high wasn't there. Nor was it with one of the sistas in their fancy off-campus apartments. It was with Courtney.

It all started one Friday in lab, as she sighed for joy at another stress-ful week being over.

"Oooh, I can't wait for later tonight! I'm gonna get high!"

"Oh yeah, what you guys got?" I asked like I was some big smoker myself.

"Well, a buddy of mine is coming down from Connecticut with some 'home-grown.'"

"What's 'home-grown'?" While I knew about "dime bags" and "nick-el bags," this was something I never heard of.

"Well, 'home-grown' means my friend grows it in his backyard. It's like a 'kind bud,' you know? It's real good stuff. Hey, you wanna come over, too?"

And though I had no clue what "kind bud" was either, all I heard now was her sweet invitation.

"Yeah, I'll come! Just tell me when and where."

"Ok, well here's my number. Just call me in a few hours."

"Cool."

So Courtney smiled, I smiled, and we both went right back to scrib-bling boring data.

Well later that night, I showed up to her smoke-filled bedroom, packed to capacity with her friends from Connecticut. Clearly, everyone was roasted already, so no wonder the bong was immediately sent my way. A bong was like a hooka without the hoses, where you put the glass tube up to your mouth, filled the chamber with weed smoke (or what-ever), and then sucked it all in. Unknown on the streets, this was my first time even seeing one.

"Okay, y'all gonna have to show me how to do this."

And of course I did my best to front like I was some weed veteran (couldn't have anyone doubting my coolness). So that night marked my very first exhale. And while I already knew that there'd be countless exhales to follow, what I didn't know was that most of those future exhales would really be nothing more than smokey, deep sighs: sighing at regrets, sighing for lack of answers, sighing for mastery over the monotony of it all.

But for now, I just wanted to be cool and more than curious.

Now with all my wanderings through Hell's Zoo and such, who would've guessed that my Ivy League bio class would host my first drug experience? And I wasn't finished making drug connections there, either.

Because it wasn't too long after that night with Courtney, when another classmate in bio lab complimented my "Philly Blunt" T-shirt.

"Dude, Philly blunts?" He smiled big.

"You know it, man." I gave him the coolest smile back.

"Dude, you wanna join us for some after lab is over?" His Grateful Dead T-shirt as much of a giveaway as mine was.

"Yeah, no doubt."

So not even knowing each other's names yet, we slapped hands and went back to our respective lab benches.

When lab was finally over, we headed straight for his spot, and I couldn't believe who was accompanying us. Because it wasn't Courtney, nor was it just one of his roommates. Why it was one of our professor's teaching assistants! And as we walked, he quickly tossed his scientific hat aside and began sharing his woes.

"Dude, I don't know what I'mma do, man. My Mom and Dad got me a beach house on this island, but I told them I don't want a beach house on that island! I want another beach house somewhere else, ya know?"

"Yeah man." The Grateful Dead T-shirt nodded like his woe was more than rational. And if that little convo didn't make a big enough financial statement, it sure did when I realized where Grateful Dead T-shirt lived—one of those exclusive frat houses on the Walk. This particular one had tall, Roman-styled columns and a huge St. Bernard galloping around as its mascot.

And I must admit, it felt great having some of my fellow black students notice me hanging outside this place as they walked by, unable to hide their wonder at how I had managed to pull it off. I mean, it was almost like my connection with these rich dudes implied that I somehow had access to all their secrets to success. So of course I soaked it all up and let people's imaginations run wild.

After standing outside for a few more minutes—meeting some of his housemates as they posed like superstars while entertaining groups of cute blondes and brunettes—we headed inside, past the kitchen where the chef cooked their meals, and up three flights to the top floor, where huge bedrooms teemed with personality and expensive hobby equipment. We went to the front bedroom, grabbed seats on the couches, and as the music started playing, out came the bong.

But mind you, this wasn't just any bong. For as Courtney was the first to show me a regular bong, Grateful Dead T-shirt was now the first to show me a six-foot bong! And like lions sensing a fresh kill, his other housemates just began popping up in the room with excited faces as well.

One of them hopped up on a chair to go first. Putting the six-foot bong to his mouth, it was so ridiculously long that someone else had to kneel down on the floor to light the weed bowl at the bottom. I watched intently, knowing it would be my turn in no time. And sure enough, after watching the first and second dudes capsize onto the couch—with their mouths exploding open with clouds of smoke—it was my turn.

Again, I didn't even know these guys. But for our age and imbecility, this was more than normal. I mean, on a drunken Friday or Saturday night, we could find ourselves sharing blunts with the most random, shady dudes—not knowing what herpes may have been living on their wet lips. So standing on the same chair now, I grabbed the top of the bong, while Grateful Dead T-shirt was more than happy to keep lighting the bowl at the bottom on the floor. I felt like a high diver before some stunt, and the bong seemed three times bigger now that I was staring down its red barrel. But no turning back, even though the fear of my lungs exploding into bloody pieces crossed my mind.

As Grateful Dead lit the bowl, I put my mouth to the bong and began sucking until I could feel the veins in my neck and temples straining. And like a giant snake emerging from its cave, sure enough, the thick white smoke began creeping up the chamber towards me.

Once the chamber was full (and as I was officially out of breath), Grateful Dead then pulled the bowl and I took the deepest breath and sucked with all my might. Boom! The six-foot white, glowing snake disappearing into my lungs, into my very soul. And like a mule kick to my chest, my lungs detonated, leaving me toppled off the chair and choking like mad.

"Way to go, dude!"

And with high-fives coming towards me through my oh-so-watery eyes, you would've thought I had just joined their frat or something.

So let's just say that when I walked down the Walk now, I didn't feel all that disconnected from these pristine frat houses anymore.

Although I got drunk and high like it was Prince's "1999," I was still maintaining a "B" average; so in my mind that made it all okay. More so, my grades even helped me justify breaking my strict vow of "weekends only," as I was now getting high in the middle of the week as well. And just as it was remarkable how I could party so hard and still get the grades, it was more remarkable the way I was so good at deceiving myself. Pretty soon, the only "strict vow" I had left, was shutting my closet door before smoking weed, so that my whitecoat wouldn't reek of it when I was on hospital rounds with Dr. Green.

Now, how was I able to pull off such grades since it was rumored that weed affected your memory and ability? Well, I didn't know. All I did know was that ever since Wardlaw, I had this knack for ingesting large amounts of info in short amounts of time. Clearly, it was a gift, which was why I could work at Dairy Queen by night and still be ready for some crazy honors test by morning. Dad would always just say that I was "smart" like him.

However, instead of being thankful and humbled by this gift, I took the most arrogant ownership of it, basically deeming myself indestructible and unstoppable. I was the humanist of all humanists, and honestly felt there was nothing I couldn't accomplish. More so, I was quick to let someone know about the childhood struggles I had endured to get where I now was—selfishly claiming the glory for it all.

Well by this point, I had teamed up with some other freshmen who lived in DuBois, and who also had this same "gift." Noodle was from Harlem and was in the Wharton Business School, while Addis—also in Wharton—was from Hollis, Queens. Both of them had spent their previous summers interning on Wall Street, and both of them were crazy and spontaneous like me. Thus, we became inseparable—"the three musketeers"—living for fly girls, cheap thrills, fashion, and ultimately to conquer the entire world, which was why we were at UPenn to begin with.

Well one Saturday night, as the three of us were drunk, high, and sick-and-tired of scrounging for food every weekend while the cafeterias were closed, we stumbled upon the "art" of shoplifting from the campus Wawas. And I'm not talking about penny-candy or gum, either. I'm talking enough food for a banquet: half-gallons of OJ, loaves of bread and hot dogs, even hoagies we'd have them prepare at the deli counter before sliding them into our puffy "goose" jackets. So stealing became as normal to us as grabbing our free copy of the university's *Daily Pennsylvanian* newspaper.

Speaking of the Daily Pennsylvanian ("DP"), after one of their columnists—an undergraduate who seemed to enjoy racial controversy—insisted on writing editorials that were insulting to the black community (and as the "DP" did nothing in response to peoples' repeated complaints), a group of us gathered in DuBois one night and strategized the confiscating of 14,000 copies of the newspaper. I mean, since they were "free" anyway, we'd just give the entire university one full day without their beloved paper, so they might better consider our protest for racial respect. But little did we know that this little protest of ours would make national news.

Well on the set morning, about thirty of us gathered way before dawn, all of us dressed in black and ready to run our routes. We had already divided the campus into sections (similar I guess to how Europe once divided Africa at the Berlin Conference), and would have upperclassmen with cars doing steady laps around the perimeter, while mountain bikers and runners were to meet them at checkpoints to unload the bundles of plundered "DP's" so they could then be driven to a dumpster far, far away. And once we began, we moved like some ninjas, political ninjas even—for at every emptied newspaper rack, we left a formal letter entitled, "a message from the black community."

But before it was all over, building security guards got involved, the UPenn police got involved, and after a police officer struck one of the black students with his stick, even CNN got involved. However, in the end, the president of the university addressed the whole thing, the racist columns ceased, and the thirty of us black students who had done the whole thing formed a bond that we'd never forget.

▲ ▼ ▲ ▼ ▲

I was just a freshman, but had already earned the respect of the "big seniors" as one who could hold his liquor. While others ran for the toilet, I ran for another bottle, and it was like I had no "off" switch. In my drunken cockiness, I'd ignorantly tell everyone that it was all because I was Indian, and how true Indians could hold their liquor like no other. Looking back, it was pitiful that I was so destitute of any of my native people's amazing history (while there was tons and tons of it), that the only thing I could look to as some symbol of fortitude was their perseverance through alcohol.

While I loved boasting about how much I could drink, I never truly examined why I drank so much. However, it was partly because of the burdens and old wounds that gnawed at me. Plus, I still had my fears too. So while the weed and liquor were the bulk of our social scene, they also acted as suppressing agents for me—dulling the noise in my head while in exchange, giving me a silly, funkadelic forest where I could laugh my life away. But it was all a lie. That's why even amidst my nonstop partying and popularity, at times I couldn't help but wonder, "Am I really happy?"

On more than one occasion, after forcing the most insane liquor and drug combinations into my body, I passed out right on the floor of my bedroom's entrance—black leather jacket, black skully-hat, and black Timberland boots. And almost supernaturally, J.J., one of my Christian roommates, was there for me every time. Getting out of his bed, he came into our hallway, scooped me up from the floor, changed me out of my jacket and boots, and even tucked me into my bed. Then, as I'd wake up in a daze later that afternoon, his smiling face would come into focus as he stood over me.

"You okay there, roomy?"

"Yeah I'm fine, man. What happened last night?"

"Man, you came in here singing some crazy R&B song, and then passed right out in the hallway, so I put you to bed. Then I slept right here on your floor, just to make sure you wouldn't choke on your vomit in your sleep."

"Wow, man. Thanks." I was shocked by this kind of friendship. I mean, not even my childhood homies had ever shown me that kind of love and respect.

"No problem, roomy!" And with that, he turned and went to his room, where his church music was playing.

▲ ▼ ▲ ▼ ▲

Though I still sometimes fantasized about how fun things might've been if I had had "cool" roommates instead, I didn't complain about my Christian roommates anymore. In fact, I had actually come to appreciate how our apartment was so peaceful all the time (even when Elvin squealed away on his trumpet). Though sadly, I wasn't the least bit concerned with giving them any peace in return.

Ron, my other roommate, knocked on my bedroom door one day.

"Hey, Aaron, I'm having a group from my church come here tomorrow for worship practice. You think you could not smoke weed or blast music while they're here, and especially not while we're singing and praying in my room?"

"Yeah okay, I won't smoke." Only for me to end up smoking as if we had never talked about it. It was disrespectful to both him and his church members, but since I was the kind of guy who regarded Bible pages as a good alternative to "rolling papers" for marijuana, what else would one expect? I was foul, for sure.

I never once bought toilet paper or soap to contribute, and I definitely never cleaned the bathroom. However, my roommates did something that I couldn't argue against, or use as ammunition the next time I got on my anti-Christian soapbox: they just kept loving me unconditionally. That's also why even though I had met droves of hypocritical Christians at UPenn, I knew J.J. was definitely the real deal.

More so, sometimes I couldn't help but imitate his "positive" ways. I mean, there were times when I'd have on my jacket and be on the way out the door to some party, only to see J.J. relaxing at his desk, and then I'd just take off my coat and stay home. This was my buddy, for sure. We studied for exams together, celebrated many good grades together, and laughed around with each other's moms on the phone. And when girls would come by to see J.J.—though strictly on a platonic level—it was nothing for J.J. and me to start wrestling right in front of them, just like two brothers.

That's why it made perfect sense when we one day decided to be roommates for the rest of our stay at Penn. And with J.J.'s life seeming so sweet—as he spoke of God so fondly—maybe I'd even consider going to church with him one day?

But then things changed. And though J.J. never seemed caught off guard by any of the nutty things I'd do, this one got him.

"Yo J.J. man, I've been meaning to tell you this, but I think I'm gonna live with Noodle and Addis next year, instead. See man, what I forgot was that we had already made an agreement to do this a long, long time ago. And I really forgot until now."

Straight lies.

"Okay. No problem." And with that, he walked back into his room. It was my first time seeing J.J. disappointed. And because I was popping this on him the very day before the big housing lottery, he wouldn't have time to find another roommate even if he wanted to. That's exactly why he ended up living alone the following year.

So yes, way back in ninth grade at my Confirmation, I got let down by church traditions, and it wasn't my fault. However, as I was now rejecting this Christian who had shown me the heart of Christ tangibly, unconditionally, and undeniably, this time, best believe it was all my fault. God had brought me to UPenn and literally surrounded my very bedroom with His love, and I had just cast Him aside like the budding hustler that I was.

And speaking of being a hustler, wasn't it about time to head back to Hell's Zoo and my cackling janitor crew?

▲ ▼ ▲ ▼ ▲

Just before freshman year was over, I got a call from Dr. Green one day. And while it was normal for him and his wife to call and check up on me, this time I could tell something was wrong.

"Hey Aaron, if you're not busy, could you come down to my apartment for a minute?"

"Sure." And since he lived right on the first floor of DuBois, I was at his door in two minutes.

His simple but elegant living room had become such a refuge over the months, a home-away-from-home where I could retreat from campus life, watch some TV, and even play with his two little kids while his wife cooked me something to eat. See, what began with Dr. Green just offering to mentor me had now blossomed into he and his wife basically adopting me like family. And we enjoyed each other so very much, too. Which is exactly why he now had to say what he needed to say.

"Aaron, now I want you to know that I'm not accusing you of anything, okay? However, I want you to know that there's rumors going around in DuBois about you doing drugs and even stealing from some of the stores around here. Now, I'm not gonna say anymore, or ask you anymore, but you need to know this: that as a professional man with a reputation to uphold, I cannot have anyone who wants to be involved in that kind of stuff working closely with me. Can you understand that?"

How gentle he was in challenging me so sternly!

"Yes, I understand," I respectfully answered.

And that was basically the end of it. So I got up and cordially left his apartment—neither of us knowing what else to do in the awkwardness of the moment.

Now, good Wardlaw boy that I was, how could I not wholeheartedly respect Dr. Green's simple wishes? I mean, I did respect Dr. Green—very much so. Only there was one problem: I respected my master plan (my selfish desires) a thousand times more. Therefore, I couldn't change for him, or anybody else, for that matter. And all I took that talk to mean was that Dr. Green could never, ever find out about my crimes or my dirt again. Besides, I wouldn't be living in "nosey-behind DuBois" next year anyway.

So with my first year officially finished, it was time to load everything back into Dad's van for the summer. But before leaving UPenn, I had to bid a romantic farewell to my new girlfriend, Natasha—a twenty-one year old junior, and by far one of the hottest gals in the Philly college scene. She was a big "Delta girl" too, and the first time I saw her stepping with her sorors at a "Greek BBQ," I nearly lost my breath, for real. At first, I didn't think she'd want to deal with a young freshman like me. But before I knew it, we became buddies, then friends, then real good friends. Then she became mine.

And of course it felt great having an "older girl." And of course I took it as the highest compliment as random men on the street would stop my Haitian princess just to tell her that she looked like Halle Berry or Toni Braxton. I mean, even white guys on campus had their crushes on her.

Then on the flipside, I got my share of stares from some upperclassmen from the different black fraternities and from other nearby colleges, too, like, "Who in the world does he think he is, anyway?" But I wasn't sweating any of them, because though I rarely bragged about it, I had a crime family in New York that was just a phone call away—and nobody wanted to see them.

So was I more than a tad bit cocky? Absolutely.

And was my master plan plus my ego more than a tad bit toxic? Absolutely.

XVI

MR. HYDE: THE ANATOMY OF A THUG

Slang: way more than "ain't" and bad grammar, every hood across America had its own version. But as far as Jersey and New York were concerned, ours was the best. And though we all knew it, it still boiled down to how it sounded when you said it. I mean, did you sound "gully" or just plain gullible? Were you wily with it, or just a wannabe? And nobody wanted to be dissed as a wannabe.

Money: cheddar, loot, greenbacks, dead presidents

Girls: females, honeys, hotties, chickenheads, skeezers

Your girlfriend: your boo, your cheese, wifey

A person: dude, cat, money-grip, n*gg*h

Relaxing/profiling: chillin', lampin', loungin', parlayin'

Your style: your steez, your technique

Your house: your crib, your pad

Drug dealing: clockin', hustlin', slingin', puttin' in work

To have drugs on you: to be dirty

Guns: gats, hammers, biscuits, burners, heat, steel, metal

To be carrying a gun: strapped, packin', holdin'

Cops: jakes, po-po, five-oh, narcos, snakes

Cars: whips, rides

Shoes: kicks

Handshake: a pound, dap

Car stereo (or any stereo): a system

If something was cool: fly, hittin', buttery, flavor, bangin', illmatic

If something wasn't cool: wack, weak, busted, booty

If something had you mad: vexed, heated, agee (agitated), salty, stressed, swole

Weed: herb, bombazee, boom, trees, lethal, izm, ganja, huff, chronic

Heroin: Diesel

Liquor: brown water

To steal: to boost, to vic

If someone got robbed: to get "got," jacked

To fight: scrap, beef, ruckus

AIDS/HIV: the Monster, Batman Forever

To leave: to murk, breeze, bounce, get Ghost or Patrick Swayze

Brooklyn-style slang: forcing a d-stutter into your words; making crib, crid-dib; black, blid-dack; slang, slid-dang; and crack, crid-dack.

The year was 1994, way before iTunes and YouTube, way before suburbanites even wanted any parts of this, back when rappers were more worried about making wack music than making millions.

▲▼▲▼▲

Back in Hell's Zoo: the rugged, but beautiful Port.

Bumming a quick light for my Newport from a passing commuter, it was bugged how quickly this place could make you forget a whole year's worth of calculus and the Kreb's Cycle. Everything was just as I had left it—even Real Estate Man, Shorty, and Loco. My janitor crew was the same, too, and as they gave me the warmest welcome back, I realized just how much we were a family.

Especially Van' Puddin'. When he saw me, his face lit right up with that deep chuckle of his.

"Fam! Haha, my son is back in New York! How you been, fool?"

Van' Puddin' loved calling people "fool," and whenever he said "New York," he said it like the king of the jungle.

"Man, I'm good. Good to be back, man."

"So you finished doing your thing down there at school, huh?"

"Yeah, but they was slavin' a kid down there, man!"

"Well Duke, it's good to have you back, n*gg*h." He loved calling everyone "duke" as well.

Some of my supervisors were happy to see me again as well, even the cool Jamaican Mr. Barrett, who I had since forgiven for that busted orientation. So yeah, people were definitely excited to see me—that is, all except for Akwei. For as my first week's assignment was to sweep the south wing perimeter with him, to Akwei's utter disappointment, I had become that very slickster-of-a-non-worker he had warned me about the year before. So as Akwei swept the nasty concrete alone while wiping his sweat under the heavy sun, I just relaxed on Eighth Avenue enjoying the summer sun, catching up with familiar faces and flirting with every fly female. Akwei would just look over at me and shake his head in deep disgust, but I didn't really care.

It dawned on me that I was becoming a real Dr. Jekyll and Mr. Hyde—a hardworking mad scientist plus experiment-gone-wild—and my pride loved the sinister paradox. I mean, on the one side, I had UPenn, home of the world's very first computer; and on the other side, I had Hell's Zoo, so esoterically evil that even some of my college classmates who were from New York couldn't fathom the stories I sometimes told. Which is why some even said behind my back that I was exaggerating about being a part of that kind of stuff. But I wasn't lying one bit. Nor was I lying over the next few weeks when warning prostitutes about the serial killer who had been abducting them right behind the Port, chopping them to pieces, and collecting their rotting flesh under the tarp of his pick-up truck. He soon got caught, but for some, it was way too late.

So standing back on the Port's roof once again, only this time with my lungs full of weed from one of the countless hustlers on the streets below, I was glad to be back.

"The New York State of Mind": the humanist's ultimate high.

▲ ▼ ▲ ▼ ▲

Van' Puddin': He was everything to me. Not to mention that he had "cool" so mastered that "coolness" should've paid him rent. I mean, he'd do certain things that challenged the basic rules of "toughness"—things you might only see a "Don" do in some mob movie. For instance, sitting with his legs crossed; most men would be scared to do that (me included), thinking they'd look like some type of girl. But here was a man so comfortable with his toughness that he was beyond feeling the need to constantly assert it—the way the rest of us might.

He'd also wear these silk, lover-boy tank-tops in bedroom colors like burgundy. Also, instead of a toothpick, he'd always pluck off a matchstick to crush between his teeth while he talked, like the early New York days of Elliot Ness and Tommy Guns. Then lastly, even though he was the size of a linebacker, he was graceful with his movements. That is, except for his walk, because the cat still had a pimp-strut you couldn't master, no matter how hard you tried.

And there was another thing of Van' Puddin's that nobody could master: his bull's-eye knockout punch that never failed in putting dudes to sleep. It was legendary. One time, this random dude came up to Van' Puddin' like he was excited to tell him something.

"Yo n*gg*h, you remember me, man? You knocked me out that one time!"

Van' Puddin' just smiled, "Duke, I done knocked so many n*gg*hs out that I can't even remember. But if you tell me I did, then I guess I did."

And that's just the aura he had. Not only did grown men follow him like remoras on a tiger shark, but even dudes he had knocked out wanted his attention. I mean, even that time he was riding the express subway and some dudes in ski masks pulled out guns, Van' Puddin' just reclined in his seat with his shades on. And as the dudes robbed every single person on the train car, like they were in the Wild West, they stepped right over Van' Puddin's outstretched legs like it applied to everyone but him. Some would call Van' Puddin' an enigma, but on the streets it simply meant that the cat "had it." That's why even Shylock—the one Van' Puddin' stripped naked that day on the subway—was back to speaking to him again.

So this was my dad on the streets, and I was officially his son. And while he had served time in prison before, I never asked him what for and he never felt the need to tell me (though if I really cared to know he would've). And though I was still learning how to hold my own ground in this colossal psych ward, Van' Puddin' was always just a holler away— and he'd pity any fool who laid their hands on me.

Like the time I had stayed up partying all night in Plainfield and ended up coming to the Port the next morning on no sleep. Well I punched in, but as soon as I got to my bathroom, I squatted on a milk-crate in the corner, buried my head in my arms, and went right to sleep. But after a few heavy snores, I suddenly felt the urge to lift my head. And when I did, there was this guy from the Meat Rack, standing directly over my head, masturbating!

Before I could even react, he dashed away while quickly fixing himself, right back to the Meat Rack where his crazy gang was waiting. I stood in plain view at the entrance of my bathroom, staring at the dude like I wanted him to die. However, as hot as I was, I knew way better than to just go over there. Because everyone knew that most Meat Rackers carried rusty razors and wouldn't hesitate to slice you up like some alley cats.

Anyway, Van' Puddin' then came walking by, and couldn't help but notice that I had major beef. So I kicked the whole story to him, and without a word, he headed straight for the Meat Rack, wearing a face like he might crack a skull. And once he got there, he calmly summoned everyone around him.

Watching from where I was, I couldn't hear what he was saying (since he alone did all the talking). But I could tell by his body language that whatever he was saying, he was only gonna be saying it once. And they were wide-eyed and attentive the whole time, like kids in the principal's office. So Van' Puddin' dismissed them and came back to where I was, the Meat Rack went back to congregating (though much more quietly and humbly), and that was that. All I knew was that I never had a problem with any of them ever again.

Now, why did Van' Puddin' even claim me as his son in the first place? For although I was good at kicking the most feisty crack addicts and homeless out of my bathroom—and as much as he loved hearing what others told him about my nuttiest street capers—if it was based on ruggedness alone, there were plenty who were more rugged than me. But the simple truth was that Van' Puddin' just liked me "for me," period.

More so, Van' Puddin' may have been a shark in these waters, but at the end of the day, he also had kids; kids whom he loved deeply, always taking them to Disney World and every other fun place. He even sent them to private school, with hopes of them going off to a big college one day and "making it big." Van' Puddin' always talked about his kids excelling in both academics as well as athletics. However, at the same time, he also wanted his kids to be "street smart." So perhaps, just as I admired Van' Puddin' for all that he commanded on the streets, he, in turn, also admired all that I commanded in living this dual life (street smarts and book smarts)—the very thing he yearned for his kids to have as well. And he always took serious note of whatever I was up to. That's why whenever some older cat at the gambling table would blurt out, "So Fam, you be away at college during the year, right?" Van' Puddin' would school them before I could even respond, "Yeah duke, he's down there at The University of Penn, studying to be a doctor."

"Oh, $%^&, for real, Fam?"

"Yup," I'd say while lighting my next Newport and asking for another hit in blackjack. And by the way, Van' Puddin' loved all my "deep" books from Black Gold's Brother Hassan. In fact, he'd even ask to borrow whichever one I had in the back pocket of my janitor jumpsuit, so that he could study it too. And nobody got to see this studious side of him but me.

We loved each other a whole lot.

▲▼▲▼▲

Payday was nothing short of a party for us. It was also when Van' Puddin' made more in a single day than a lot of lawyers and doctors. For payday was also when people "paid the piper." And though Van' Puddin's rates were high, sadly enough, it was nothing that people hadn't agreed to when they first sought him out and begged for the loan.

For starters, we always gathered at our regular restaurant, behind tinted windows, while sitting around the table like a crime family. Everyone would be there. There was Audio, the older Brooklyn cat who watched Van' Puddin's back with such sharpness you would've thought he was back in his prime again. Then there was Pilot, the cool jester of the crew, who one day, when standing at the Meat Rack urinal and realizing that the guy next to him was glaring over at his privates, he turned and finished peeing right on the dude's leg.

Then there was Big Husky, the Queens cat who was Van' Puddin's partner in the whole operation. And while he wasn't as quick to knock someone out as Van' Puddin', he still had this stone-cold look that made you not want to find out what he just might do. Then lastly, there was Cat Daddy and Pedro, though they rarely sat at the table with the rest of us. Instead, they sat at the bar right behind us, taking endless whiskey shots. And while our big, round table had no "head" to sit at, it was clear that Van' Puddin' was the one. That's why when debtors came in to pay up, he was the only one they really looked at.

One particular payday, Cat Daddy rose up from the bar and stepped over to Van' Puddin's side.

"Look, man! There's that dude Low-Life right over there! Man, look at him, walking up the street, trying to be all slick like he don't owe you nothin'!" Cat Daddy was a cool, spunky old man, and would do just about anything for Van' Puddin'.

Van' Puddin' calmly looked that way and sucked his teeth. "Yeah, I see him. That Low-Life is so low, he could walk under a snake wearing a top-hat. Man, go get that fool!"

In no time flat, Cat Daddy was back with Low-Life in tow. Already knowing he was wrong, Low-Life came right to the table and dropped a lump of cash next to Van' Puddin's dinner plate. Patiently disgusted, Van' Puddin' looked him up and down like he was a giant crack vile, and then banished him by looking in the other direction.

Man, it felt so good being a part of all this! Smacking extra loud on our food while taking turns telling stories and laughing our heads off. We were like a big thick-skinned, hard-hearted wolf pack. And though I was still years behind some of these veterans (a mere wolf-pup, in many ways), let's just say that by this point, I was hardly a square among circles. And as far as wondering what some Plainfielders from my childhood might've thought if they saw me now, honestly, I wasn't even thinking about them. Like I said, "The New York State of Mind" was the humanist's ultimate high. And not only was I super high, but Nas' song just about paralleled my life:

> *The City never sleeps, full of villains and creeps,*
> *That's where I learned to do my hustle, had to scuffle with freaks,*
> *I never sleep, 'cause sleep is the cousin of death.*
> *Beyond the walls of intelligence, life is defined,*
> *I think of crime, when I'm in a New York state of mind . . .*

Well, after we finished grubbing, and watching Van' Puddin's pockets get pregnant with cash, it was over to our favorite street corner for some gambling (even though we basically gambled all day). Our favorite game of all was Cee-lo. It was a dice game and actually Chinese in origin— "Cee-lo" being short for the Chinese words *"Si Wu Liu,"* meaning "4-5-6." Though the only Chinese connection any of us now had with it was that one of us was always chowing down on some fried wings and fries from the Chinese take-out.

Like a rabbit out of a hat, the dice would always appear as soon as we formed our circle. And the rules were as follows: one person at a time rolled the three dice. If you got a "4-5-6," that was called "headcracks," and you automatically won the whole pot of money. But on the flip side, if you rolled a "1-2-3," that was called "crackhouse" (123rd Street), and you'd automatically lose. Now rolling three of the same number was called "trips"—which also took all bets—that is, as long as someone didn't beat it with a "headcracks."

Now outside of rolling a trips, headcracks, or crackhouse, you basically kept rolling until you got doubles with any of the two dice, while your third die set your final score. So while any set of doubles and a "1" was an automatic loss—just like "crackhouse"—any set of doubles and a "2" was called "deuce;" any set of doubles and a "3" was "tre;" "4" was "box;" "5" was "feva';" and "6" was "star."

Lastly, the money pot was "the bank," where only one person held "bank" at a time, announcing to everyone else how high he was willing to bet. And then once all the fast-talking bets equalled his max, he'd announce that the bank was "plugged," and nobody else could jump in for that round. Then the banker would set it off with his first roll, with everyone else then rolling against him, in a one-on-one fashion.

So there you'd find us, clustered together on a Hell's Kitchen corner with a big pile of money on the sidewalk and not a single worry about some fool trying to rob us. People stared as they went by because this wasn't something you saw on every midtown block in the midst of traffic. The invincible feeling was more intoxicating than the third or fourth Heineken I'd be working on. On days like these, I wouldn't make it back to Plainfield until way after dark. And by the way, Mom didn't worry about me anymore; I guess she could see on my face how effortless this was for me.

Anyway, more than being hooked on Cee-lo, I even started carrying a pair of "loaded dice" that guaranteed a headcracks every time, because one die had nothing but "4's" all over it, the other nothing but "5's," and the third, nothing but "6's." And the trick was to roll them, get your headcracks real quick, and then scoop them back up before anyone could notice you switching them with a regular pair (same size and color) in your other hand.

However, those loaded dice were never for my crew—I mean, never. Love and loyalty was everything to us. For while we might've taken each other's cash in a heartbeat, that was only when we won it fair-and-square.

My loaded dice were strictly for the crack addicts, homeless, and loners whenever I was bored. And could using loaded dice with the wrong person get you killed? Why of course it could. But then again, running around the Port for over eight hours a day could get you killed just the same. (I almost poked my hand on a bunch of used needles some addict had tossed in my cleaning bag.) So again, my crime family was my family for sure. "Thick as thieves," you could say, because each of us was a thief.

So with my master plan gaining momentum, my cocoon was now open and my dark and colorful wings looked lovelier than I would have imagined. And now, if you had asked me if I was happy, I would've looked at you like you were stupid for even thinking I might not be.

▲ ▼ ▲ ▼ ▲

But doggone it!

Because for every forty acres I claimed in this aggressive game, something would always come along and make me feel like that same soft punk, all over again. And I'm not talking so much about public humiliation as I am about personal condemnation, leading to more self-hatred, and more vows to become even more hardened and evil—since that's what seemed like the only solution.

Well one day, I was driving home from the Port with Chico, my childhood best friend who, by now, also worked at the Port. (The same Chico who wiped the oil off my forehead at my Confirmation.) We were riding in my dad's utility van that he had just given me, and I was making one last loop around the Port before heading for the Lincoln Tunnel back to Jersey. And there was crazy traffic that day, all because of Wyland, some famous muralist and whale preservationist who had just finished his colossal mural on the Forty-first Street wall of the Port. So it was a big event and everyone was out there taking pictures—even New York City's black mayor, David Dinkins.

So as we sat there in the most obnoxious traffic, I started honking at the limo that was stalling in front of me. Well, the limo ended up moving to the side, but as I drove forward a bit, a penny suddenly flew through my driver's window, just missing my face. Chico reacted before I could even pin-point who had done it. Grabbing a handful of dirty pennies from my van's console, he jumped out of the van, literally climbed over top of it, and spiked them across the limo's hood—leaving as many nicks in its paint as there were coins in his hand.

Now, have you ever heard of someone dying over mere pennies? Because before I knew it, that's exactly what started unfolding. Four older black dudes—three of them outweighing us by a solid one hundred pounds—were now storming toward us with volcanos in their eyes. They must've been someone's bodyguards.

And what did we do? We rolled up our windows and locked our doors as fast as we could. (We may have been dumb—and Chico even more dumb for doing it—but we weren't stupid.) And we locked everything just in time too. Because like some gorillas whose babies had been smacked, they not only surrounded us, but they began clobbering the windows with all their might. Never had I seen a vehicle get attacked in this way.

"Yo, chill out! Chill out!" I yelled as loud as I could. But it seemed like the more I yelled, the more bent they were on breaking inside and bludgeoning us.

One of them was punching the driver's window right next to my face, to the point where his knuckles looked like they were bleeding. All the while, he was gritting his teeth and spitting every threat imaginable, dead in my eyes.

Another one stepped in front of the van, and like King Kong actually ripped both windshield-wipers right off at the hinges! I was in shock off that one; Chico was, too. But as easy as it could've been to just sit frozen and keep begging for mercy, I was still just another dude infected with the insanity of Hell's Zoo. So I did something I would've never imagined doing.

Quickly throwing the van's gear shifter into drive, I floored the gas pedal. I was determined to crush his legs and mid-section between my van and the vehicle in front of me. My eyes to his eyes, my impulse to be a man to this grown man's wrath—and most personal, too. And this wasn't so much what I wanted to do, as much as it was what I felt I had to do—and couldn't even seem to say "no" to.

Isn't it crazy how one's entire "bright" future can change in just a handful of seconds—over just a handful of pennies?

Vrmmmmmmm, the van's old engine screamed for extra horsepower.

However, in the fury of it all, I had mistakenly thrown the gear into neutral instead.

"Aw, you just tried to kill me, n*gg*h! Ahhhh!"

Jumping from in front of the van now (as he could see that that was no bluff), all four of them were now trying to break in triple-time. All I could do now was brace myself for the inevitable, suddenly picturing myself in a coma.

"Man, where's the cops at? Where's Van' Puddin'?" Nobody to save us. But then, they just stopped all of a sudden and stormed away. I mean, almost as if someone had finally called them off of us.

Dag.

I sat with Chico in absolute silence and I didn't know whether to light a Newport or what. But I sure knew better than to risk rolling down my window, at least not until traffic opened up and we were on our way. And speaking of traffic, as I looked around, the commuters in the neighboring cars actually looked more traumatized than we were.

Well, as much as I wanted to forget about the whole thing, I really couldn't. Because what had me worried was that before one of the dudes walked away (the one whose legs I tried to crush), I could've swore I saw him glance at my red janitor uniform and then give a nod, like he knew just where to find me again. And how in the world could I watch my back at every moment, for eight hours straight, on these kookoo-crowded streets?

Later that night, I even thought about quitting. But then I realized that as shook as I was, I couldn't quit. For one thing, I hadn't yet put aside a dime for my meal plan in the fall. And then secondly, beyond my meal plan was my master plan: still on a quest for that ultimate street status that I was definitely on the right track for. "The New York state of mind" was addictive.

So the very next morning, I returned to the Port and told Van' Puddin' everything.

"Man, them cats know I work here, man! And they know I'mma have on this big red monkey suit, too! Yo, I'm walking around this joint with my back straight against the walls for a while, knowhutimsayin'? Because ain't nobody just gonna sneak up on me. I'mma see 'em comin' first!"

Van' Puddin' was bothered because I was bothered, but he wasn't stressed one bit. "Well Fam, first thing you need to know is I got your back, ya' dig! But if you want, I'll let you hold one of my burners. I got the Sig?"

And there I was, so stressed out, that I didn't even notice how special this moment was. For here Van' Puddin' was all but "knighting me," by offering me his favorite tool: the 9mm Sig-Sauer.

"Cool, thanks man."

"You know it, Duke."

So while this was a time when I realized how much Van' Puddin' loved me, this was also a time when I realized how weak I still was. And you know what? I hated myself for that. Because if I remembered correctly from grammar school, "strong" and "weak" were total opposites, right? And there was no room for weakness in my master plan. This all reminded me of how in the movie *Juice*, the late Tupac's character finally got a gun after saying he was tired of always running scared.

▲▼▲▼▲

So then, what exactly was a thug then? Was it being perfectly strong and never, ever weak? Was it never backing down from a single thing? Was it never being scared? Was it having someone like Van' Puddin' in your corner? Was it carrying a gun?

Or rather, was it having a hard upbringing as a kid? Or was it just something you imitated from your favorite rapper? Well by this point, I'd seen some well-known "thug" rappers as they were cutting through the Port, and for one thing, they weren't nearly as tough-acting in these waters as they were in their music videos.

More so, did Cee-lo, forties, and blunts make someone a thug? Did being black or Latino make someone a thug? Well obviously not, because one of my fellow janitors was a "white boy" nicknamed Vanilla Ice—one of the coolest brothers around. And while many white dudes were accused of trying to "act black" (just as many black dudes were accused of trying to "act white"), Vanilla Ice seemed content with whatever in the world he was—cool, crazy, and pretty. With brownish-blonde hair combed into a cow-lick with a crew-cut on the sides, Vanilla Ice had done time in prison, as well. One day he told me about all the different homemade weapons he'd sneak into the prison yard; and how this other inmate (whose head Vanilla Ice cracked open with a frying pan) had paid someone to give him the infamous "buck fifty"—which was when someone cut open your face so badly, you'd need a hundred and fifty stitches to sew it back up. Well, Vanilla Ice never got that buck fifty; he was too slick. And speaking of slick, he always talked slick, too—always out of the side of his mouth, and always extra low, in case someone was being nosey (obviously a jail habit). So did all Vanilla Ice's experiences make him a thug?

So while thugs clearly came in all shapes and sizes, and could be summed up by much of the above, at the end of the day, there was still no set code of qualifiers. However, along with that necessary "coolness," there did in fact seem to be at least one common denominator: pain. For as abstract and esoteric as much of it seemed, a lot of thug-life was simply learning to channel your pains until they produced fangs. And just like pain could pretty much recognize pain, thugs could pretty much recognize other thugs. I mean, it was almost like when a new dance came out—you simply either "had it" or you didn't. And if you didn't, then you obviously had to work on your dance moves some more. So needless to say, there were tons of dudes working on their thug "dance moves" some more, too. Because the streets made it quite clear—being a thug was being a man.

And it seemed like there were always higher levels to reach in this thing. I mean, it's not like these levels had different names or anything corny like that, it's just that there were indeed levels—just like wolf packs have their "alpha males." Then, if you at last graduated to being so comfortable with it all, that, even with your guard completely down, you still gave off the vibe that you were running things, then you were perhaps on the track to becoming a gangster. And by the way, all this had nothing to do with fashion, money, or who you could pay to fight your battles for you, because any Tom, Dick, or Harry could manage that. This was a heart and mind thing; and yeah, it could be stressful. Factor in the jealous dudes around you, and it could become even more stressful at times.

So with legs crossed, lover-boy tank tops, graceful mannerisms, big fists, an even bigger Sig-Sauer, and a fleet of trigger-happy hooligans who, when he said "jump," asked "on who's head," Van' Puddin' was a gangster, for sure. He seemingly had no wants. I too, wanted a life of no wants. I wanted that money, power, and respect, and to be delivered from the disease of weakness and fear. I wanted to be that successful doctor who still had a fabulous amount of stock with the streets.

Really, I just wanted to be happy.

XVII

DR. JEKYLL: THE WISTAR INSTITUTE

Sophomore year back at UPenn, and off to the races once again. Having ditched my ever-faithful roommate, J.J. (and DuBois College House), I was living in one of the campus high-rises with Noodle and Addis, where the three of us built on our reputations for being "bugged-out and crazy"—an admirable identity in our Hip Hop culture. We were so convinced that our partying would never clash with our school performance: Addis stayed on top of his Wharton classes, Noodle stayed on top of his Japanese, and I stayed on top of my chemistry. But in reality, it was clashing already, because even if we were still getting the grades, we often had to hit the books twice as hard, since we were usually high or hung over. The weed and liquor were quite deceitful. My heart was even more deceitful.

However, there was no deceit when a friend called us from our high-rise lobby one night, saying he had just passed some cops on their way to the elevators and overheard our apartment number over their walkie-talkies. Obviously, too much of our weed smoke was seeping into the hallways, and clearly it was time to sober-up and be scared. But instead, we just thought it was the funniest thing. I mean, almost like it was a test: seeing how fast and slick we could be under police pressure.

Well since Addis was too "tore up" to flee our apartment with us, we decided to lay him in our dirty bathtub, begged him to stop laughing (while still laughing ourselves), warned him not to breath too loud, grabbed whatever weed stash was left, and bolted up the fire steps just before the cops reached our door with their master keys and cuffs. Yeah, another escape by the skin of our teeth, and how we loved it! However, the next time the cops came, I wouldn't get the chance to flee or laugh. But since I had quickly tossed all the evidence out of my seventh-floor window, all they could do was berate me like I was the biggest moron.

So make way for three of UPenn's bad boys! Though when it was time for our tough classes, we still might've preferred being called nerds. More so, we always justified our insanity by pointing out how one of the most historic fraternities on campus had just gotten busted for smoking crack. And our logic seemed simple: since we never smoked crack, that still made us more moral than them, which therefore meant we still had morals, which therefore meant we were still "good people." So boiling it all down, if living wild was the chickenpox, then me and my roommates were one big, self-righteous scab—itching for drama.

▲▼▲▼▲

Now along with spending my entire summer in Hell's Kitchen, as I'd return to Plainfield each day, I was also spending many evenings back at Black Gold with Brother Hassan. And at this point, he was teaching me "Mdu Ntr" (Mid-doo Netcher), the language of ancient Egypt (or "Kemet," as it was called). Said to be the oldest language in Africa, how fascinating it was learning to read hieroglyphics right off the pyramid walls! I was learning to speak it and write it, too. And in my exploration for some type of spirituality and truth (trying to figure out what that even meant), Mdu Ntr was my first major stop after that letdown with my Catholic confirmation.

Because apart from my master plan with UPenn and the Port, there seemed to be this unarticulated, spiritual master plan as well: finding out who in the world I was, and where I even came from. So in my meandering, I was now into Gnosticism—the view that all of life's meaning and "salvation" comes by liberating your mind through knowledge. And the more "deep" or hidden the knowledge was, the more precious it felt.

Therefore, when I wasn't cramming for some big exam, partying my lungs and liver away, or scheming on some girl (as I was having the hardest time being faithful to my Natasha), ancient Egypt was where I focused my energy, especially as I now believed that all truth originated there. So while my bedroom was as plush as could be with its king-sized bed, extravagant stereo, and funkadelic black-light to make it all glow, I had Egyptian relics all over the place. "Nice art," girls would comment as they'd enter my lair, but to me, it was religion. My religion.

On a small shelf directly above my bed was a wood-carved statuette (idol) of Ptah, the self-created Egyptian god said to have dreamed all of creation in his heart. Represented as a mummified man with crossed arms and that traditional, Egyptian "beard," some even said Ptah was one with the god Osiris. Then above Ptah, I had a parchment "relief" of the god Shu, meaning "air," separating the god Nut, the "skies," from the god Geb, the "ground"—the Egyptian account of many gods creating the earth. So I guess I was now a polytheist.

Then at the top of the same wall were two large, wood-carved eyes: the Eye of Djuhuti and the Eye of Horus. These were my prized possessions, and every time I gazed at them, I'd get inspired to grab my composition book and practice my hieroglyphics some more. And once I learned that UPenn had an ancient Egyptian history course that included students roaming UPenn's world-renowned museum, my inspiration went through the clouds. So come Tuesday afternoons, you'd find me surrounded by mummies and limestone artifacts, feeling so enlightened as I was the only one in the class able to decipher some of the ancient and weathered writings.

All the while daydreaming about living on the Nile back in the 18th Dynasty.

For Mdu Ntr was all about achieving "balance" in one's life—or *Ma'at*, as it was called. *Ma'at* was represented as a kneeling woman with outstretched, feathered arms. I longed for that balance, even thinking that if I tattooed her image across my entire back it might somehow bring me closer to achieving it. Then, I might even graduate to "perfection"— or *Khepr*, as it was called—represented by a majestic-looking dung beetle. And of course I wanted "eternal life" as well, represented by the large wooden Ankh that I kept right next to my idol of Ptah.

However, with all these fond hopes of an eternal paradise one day, I eventually learned that in the end, none of it was certain. Because based on the ancient Egyptian funerary text known as *The Book of the Dead*, once I died I'd have to stand before Thoth—the ibis-headed scribe of the gods—where my heart would be weighed on the scales of *Ma'at* to see if it was lighter than a feather. And if my heart was indeed lighter, I'd be permitted into the afterlife. However, if it wasn't, my soul would be devoured by the ferocious chimera—part lion, part crocodile, and part hippo. So then, how could I ever be sure that my heart would be lighter than a feather on that day of judgment? Especially when my heart was already pricked with the guilt from so many wrongs I had already committed? Not to mention that I secretly enjoyed so many of those wrongs.

I found no definite answers, but I stayed with Mdu Ntr anyway, figuring my ardent search for knowledge would eventually bring me to something else when it was time. Thus, Gnosticism remained my thing.

▲▼▲▼▲

First semester went by like a flash. And at the end of Sociology 101, we all had to do this big final project: an in-depth study of any segment of society, to be presented to the entire class. Some of my classmates whispered to safeguard their "great ideas," but I had zero worries about anyone possibly stealing mine. Grabbing my walkman, my backpack, and a train schedule, my plan was to head "home"—not to Plainfield, but to the Port. Yup, I'd give UPenn something they'd not soon forget.

"Fam!" Van' Puddin' was shocked to see me popping up in the middle of the week like this. "What you doin' up here, son?"

"Man, I got this project where you gotta pick somewhere and break it all down on some sociology stuff. Man, that professor and them students think they be knowin' some stuff, but I'mma give 'em our world, knowhutimsayin'?"

"Duke, give it to 'em , baby." He said it like he would've paid money to see their reactions.

So after catching up with more of my janitor family over a Newport or two, I got right down to business. I grabbed some choice homeless dudes, took them into one of the mechanical rooms where we janitors always hid out, and video-recorded each of them as they shared about life in Hell's Zoo. (I could smell that professor's "A+" already.) Then one week later, there I was, standing in front of my sociology class with the lecture-hall lights dimmed. Excited and ready, I gave them a quick introduction, and then popped my tape into the VCR beneath the giant TV.

My documentary began with me walking through Hell's Kitchen, just as comfortably as if I was in my own kitchen. And though the streets of New York already had my classmates' undivided attention, they hadn't seen anything yet. So after capturing everything from the yellow cabs to the typical stone-cold, commuter rush, the scene switched to a white homeless guy smiling away at the camera with a drunken smirk. Smiley was the nickname I had given him, and everyone called him that, too. However, as I began asking him pointed questions about his life, Smiley sobered right up, and it was the most serious I'd ever seen him.

"I was a cook. A gourmet cook! I've always loved to cook, and everyone always loved my food. But then, one day, I broke my arm, and my job let me go because of it. Then after that, I couldn't get work no more, so I ended up losing everything. Now, all I got left is this liquor . . . ."

And as Smiley hung his head and scratched his scruff, you could've heard a pin drop in my lecture hall.

So after a few more heart-arresting interviews, I topped it off with this Latino homeless guy from the Meat Rack, giving a detailed description of how he'd go into bathrooms every day and profile at the urinals to pick up other guys. He even shared how rich executives were a part of this whole game. And while I knew I was pushing the envelope with this last interview, I was only doing what the assignment called for—bringing untapped segments of our society to light. Needless to say, I got an "A" (along with an "A" on my stinking pride, too); and in academics, this is what we called a "power move."

And speaking of power moves, even though I stopped living in DuBois, I was still donning my resident whitecoat and doing my hospital rounds with Dr. Green. And since he never brought up what we had discussed that night in his apartment, I never gave him any reasons to think about it. Our level of intimacy was much more shallow now—which was all my fault, because I had once enjoyed regular dinners at his home, but now I smelled so much like weed all the time, that I couldn't. And every time I bumped into his sweet wife on campus, I could tell she missed those times. But again, I was too wrapped up in myself to stay dwelling on it.

▲ ▼ ▲ ▼ ▲

Then, to my most pleasant surprise, I got the letter of a lifetime. In light of my grades and other positive factors, I had been selected as a finalist to receive UPenn's prestigious Pew Fellowship. If I were chosen for it, not only would I get all my tuition paid for the remainder of my undergraduate studies (since borrowing all this money was too scary to even add up), but I'd even get my own office space in the vice provost's building, a new computer, and truckloads of other perks.

So with tan khakis, a white shirt and tie, and plenty of last-minute phone calls from Mom who was beside herself with joy, I hustled across campus to the big, evening interview. It was held in this fancy conference room in a building I'd never been in before. And while nervousness wasn't exactly my thing, as I sat at the head of this long, lacquered table with close to ten people asking me whatever came to their minds while scribbling notes on their secretive legal pads, I almost felt like a baby in a high-chair.

What was my idea of success? What were my future plans and why? How would the Pew Fellowship further the pursuit of my ambitions? Where did I plan to travel and why? Some of these I had never considered before. Because for us pre-meds—who really only had eight semesters to take some twelve semester's worth of required math and science classes—the closest most of us ever got to "studying abroad" was going home for the weekend to cram for an exam.

But when the interviewing committee asked me about any projects I had worked on, I thought of my recent documentary in New York. "Field work" was the catch-phrase I knew would tickle their ears; and I told them about it all: nine and ten-year-olds living on the streets with hearts rock-hard like the sidewalks, along with Smiley and others who became "bums" only because of one unfortunate event in their lives. And of course they were shocked to hear about the reality of homeless cannibalism. Lastly, I even told them about the Latino guy from the Meat Rack. Needless to say, when I was finished, it was clear they were impressed. All except for one of them.

"So tell me more about the homosexual from that Meat Rack place, and your findings therein?"

Suddenly realizing that this genteel, Latino grad student at the far end of the table might be gay himself, I began rambling to cover up any offenses that might murder this sweet deal. (Though he still looked just as perturbed when I was through.) So with this hour-long inquisition finally over, I rose to my feet, warmly thanked each of them for their time, and walked back to my apartment hoping for the best.

Well, I didn't get the Pew Fellowship. But amidst all these geniuses, I still considered it an honor that I got that far in the process. Though believe it or not, me making it that far was a bad thing, too. Because in a twisted way, it helped me rationalize my "Mr. Hydish," shady proclivities—figuring that if I could make such power moves on such little effort and such loco living, why ever change?

▲ ▼ ▲ ▼ ▲

Then came Wu-Tang Clan—hitting the Hip Hop scene as hard as the Beatles once hit the baby-boomers. Straight out of Staten Island (which they had dubbed "Shaolin"), it was the first time in Hip Hop's history that an army of hustlers had more dudes rhyming than you could count. "Ten times ten men, committin' mad sin," is what the leader of Wu-Tang boasted. And with countless samples from John Liu's classic Kung Fu films, nearly all of Wu-Tang's members had taken the names and personas of their favorite kung-fu characters—from Ghost Face Killer to Master Killer to Golden Arms.

More so, just as the rap group Public Enemy had their zany Flavor Flav, Wu-Tang Clan had their infinitely crazier Ol' Dirty Bastard (his name also taken from a character in a kung-fu flick). He did stuff that made Parliament's George Clinton seem shy. Matter of fact, I even worked with Ol' Dirty's favorite uncle back at the Port, and it was the funniest thing because they looked and acted just alike. One day, his uncle even broke it all down for us as we stood on the corner of Fortieth and Ninth. His squeaky Brooklyn accent and beady eyes held us captive.

"See, listen here now! Y'all calls him 'Ol' Dirty' and whatnot. But me, I just calls him Russell! So whatch'all wanna know about Russell? And you see the way he be singing all wild and high and low like that? Well, he got all that from me! See, I been singing like that since he was a little kid, and he always loved it!"

And as he finished (wearing this cocky smirk that said, "so there!"), you could see that he was so proud that his nephew from the projects had become a rising American icon. And I say "American" icon, because along with revolutionizing so much of urban culture, the suburbs also got swept up in the Wu-Tang hysteria.

Now from Sudanese Willis, to "Strong Island" Biggie, to (Brooklyn's) Red Hook Poopie, to Jamaican Phife, I had a UPenn crew who were just as book-smart, but just as bananas as I was. In fact, "Crew" is exactly what we called ourselves. Made up of at least thirty of us (plus all our homies from our hoods back home), we were as "deep" as any fraternity and even had our very own logo. It was an "Irie Rastaman" with thick dreads and the biggest blunt burning away in his smiling mouth. We had an unofficial mascot, too: my new four-foot python that I wore around my neck wherever I went—even blowing weed smoke into his tank first, so that we could be high together.

Setting up domino tables in the middle of campus and devilishly mixing rum with our Snapples before walking into class, it was really only a matter of time before we teamed up with the notorious Pi Kappa Alpha ("Pika")—the mostly-white, rogue fraternity on a two-year campus suspension because of hazing. Together, we threw some of the biggest and craziest parties of our undergrad era, drawing people from nearby campuses and hoods alike—guns often included.

So with my school crew more than established, my thoughts headed back home to my childhood homies. After all, nobody could replace them. I mean, who else made you feel comfortable enough to do a random Michael Jackson spin for no reason at all? Who else could you reminisce with like there was no tomorrow? Who else could you confide in that you felt like you might be "losing it?" And as the stakes in all our lives were getting higher, we needed each other more than ever. I mean, we may have worn "man-sized" Timberlands, took "man-sized" pulls from our Newports, and drove cars that made grown men stare, but we were barely twenty years old.

And this black-on-black crime stuff was no joke to be navigating nonstop. From the crack corners of North Jersey, to our West Philly college parties, even to a harmless walk down the street or ride on the subway, the stress was as subtle as high blood pressure, but as pervasive as the plague. Muggings, carjackings, and imprisonments could at least be gauged by statistics, but there was really no way to gauge the nagging pressure of this crabs-in-a-barrel, pitbull-eat-pitbull dynamic. Though you could somewhat gauge it by peeping the insane amounts of weed and liquor we consumed before hitting the dicey streets. And how did you know when you had consumed enough? When your heart was as calloused as barnacles, and your thoughts as low as a sunken ship with eels. Basically, when you had no more of that nagging fear inside. So yeah, the whole thing took its toll on us, for sure. However, this was our normalcy.

By this point, most of my homies back home were selling crack, and they had the flyest cars to show for it. Keell, who was hustling with Plainfield's infamous "Arlington Ave," had just copped a cherry-red Acura. Pooh had a Saab with "cookie-hole," chrome Atev rims. And Deuce, the one making the most money out of everyone, had an Acura Legend with Antera rims. It was obvious that we loved cars, but we loved fly rims just as much. Whenever my homies came down to Philly to see me, they would cruise onto campus like a real rap video was in the making, and even the richest students would have to stop and stare.

I felt so complete having my childhood crew in West Philly. Not to mention how much things had changed from back in the day—back when I was the "private school kid" of the crew and the last one to experience everything. For although UPenn was just as "private" as Wardlaw, I had been away at another "school" as well—the university of Hell's Zoo. When it came to drinking, smoking, and running crimes, I was now a ringleader. I would run into some of my old childhood bullies back home, and they'd have nothing to say now. (Some didn't even recognize me!) All they could do was notice that my gold jewelry was bigger than theirs, my car meaner than theirs, and my girls more lovely. Man, it was like my very own "rags-to-riches" story!

To top it all off, one night when I was at this big UPenn party, I saw someone I would never have imagined in a million years. Looking over in the distance, there was my old, seventh grade crush—fly Melinda from Plainfield (and she was still just as fly)—bopping her head to the music. It had been six or seven years since I last saw her. Basically, ever since she dissed me. So of course I had no clue that she had matriculated at Drexel University, right next door. Come to find out, she had even been accepted at UPenn, only since they didn't give her enough financial aid, it didn't work out.

Anyway, Melinda recognized me at about the same time, and it was nice giving her the coolest hug, tore up as I was. We did our best to talk in each other's ears amidst the loud music, and as people kept walking by and giving me love (pounds from my dudes, and hugs from my girls), it was obvious that I knew almost everyone in the joint. And with my

Guess and Polo commanding respect from even the biggest Brooklyn clothes critics, it was obvious that I had retired those seventh grade corduroy pants too! So we exchanged numbers, hugged again, and were soon having long phone convos. In no time, we were kicking back way harder than we ever had on her front porch with L.L. Cool J's "I Need Love"—sharing blunts that had us high like Jimmy Hendrix.

Well, after coming to her off-campus apartment on different mountain bikes and with fly new clothes every two minutes, Melinda soon learned how good I was at boostin' (stealing), so we plotted our own little hustle together. The set up would be some piece-of-cake "inside job," where I'd be boostin' clothes from a department store. She and her girlfriend were providing the place and the platform, and I was providing the skill and the fearlessness. The only condition was that I had to grab some outfits for her and her girlfriend, too. Easy enough, right? Only there was one problem: by this point, everything I did was a hustle—even the hustling that took place around my hustles. And Melinda sadly learned that.

"So wassup Aaron, you make out good?"

"Oh yeah, no doubt." (I always made out good.)

"So, you got the stuff?"

"Ummm, well naw, yo! See, what had happened was that I had your stuff, and was waiting to give it to you, but then somebody robbed me. It was crazy!"

The truth, of course, being that I returned half of her clothing back to the store for cash, while giving the other half to my Natasha—who I had no business cheating on anyway.

Well, smelling my lazy lie over the phone, Melinda suddenly had to go.

"Ai-ight, well I gotta go."

"Ai-ight." I hung up as well, and then chuckled:

"Well sweetheart, you'll just have to forgive me the same way I forgave you for dissin' me back in seventh grade!"

Besides, while that inside job might've been big to Melinda, to me it was as simple as grabbing extra napkins from a fast food spot. And that's exactly how it was with "napkins"—easy come, easy go. Not to mention that my basic morals concerning other people's property was easy come, easy go, too! For what had all started with me, Addis, and Noodle pocketing snacks from Wawa, was now becoming sheer kleptomania. And although "kleptomania" was a term I had always heard of, never did I realize that it could be so real—that I could become so addicted to the rush!

It made me feel like a king the way I now had this power to take almost anything I wanted—especially when I was on risky missions and saw how other dudes folded under the pressure and got nabbed. For me, it was just the opposite: the higher the stakes were, the more cool I'd actually become. And at times, I'm sure my cockiness alone drew attention. That's probably why the dude in the hardware store gave me that suspecting look when I walked in and asked for a small propane torch. So yes, I was more than "good" at it; and the way people sang my praises and shared my stories like legends made me feel fantastic.

However in truth, I was becoming a monster—an experiment-gone-wild; a savage losing his sophistication, just like those private school boys in *Lord of the Flies*.

Then one night, for no reason at all, I "woke up" (like an out-of-body experience), growled like some sort of werewolf, and bit my sleeping girlfriend's shoulder hard enough to make her jump right out of bed. Only it wasn't me! (I mean, the whole time, I was actually wondering who had just growled like that!) Then as Natasha began punching me all over, crying and demanding some sort of explanation, I just lied there in the darkness, absorbing the blows with this sinister smile. So did this mean that I was demon possessed now?

▲ ▼ ▲ ▼ ▲

You know, back in the early 80's, we all loved the board game, "Chutes and Ladders," where you could be close to winning and then suddenly hitting a giant "chute" that would slide you right back to the beginning. Well, that's exactly how my life now was. Except in this "game," the chutes were most alluring—and they could take you to far worse places than just "the beginning."

"Freedom" is what I still called it, though (my head as hard as any coconut). Stereo speakers full of bass, a refrigerator full of "forties," a closet full of Polo, and an apartment full of UPenn cats, from Camden to Cali. There were even local West Philly cats, who didn't go to UPenn, but loved running with us and would randomly pop up on campus and then pass their guns around for everyone to admire, while we rolled blunts and bopped our heads to Trendz of Culture's "Who's Got My Back?"

And every time that song played, I couldn't help but wonder who in my room (sprawled across my king-sized bed with their big Timberlands) would really have my back in any situation? I mean, who truly had love for me? And in turn, who did I truly have love for? Because while more "homies" came through our apartment than me and my roommates could count, so much of it was only because we loved weed (along with hasheesh and opium). And although most UPenn students wanted no parts of drugs, there were still truckloads who did—and even truckloads more who "experimented" (whatever that meant). And wherever you had all the above, of course you'd have those seizing the opportunity to be "entrepreneurs"—a.k.a. drug dealers.

Well, not only did more than a few from Crew sell weed, but my roommate Addis did, too. But not so with me; one thing I had learned from Van' Puddin' was to focus on one hustle and master it, and my hustle was already boostin'. However, since I was the one who knew so many people on campus—from blacks to whites to Asians (I could thank Wardlaw for that)—I was always directing people whenever they asked where they could get something. So while I didn't deal drugs regularly, I was definitely the one who could add depth to a dealer's client list. Especially my roommate. I mean, why not help the very one I shared the same toilet with?

However, I soon started getting vexed. Because even with all these referrals I was giving Addis, here he was still charging me full price whenever I wanted weed for myself. And my logic was that if all the people I referred to him saw fit to tell me, "hey, thanks," then why couldn't Addis also say an occasional "thanks" with at least a small discount for me? So I felt that he was greedy, and I had a plan. (Though in truth, we were both as greedy as could be.)

"Yo Addis, remember that rich dude who wanted to buy that weight from you, man? Well, you don't gotta worry about that one, no more." See, I had just hooked him up with a deal to sell a pound of weed to someone, but now I was gonna teach him a lesson by keeping it for myself.

"Really, man? I just got the weed for that, too!" He was suspicious already.

"Yeah man, it's cool. You don't gotta worry about that one. They cancelled."

Looking at me a moment longer, Addis just walked into his room. While I, on the other hand, shut my door and jumped on the phone.

"Yup, just come through tomorrow night as planned. You know I got you."

Then as I stood in one of the campus' dark parking lots that next night, waiting for the big-body Benz to pull in for the trade off, I could've sworn I spotted Addis spying on me again. It seemed like he had been doing that all afternoon, almost like he was reading my mind. I mean, both of us were some kleptos, and both of us were just as sly and sharp when it came to hustling; so here, it was almost like two chess masters facing off—Queens vs. North Jersey. However, as I finally made the exchange in the wake of the Benz' brake lights, not even counting the handful of cash because I knew it was all there, I had obviously won. But the sad reality was me and Addis both lost miserably; on that night, the closest of friends became enemies over a measly $1,500. Yup, pride and paper ruined it all!

After that, we didn't speak anymore, let alone give each other any phone messages from whatever girls had called. And as for our sweet apartment that we had even nicknamed "seventh heaven," it now felt more like the seventh circle of Hell from Dante's *Inferno*. We even refused to clean up after each other. So while our living room would continue to hold our stolen goods, it was putridly littered with empty liquor and St. Ides bottles, food wrappers, and all types of mystery perishables buried in the muddle. And as for our dishes, they stayed unwashed for so many months, that they were soon covered in the nastiest, slimiest sink water reduction, with "fungus pads" like lily pads. Our whole kitchenette smelled like an unflushed toilet. And speaking of the toilet, our bathroom got so hairy, soiled, and germy—with only a ruffled stack of Wawa napkins in the place of toilet paper—that when any of us had girls over, they wouldn't even set foot in there without putting on our biggest Timberlands.

So with all this going on now, I'd be heading to class some mornings and bump into J.J.—my Christian roommate from freshman year! Well of course we'd take time to hug and fill each other in on our pre-med endeavors. But I knew he could still see that my life was most trifling.

And as we'd hug again and part ways, I began wondering how different and peaceful my life would have been if I had never ditched J.J. for Addis and Noodle.

So talk about master plan turbulence? By this point, things weren't nearly as fly as I had planned. I even started having bouts with unmitigated paranoia, feeling like Addis was turning fickle hearts against me. I became distrustful of almost everyone, except for my girlfriend, my crew from home (whom I now started having down all the time), and all the other girls whose flatteries I needed at this point in my life.

On a couple of nights, I woke up swearing I was having a heart attack, so I'd run down the street to the UPenn emergency room. But as the all the tests kept coming back negative, one of the doctors finally gave me a pamphlet to read: "Anxiety Disorder."

"Anxiety disorder? Me?" I sucked my teeth as I flung the pamphlet on the ground. *"Man, does this doctor know who I am? Straight-up 'survivors' like me don't get crazy stuff like that! I ain't weak! I'm too strong to be weak!"*

So of course I still profiled to protect my gorgeous reputation that I had worked so hard to build, and I kept pursuing this master plan too, since I was no "quitter." But if I were being completely honest, I'd have to confess that I was no longer having fun. All my "freedoms" were now starting to show their true colors as the bondage they really were. I was addicted to boostin', addicted to being conceited, addicted to getting drunk, and addicted to fashion. If I had $20 for every time I had tried to quit smoking weed, I would have had enough money to pay for a weekend retreat somewhere.

▲ ▼ ▲ ▼ ▲

This was why my research job at Wistar couldn't have come along at a better time! Right on UPenn's campus, The Wistar Institute was the oldest independent biomedical research institution in the entire country, and getting a job there was like a dream. I mean, if doing hospital rounds with Dr. Green was a slam dunk, then working at Wistar was like buying the whole basketball team. And it all happened so spontaneously. One day, I was sitting somewhere on campus smoking a Newport, when I saw Tiffany, another pre-med who was my same year. I said hello, asked her where she was headed, learned of her job at Wistar, asked if she wouldn't mind checking on an opening for me as well, and then voilà!

Many floors high, with security personnel and countless labs (even the feared "rabies lab" where people wore "spacesuits" behind double-doors), I quickly found Wistar to be the ideal place to get away from all the negativity—the very negativity I was still craving and enslaved to. Sometimes, I'd spend close to thirty hours a week there: loading and unloading the autoclave, making 5% agar gels, running the centrifuge, and walking slowly and steadily as I'd carry large rubber bowls of liquid nitrogen down the hallways. After all, I still hadn't given up on my master plan, one bit. And just as I stayed studying the whole street game, I was still studying the whole "get-into-med-school" game even more. Not to mention how Dr. Herlyn, the world-renowned German doctor I worked for, was known for writing medical school recommendations that didn't just "open doors"—they blew them right off the hinges:

The Wistar Institute, 1892
Meenhard Herlyn, D.V.M.
Professor and Chairman
Program of Molecular and Cellular Biology

February 21, 1996   NONCONFIDENTIAL

I have known Mr. Aaron Campbell since the Fall of 1994 when he first came to my laboratory to work as a work study student. He worked under the supervision of the Senior Molecular Biologist in my laboratory, Dr. Kapaettu Satyamoorthy. Aaron is a dedicated young student who has volunteered to work in the laboratory far and way beyond the time requested and expected. He is quiet but attentive, has a quick mind, and is interested and motivated. He committed himself to work extra workdays, and was often in the laboratory until late at night and on weekends. He performed all assigned duties to our full satisfaction. He was always reliable and dependable. Thus, I have full confidence in him, in the work he is doing, and in his overall work performance. He appears to like our experimental cancer biology work and participated in laboratory meetings. Although listening only, he was always fully attentive. Dr. Satyamoorthy is full of praise for Aaron, and they are a good team.

Aaron's main task was to perform Southern analyses for the presence of specific sequences for human growth factor genes that we constructed for insertion into adenoviruses for gene transfer studies. His assays are meticulous, he is inquisitive and has the desire to understand the complex biological events that underlie our investigations.

Aaron is well liked by all in the laboratory in his quiet but assertive way. He was polite, and only slightly shy. I appreciate him as a good colleague, well in the upper third of his group of undergraduate students that I have experienced.

Please feel free to contact me with any further questions.

Sincerely yours,
Meenhard Herlyn

Swiping my Wistar badge and waving at security, I loved having this place in my life. I quickly excelled beyond the doctors' expectations; in a year's time, I was promoted to training UPenn's fourth-year medical students in lab protocol before they could graduate. I was even asked to train Dr. Oka San, who had just touched down in the U.S. from Japan so he could learn American lab protocol, along with some English. So we were like one big "lab family;" and since pretty much every one of us smoked like chimneys and drank coffee like Gatorade, we could almost read each other's minds when it came to suggesting cigarette breaks. And even though one of the doctors loved making laughs over how incredibly thick my new Rolex-link gold chain was that I kept under my sweatshirt, I was still the one student he ended up picking to head one of the most cutting-edge and time-demanding experiments in the entire lab.

So now with my mixtapes playing in the lab's box at three in the morning, as I'd pretty much be the only one in the building, I never betrayed my lab family's trust. (Though I must admit, the Mr. Hyde in me stayed plotting on how I could steal some of that liquid nitrogen from the basement, so I could freeze-bust locks and taking my thievery to a whole new level.)

But no, I never took a drop of liquid nitrogen, nor anything else from Wistar, because come Monday mornings, as I walked into the large, fancy conference room complete with cherry wood tables and fresh bagels with all the fixings, it felt good having this one special place where I was still "straight legit."

Wistar: and as I'd be heading back to the lab after running over to the hospital to pick up some freshly-removed skin cancers in little sandwich baggies, I'd pass UPenn's medical school and mumble under my breath, "I'm still coming for you!"

XVIII

SWEAT LODGE

Of all the liars in the world, sometimes the worst are our own fears.

—Rudyard Kipling

"Salut!"

That's what my two older Puerto Rican janitors taught me to say as we'd take shots of 151 proof rum from the same dirty shot glass in one of the Port's countless closets. And while spurring each other on down at UPenn with shots of Jamaican overproof rum, we'd always say, "Yeah, n*gg*h!"

See, it was the same stuff now, just different places. Same insane tolerance for alcohol, too. That's why when this new freshman kid from Harlem tried partying with us and ended up unconscious with blood oozing from his orifices, we weren't surprised. In fact, in the most calloused way, we even claimed his tube-fed body as a type of "toast" to our craziness (though his nurse in the hospital called us a bunch of stupid jerks when we showed up to see him).

I was twenty-one years old now. If you saw me standing with my crime family on the street corners of New York with a Newport hanging off my lip, you would never have guessed that I was an Ivy Leaguer working for a world-renowned scientist. Conversely, when standing with my lab family outside of Wistar with a Newport hanging off my lip, you would never have guessed that I slurped "E & J" on the dark streets of the Port's graveyard shift as Van' Puddin's "son." Dr. Jekyll and Mr. Hyde, Cliff Huxtable and Miles Davis, respectable and reckless, I pretty much had both sides "down packed" by now. However, what was once so "black-and-white"—in terms of proper time and place to do or say whatever—was now becoming increasingly gray. That slate-gray that always meant a horrible storm was brewing.

For starters, years of me and my homies "sowing" whatever in the world we wanted (without fear of any consequences) was finally delivering that harvest of "just deserts." So now, not only were childhood friends getting arrested, but there were more than a few UPenn homies flunking out and vanishing back to their respective hometowns like they had never been part of this intellectual elite to begin with. It was sad, and of course, everyone hurt deeply whenever any of this happened. So then, why was it still so easy for the rest of us to continue on the same destructive courses as if we were somehow immune?

To be honest, this whole "fast life" thing was now losing it's hype. I mean of course I still loved all the attention I got, still loved my mixed drinks, and still loved my "hydro," courtesy of my white homies who had long since introduced me to the expensive stuff they grew in their humid, foil-covered rooms with the carbon tanks and crazy electric bills. I also still loved how my "boostin'" skills were so slick that thug after thug and gangster after gangster would sit quietly as I recounted my craziest capers before giving out tips. In fact, "Cat Burglar" was another nickname I had earned—"Cat" for short—and I loved that, too. But the only thing was, if my other nickname was "A-Dog" (for being a "dog" when it came to girls), then weren't the two nicknames a contradiction? But you see, my whole life had become one big contradiction. And like I said, I realized I was getting bored.

Though I still couldn't put my finger on what was wrong. For while it was obvious that I wasn't being fulfilled, it's just that the word "unfulfilled" never crossed my mind. I mean, even my snake became "played out" to me. So one day, as I noticed this broke dad and his boy window-shopping at the pet store a few blocks from campus, I simply told him to follow me back to my apartment, where I put my snake in a pillowcase and just handed it to him. And while he couldn't thank me enough, I actually felt like I needed to be thanking him! Because as I now realized that I needed some major change in my life, I figured that any little changes in the meantime would at least be a step in the right direction—like tossing cargo to lighten the load on a sinking ship. But why couldn't I also finally "toss" my Newport and blunt habits—especially since they now had me spitting up blood in my morning showers?

See, UPenn was supposed to have provided some ultimate sense of stability by now, while the Port, on the other hand, was supposed to have provided some ultimate sense of manhood. So now that I was as Ivy League as one could be—with both Wistar and a strong contact list to prove it—well why wasn't I experiencing that ultimate sense of stability? And now that the Port was like my personal playground with monkey-bars, why wasn't I yet feeling that King Kong sense of manhood? I mean, yeah, I was as cocky as one could be, but we all know that cockiness and contentment are two totally different things.

More so, even though I had reached a point where I could chill in almost any hood, do dirt with the dirtiest, and drink the rest clear under the table, I was still plagued by many of those same insecurities, questions, and fears from long ago. That same emptiness, too. So no wonder then, that one night as I was slamming down a bottle of Bacardi Black while staring at my shirtless self in my mirror, I had to do a double-take as I suddenly saw that same scared little boy looking right back at me— just an older and more fly version with muscles, jewelry, and blunt-burnt lips. And what scared me the most was what I saw the most: weakness. And having already tried everything I could to make that weakness go away, I felt so impotent in the face of it.

And on top of weakness, I still had plenty of fears, too: fears of still not "meeting the mark" in this black-on-black climate (which mind you, was constantly rising like mercury in a thermometer). Most of all, there was the fear of someone else seeing or thinking that I was ever afraid! And I wasn't alone with these struggles, either. Because the more I got embraced into the illest of circles, the more I saw the way others wrestled with the same stuff. And like deep-sea diving, the pressure was intense. That's why some homies had nervous breakdowns and had to spend time in mental hospitals. And though none of us would really talk much about it whenever it happened, it's like we didn't have to. I mean, there was just this common understanding that the streets could mentally kill a cat; as even our favorite raps always talked about trying to "maintain."

This was why a lot of dudes carried guns to begin with. Yeah, to do dirt or whatever, but also because of this very fear, as we all constantly felt that invisible evil in the air. Even the late Tupac Shakur shocked everyone when candidly admitting that "we" were scared of the same crime element that white people were scared of. So all of these subconscious wrestlings could easily explain why the night after I fired my first 9mm (and got a taste of its sheer power), I stayed with a *Guns and Ammo* magazine, playing "eenie-meenie-minie" daily.

"And maybe I'll do just a few late-night stick-ups too? Easy money, right?"

So again, I still had my weakness and I still had my fears. But at the same time, I was now such a pro at suppressing things and lying to myself, that I still believed I was "rock-hard" and ready to do just about anything my mouth blabbed. So when I'd get heated and run off at the mouth about shooting someone, I totally believed I would do it.

Though I'd still never forget that lonely night with the "man in the mirror."

▲▼▲▼▲

By this point, I was still at UPenn full-time of course, but would not only go to the Port during summers, but during any extended breaks in the school year, as well. Well, late one night in New York, I was leaning against the wall on murky Ninth Ave, when Diamond came along.

Diamond was this full-blooded Cherokee dude who used to be a pimp on "Forty-deuce," but now just walked these human-fluid-stained streets like the mayor of the underworld. Not only did he seem to know every addict and deranged homeless person by name, but whenever there was a beef, it was like he'd already know both sides of the story before even stepping between them. Diamond was raised on an Indian reservation in the South and could still speak the Cherokee language fluently, and what a beautiful language it was. And it warmed my heart that he could tell I was a fellow native before I even had the chance to say so. Needless to say, we quickly became friends. And though Diamond was well in his forties, he didn't look a day over twenty-five; and though Diamond had a baby-face with no facial hair (just like me), he was nobody to mess with.

"Yeah, I did a lot of time in prison."

"Yeah, what did you do?"

And while it was an unspoken rule that you never asked somebody what they "went away" for, Diamond and I had become like brothers. In fact, he'd only greet me by the Cherokee word for "brother." He continued.

"Well, once the mob killed a man, and my baby brother witnessed them doing it. Some snitch went and told the mob how my baby brother had witnessed it all. So the mob turned around and killed my baby brother, too . . ."

His sudden silence made clear how much he was still mourning. But then he took a deep breath and said the rest in one exhale. "So anyway, I tracked the snitch down, cut his tongue right out of his dirty mouth, and put it in a jar of alcohol on my mantle, and that was that; I didn't even deny it when the cops came; I just confessed and walked right into prison." And he said it like he still had zero regrets.

"By the way, when I was locked up, I was actually put in with the 'Son of Sam.' He was a really nice guy!"

So Diamond and I would talk in pissy alleyways for hours. And as he'd share his heart with me, I'd also share with him how I was searching for something more to life than just material things and being "successful." And while these street meetings of ours were never planned, Diamond would tell me that it was all just the movings of The Great Spirit—or Wakan.

As the son of a true medicine man, Diamond began schooling me on Native-American spirituality: the proper use of sweat lodges, making drums and sacred staffs with animal skins and bones, and even how he felt he could converse with his deceased grandfather. Then there was one last thing he liked talking about, and it was actually something he wanted me to experience with him.

"Hey man, to reach the next level of your spiritual journey, you've gotta try peyote with me some time!"

"Naw, I don't know about that, man!" I spewed a quick chuckle, having no problem showing my healthy fear of it.

"No, really it's not that bad."

Not that bad? Why, I had just finished hearing about someone's ordeal with peyote. Arizona was his name, a philosophy major at UPenn who was one year behind me. (By this point, I was hanging with a good number of philosophy majors.) With bright blue eyes and shoulder-length blondish hair, Arizona was also on his own quest for "answers" beyond the material, the mundane, and the petty. And I'd never forget about his death-defying encounter with peyote—that mysterious little seed from the cactus plant. I mean, I could still hear his every inflection like he had just told me an hour ago:

"Dude, I took that peyote once!" Then laughing with that obnoxiously loud, but semi-enjoyable laugh of his, "Maaan, I thought I was gonna die, dude! Man, I was all balled up on the ground in the fetal position, puking, pissing on myself, and almost crapping on myself. Then this evil spirit came, and just hovered over top of me in this dark cloud, man! It was trying to take my soul, dude! So I just laid there, screaming and covering my solar-plexus with a pillow. Now they say that once you get past that bad part, you make it into the sweetness of the journey. It's just that I never made it past that part, dude!"

Then Arizona laughed like he was just thankful to be alive, all over again. So this was exactly why I now looked at Diamond like it would never happen. I mean, I'd "trip" on some mushrooms like it was nothing; I'd sell a quick pound of it to someone, too. But to me, peyote was as scary as crack.

So with Egyptian relics and even hieroglyphics markered all over my walls (as well as all my homies' best graffiti "tags"), a green light bulb for seances, and dozens of books lining my shelves—from Lao Tzu, to Khalil Gibran, to "No-Eyes" and other Native-American sages—my off-campus efficiency now felt more like a personal sweat lodge. And the motivation in this search was never about following what was trendy, or what some rapper or singer was now "droppin'" in their music; this was my sincere groping for change and real "truth." Because I could now whole-heartedly say that I had "been there and done that," and while people would say that I was definitely "chillin'," this peace-deprived life was no longer cutting the mustard for me.

So sitting in my favorite, broken IKEA chair with books all over the floor and a Newport between my fingers, I'd study for hours a day now, even to the point where I'd dread having to stop to go work at Wistar or study for some physics exams. Not to mention that I was going to class much less these days, because as far as I was concerned, the main "classroom" I needed right now was my sweat lodge. And for the first time, I understood why men like Plato, Aristotle, and Socrates found their truest "hard work" in studying and pontificating the depths of this thing called life.

▲ ▼ ▲ ▼ ▲

Now if you saw me flirting away outside of some New York City club, or watched who I was "creepin'" with in the wee-hours, it might not have looked like it, but the fact remained that I did have a long-term girlfriend, my beautiful Natasha. And as her Scotch-Irish mom and Port-au-Prince dad definitely dug me, it was also pretty clear that one day we would most likely marry.

Well, as Natasha was a junior back when we first got together my freshman year, she had now graduated from UPenn and was off at Georgetown Law School, down in D.C. And though our relationship was now long distance, we still called on each other for everything. So whether it was her giving me the keys to the fancy new car her dad had just bought her, or me all-but-forcing her to apply to Georgetown Law when I saw that she was afraid to aim high and settling for lower choices, that's just how we rolled. And the very first time I brought her around my crime family, Van' Puddin' just looked at me and said, "Duke, don't lose that one there! That's wifey, son."

With sweet brown eyes, that "mixed kid" caramel skin, and natural-ly-highlighted hair that she kept styled just like Halle Berry, not only did she stop traffic when walking down the street, but she could talk herself out of a speeding ticket with a state trooper, too. And what made her most gorgeous was how she didn't even think she was all that beautiful. In fact, she had always been slow in giving herself a compliment.

And it was a crime how unfaithful I was to her. I mean, not only was she head-and-shoulders above any girl I ever cheated with, and the cool-est "ride or die chic" I'd ever known, but she was also my best friend. The one person I'd tell things that I never told any other human—from that night with Big-fat-Ron to this dire spiritual search I was now on. That's why, without feeling the least bit "uncool," I'd get right on the floor and do all my esoteric rituals right in front of her, even calling her right away when that time I thought I had just conversed with my deceased Chero-kee great-grandmother during one of my seances.

So if "Tash" was sweeter than a lifetime supply of Lemonheads, and more fun than a bag of BBQ corn chips on a summer day, then why did I cheat on her anyway? Well, if you had asked me, I would've just told you that I just loved girls. However, on a deeper level, it seemed that my manifold insecurities needed as many fly girls validating my "manhood" as possible—showing me that I still "had it." (I mean, it had been that way since high school, as I couldn't remember a time when I didn't have at least one.) And the reality was that I couldn't stop cheating now, no matter how hard I tried.

But anyway, as Tash and I had come to know so much about each other, it was obvious that we both desperately needed healing and change. For while it might've appeared to distant onlookers that I was this "bad boy" dragging this "innocent girl" through so much drama, the reality was that she had her own life full of drama and "unfulfill-ment"—doing things that she also deeply regretted, while frustrated by the lie of her own master plan for happiness. So as two best friends (where even Tupac once said, "all I need in this life of sin is me and my girlfriend"), Tash now leaned on me so heavily that whatever belief system I was currently studying, she'd come behind me and read whatever I was jotting in my journal.

▲ ▼ ▲ ▼ ▲

So in my increasing disenchantment with worldly distractions (many of which I was grossly addicted to), I started reading Herman Hesse's, *Siddhartha*. Written in the 1950's, it's the story of a young man named Siddhartha, from a respected Brahmin family, who's growing increasingly discontent with the monotony of life and empty religious ritual. True happiness and peace is what he's after, and he's even willing to lose his family and social respectability to find it. And I could definitely relate to that.

So first, Siddhartha attaches himself to a group of ascetics, who believe that enlightenment can be found only by completely eliminating "self." However, the only problem is that even after losing all his material possessions, along with his desire for sex and food, Siddhartha still feels just as empty. So he's then drawn to a holy man named Gotama the Buddha, a man said to have attained this true spiritual enlightenment called "Nirvana." However, finding contradictions about how one is supposed to relate to the physical world, Siddhartha eventually moves from that teaching as well. In fact, Siddhartha soon becomes so disenchanted with his search that he simply gives up and goes right back to the world of materialism—deciding to just "play the game" like everyone else.

So he becomes a successful business man. However, even then, he realizes that he's as discontent as ever. Until one day, he finds himself standing at the edge of the river, contemplating whether to just jump in, drown himself, and end it all. But it's then that he meets this peaceful, simple-living ferryman, who begins instructing Siddhartha on how to be still and "listen to the river speak." So Siddhartha does it, and to his surprise, the river eventually speaks.

The river speaks to him of how all things in life simply "must be"— the evaporation of water followed by rainfall, life and death, joy and sorrow, good and evil—so that everything can continue flowing in one grand cycle, the "circle of life." And having received that revelation, it's at that very river that Siddhartha decides to remain, even becoming a peaceful, simple-living ferryman himself—ready to greet other seekers who may come along the way. Ultimately, *Siddhartha* is a Buddhist diatribe on how everything is connected, and how receiving the revelation of this unity is what brings true enlightenment.

So sitting in a broken IKEA chair in my sweat lodge, with *Siddhartha* in hand, I couldn't help but frown, as the end of the story left me feeling much like Siddhartha did at the beginning of the story. Because as I tried applying it to my own life now, it still gave me no type of clarity, resolve, or boldness with which to face my hardest difficulties:

"So this means that my baby-sitter beating me down like a sick dog and then sexually abusing me and messing my head up for years on account of it was all just a part of some impersonal and arbitrary 'circle of life'?"

Sorry, but I just couldn't jive with it. So lighting yet another Newport with the soon-to-expire one in my hand, I studied some more.

Speaking of my old baby-sitter, I badly wanted revenge on him now. I mean, didn't it ever cross his sick mind back then, that one day I might grow up and become "sick" myself? The type of sick where I just might "Cape Fear" his behind? Sometimes I'd plot against him so badly in my sweat lodge, that on one or two occasions I literally had to wipe the drool from my rummy lips. And did I want to kill Big-fat-Ron? No, not necessarily. I just wanted to "scar" him back a hundred times worse than he had scarred me. And what if I were to round up some of my fellow nut cases, kidnap him, take him deep into Hell's Kitchen, and have some loonies from the Meat Rack show him a thing or two that he'd never forget? And scariest of all, was that this was something I actually could've done—Hell's Zoo was that sick and I knew Hell's Zoo that well.

So make way for this runaway train! A runaway train loaded with bassy music, weed smoke, mushrooms, black rum, and philosophy books. I'd continue my search.

▲ ▼ ▲ ▼ ▲

I heard the brook lamenting like a widow mourning her dead child and I asked, "Why do you weep, my pure brook?" And the brook replied, "Because I am compelled to go to the city where Man contemns me and spurns me for stronger drinks and makes of me a scavenger for his offal, pollutes my purity, and turns my goodness to filth.

—Khalil Gibran, Lebanese philosopher

Whether it was rivers, streams, or waterfalls, I just loved being around running water, and deep in the woods, too. And I had Mom to thank for that, because since we could never afford a family vacation back when I was little, she'd always plan day trips to some of the sweetest beaches and state parks in our part of Jersey. And as she'd lay on her blanket and relax, Brett and I would roam and explore nature for hours, even building fishing poles from sticks and using safety-pins for hooks. So that's why as my search now had me in the woods, I felt right at home.

My knapsack filled with weed and books, I was climbing mountains in upstate New York, embarking on what Native-Americans referred to as "vision quests." Basically, a vision quest was when one journeyed into the wilderness to find one's "self" and spiritual direction, even looking to nature for signs from The Great Spirit. And on these quests, anything you came across could mean something—from a hawk flying overhead to a deer hurdling past.

Well by this point, I was heavily into Carlos Castenada's teachings from a Native-American sage named Don Juan. His writings got me especially excited to search for my own personal spirit guide. And would this spirit guide be elusive or accessible, gentle or rough? I couldn't help but let my curiosity wonder. I mean, just the thought of having my own immortal guide to never leave me or forsake me? It sounded too good to be true, but I sure wanted it. Most of all, I just wanted truth.

So sitting atop my favorite mountain, overlooking that same majestic Hudson River that became the decrepit Harlem River to the south, I'd feel like I could stay up there forever. There was no stress, no noise, and nobody to interrupt. Then I'd look over at Tash sitting on a nearby rock, relaxing and warming herself in the autumn sun. She always looked so at home up there, mostly because the base of this very mountain actually began at the edge of her big backyard. For as Natasha's father was a genius of an architect—designing some of New York City's most cutting-edge structures—he had moved them from Manhattan's Upper West Side to upstate New York back when she was a teenager.

So against this windy overcast sky I'd sit in serene silence for hours—waiting, listening, trying to make my mind as pure and peaceful as one of the little waterfalls I had stopped to drink from on my way up there. Then eureka, one day I did it! It seemed like I had finally succeeded in making my thoughts as pure and peaceful as the sweet-flowing waters. I mean, I felt no negative feelings whatsoever, and everything felt absolutely perfect all of a sudden. And though I couldn't put it into words, life seemed so amazingly simple and easy now. Yes, happiness was finally and undoubtedly mine!

Well as much as I didn't want to leave this mountaintop, the sun was starting to set, plus this place was known to host bears and bobcats. And as I began the long hike down, I couldn't wait for everyone to see how different my life would be now. No more egotistical jerk for me! I'd now be a "righteous man," only giving the very best of things to people. Yup, that's how I felt, and that's just how I pictured it. And that picture had me smiling real big as I finally emerged from the thicket.

However, just as even the most gorgeous rainbows begin to fade, so did those colorful feelings of peace I had discovered in those woods; and it didn't even take the entire evening for it to happen. Was it the dumb phone calls waiting for me? Was it the fact that there was no more beer and the stores were now closed? Was it that I ran out of weed? I didn't know. All I did know was that what I thought was true change on that mountaintop was really nothing more than "having a great day"—nice to enjoy, of course, but completely void of supernatural power. The very power I needed.

Bummer.

More so, as much as I enjoyed Lao Tzu's and Kahlil Gibran's quotes, I also found them to be just as powerless in breaking my shackles. Thus, the egotistical jerk within would continue his dictatorship.

XIX

THINGS FALL APART

Tarot cards: I'd steal almost every pack the bookstore had. Egyptian decks, Celtic decks, Chinese decks, and more, always to be found in the "Occult" or "Witchcraft" sections. But I still didn't feel that made me some "crazy witch" or anything; that's why I refused to be labelled as "occultic." However, as I now sat in my apartment, "breathing my spirit" into my tarot cards before spreading them across my bed, I most definitely was.

You know, the academic hallways of UPenn and Wistar might've laughed aloud had someone asserted the existence of a devil. But for me, there were too many strange things I just couldn't explain away. Not only had I seen some haunting things at the Port (like that powdery, deathly white woman in the long, white flowing gown who glided past me one day like she had no feet), I had experienced stuff at UPenn, too. Once during freshman year, I was getting under my covers for bed one night, when suddenly they got super tight like a giant pair of hands was yanking them. I got so scared, that I jumped up, ran out my apartment and down the hall, and knocked on my homegirl Athena's door to sleep in her bed. Crazy, I know, but I was dead serious. However, compared to what happened recently, that was just child's play.

Well, I was getting high with some of the regular guys and gals from the crew one day when something hit me all of a sudden. At first, I just figured the weed had been laced with roach-spray, oven cleaner, or even a little crack, as we all knew that some hustlers did all types of jacked-up stuff to their product to make it more "bomb." Though seeing how I had definitely smoked my share of tampered-with-weed before (experiencing almost every type of insane reaction and bizarre sensation), there had to be something else going on. But whatever this was, it was like nothing I had ever known. Things got real dark—real fast.

Lowering my head in my hands, this was bad. And more than scared, I seemed to be going into a type of shock. It felt like I was losing my mind. Then out of nowhere, this evil voice told me to just get up, walk to my off-campus apartment, and die. And like the voice's little puppet or sidekick, that's exactly what I did. Without warning, I jumped up in the middle of our mid-afternoon "cypher" and deserted everyone with no goodbyes. Too much mental pain to say a word to anyone.

From the elevators, to the high-rise dorm lobby, to outside on campus, I remained a slave to this evil voice. There I was, looking so much like "the man" on the outside—"Mr. Popular" in the flesh—while indescribably horrified and dying on the inside. And what I really wanted to do was turn right around and race for the emergency room. But again, I was too much of a slave. I mean, it's like I was under some type of spell. Besides, what would I tell them at the hospital anyway? That the devil was shepherding me to my death?

Trotting up the street, it seemed like there were sirens and ambulances everywhere. *"What's this, some type of omen?"* I wondered. Everything seemed so dreary (even though the day itself was sweet and sunny). Yeah, I was gonna die, for sure. And I couldn't stop having visions of cadavers being shredded right before my eyes. Yeah, I was gonna lose my mind, too.

Running up the steps to my second-floor sweat lodge, I dropped my backpack like I no longer had arms and staggered over to my stereo. Proving once and for all that I wasn't in command here, instead of me playing something soothing like Sade, I put on "Diary of a Madman"—the horror-rap by Wu-Tang's latest group, Gravediggaz. Turning it all the way up, the bass began pounding (hard like my heartbeat), the girl's eerie opera began screaming, and along came the lyrics as I collapsed on my bed.

> Stroll through the dark conditions,
> I'll stone ya' until I see sparks of friction.
> I'll chop ya' like a coal miner,
> Then combine your blood and mix it with the drug.
> Some more, I'll give ya' some more and watch ya crawl,
> Guts hit the floor,
> Worms that dig your pores,
> I'll trick ya, ha, then I'm quick to syringe,
> Deep into your thoughts and bust out your skin.

Flopping around in my scared sweat, I struggled to breathe. *"Man, is this really how I'm gonna die? All alone like this?"*

Reaching across my bed, I grabbed my cordless phone, dialed Tash down in D.C., and left her a voicemail to rush to Philly right away. Though the music was so loud, all she'd end up hearing was "Diary of a Madman." I had no sense of time whatsoever, especially since the song had been set on "repeat." And whatever Arizona and Diamond had said about peyote, this had to be a dozen times worse.

And I wasn't alone in my sweat lodge, either. Something was enjoying watching me suffer like this. It felt like demons were dancing around my bed. Impish and shadowy and quite a few of them, too. Squeezing my eyes shut in anguish, I refused to look. I was sinking, and it was getting harder to breathe.

The strongest urge to sleep now hit me. *"Oh no,"* because I was afraid that if I did, I'd never wake back up. Surely Death was coming for me, even walking up my hallway steps to make its undeniable entrance. And to think of how many times my homies and I had mocked Death while spitting the brashest lyrics from Biggie's *Ready to Die* album. But I wasn't mocking anything now. In fact, I was the one being mocked!

"Man, I'm fading..."

"Please, God," I whimpered. I sure wasn't an atheist now.

Fading for sure . . .

Gone.

Well, it was quiet now—dead quiet. But at least I wasn't dead (though at first, a part of me wondered if I was). And I knew it was hours later because it was completely dark outside. My room was pitch black, too; except for my stereo—sitting idle with its lights on, like a truck that had just hauled through Hell.

The silence was too ambiguous to lay still. I mean, did it mean rest now, or continue losing my mind? Groaning to my feet, I stumbled to the bathroom and splashed some water on my face. I was discombobulated, but as soon as I had my balance, I grabbed my jacket and headed outside to the streets. I felt like a hermit emerging from the depths, or even an escaped prisoner from the French Chateau D'If. I went to one of the regular Chinese food spots, ordered some General Tso's Chicken, and walked around some more while gobbling it down from the carton. Would I ever be the same again? I mean, a part of me still wondered if it was the same day. I eventually went back home and passed back out.

Needless to say, I had tons (on top of my already-existing "tons") to think about. For one thing—big pre-med thinker that I was—I had no idea how to intellectually categorize this experience. And again, blaming it on the drugs was too hard to believe, especially since I had only taken three or four puffs at the most (compared to my normal amount which could be well in the hundreds). So then, was it really the Evil? My conclusions equalled "most definitely"—and with an onslaught like I never imagined possible. Because instead of my childhood back door, this one was at the back door of my very mind and soul!

So what was I gonna do now? Well, as it quickly began circulating how "Aaron had a fight with the devil," I actually didn't change much at all. But that was only because I had no clue how to change anyway (or where to find the answers I was groping after). However, there was at least one thing that changed inside of me. As for that super hero, "New York State of Mind" humanism of mine (fueled by how much "I" had survived, and how much "I" had braved all of my life), I now knew for certain that in the blink of an eye, "I" could become weaker than a legless beetle. I was way more fragile than I ever thought. That's why as I did my next tarot card spread and saw that "Devil" card pop back up, I cursed it under my breath and started watching my back all over again.

Paranoid.

▲ ▼ ▲ ▼ ▲

But guess what? As contradictory as it seemed, I still loved that sinister rush that surged through my body and left me feeling untouchable (demonic onslaughts aside). It especially made me feel powerful in the face of black-on-black crime—the ubiquitous pitbull-eat-pitbull. Because our streets were only getting darker. I mean, just recently some dudes my age had stopped off at a random ATM machine in Newark, when suddenly some dudes with guns jumped into their car, abducted them to some abandoned housing projects, stripped them naked, beat them, and even threatened to kill them if they didn't give each of them "mic checks!" And since I loved creeping through these same dark streets—spray-painting my name in Egyptian hieroglyphics for everyone to see—it seemed like the only way to ward off such evil was with an evil heart.

But man, what a price I had paid to arrive at this place! I mean, the countless hours I had spent hunting the darkness, studying the darkness, and guzzling the darkness—"raw with no chaser." But then again, wasn't this what we all coveted as teenagers in our lust for manhood? Wasn't this part of my glorious master plan? Only now that I had finally "arrived," if you will, I had no idea that it could get so doggone dark (and the bondage so doggone strong)—and at the same time, be so doggone unfulfilling. So lights, cameras, and action aside, I started facing up to the fact that I was miserable (even with my overwhelming success at Wistar). Only I'd never show any of this, because our society had taught me to hide such feelings. "Never let 'em see you sweat," as the famous deodorant commercial once said.

And to think of how much worry I was subjecting my family to—not nearly as good at hiding Mr. Hyde as I thought. Dad, for one, had his deep suspicions: the gallons of liquor that went missing from his cabinet, the way I'd reference notoriously bad places as if they were normal, even the time during my freshman year when I called him from school while tore up, then never showed up at the train station in Jersey the next morning as he sat there, waiting. And as for Mom, she just held it all in—her typical reaction whenever something worried her to the core. However, since she had watched me beat so many odds in my life—from elements of my childhood, to Wardlaw, to UPenn—she just believed that whatever this now was, I'd eventually "beat it" in the same way. But if only she knew how badly I was being beaten.

Then there was my mom's younger sister, Aunt Carol, and her husband from Greece, my Uncle Andreas—the one who first inspired me to become a doctor. As he had been growing so impressed with my strides at UPenn and Wistar, he recently offered me the opportunity of a lifetime: becoming a partner with him at his private medical practice, which by the way, had become one of the most noted oncology practices in all of North Jersey. All I had to do was get into medical school—any med school, for that matter—and I'd be "set for life."

"Hey, what do you think of that, Aaron?" My family smiled big, so excited for me.

"Wow, that's awesome! Thanks so much, Uncle Andreas!"

I was touched, excited, and could even picture it happening—me and my Uncle Andreas standing over a patient's hospital bed, deliberating on what crucial steps to take next. But in reality, I was too caught up in my own drama to be as ecstatic as I would've been as much as a year ago (reaching across the Thanksgiving dinner table for the gin so I could pour my fourth or fifth "straight" glass—which of course had my family talking on the phone the next morning).

Thus, I was in some pretty deep waters. And as my addiction was to the darkness, you could say they were dark waters, too.

▲ ▼ ▲ ▼ ▲

As for my childhood friends, it felt like we were split up now. However, not because we had "beef" or had stopped loving each other, but only because we were off in our own stormy seas, fighting to stay afloat.

Having been "knocked" by undercovers too many times, Keell was now on the run down in Gary, Indiana. And as for Deuce, having already served two bids by this point, he was on the run from two big bounty hunters with .45's on their hips. And things actually got so crazy for Deuce, that he'd be hiding out at some relative's house, only to answer the phone, hear nothing on the other end, and then dip out the door just before the bounty hunters came crashing through. But eventually, both Keell and Deuce got caught and locked up. And they were both locked up for a while.

No matter how hard I'd be cramming for my brain and behavior class, I'd always stop for one of Keell's "collect calls" from Union County Prison in Elizabeth, a city between Plainfield and Newark. But of course his very first phone call I'd never forget.

"Yo Aaron man, don't ever get locked up, man! You don't wanna be in here. This is a cage for freakin' animals, man! This ain't no place for no human being. Man, my first day here, I was walking around with a towel over my head, 'cause I was cryin', man, because I couldn't believe I was locked up! Man, when I get out, I ain't never comin' back here!

"But man, as for my 'celly,' though? Man, you can tell this cat be in and out of jail all the time. This cat got a clothes-line in our cell! He knows how to get weed up in here, too. Man, this cat even knows how to take baby powder and toilet paper and twist it up and make real incense!

But man, that can't be me, though. I ain't gonna be up in here just makin' incense for the rest of my life!"

And to think, back when Keell and I were little kids doing push-ups in his basement to earn our first boy-scout badges, who would've predicted all this? So I'd always try to cheer him up as best I could during these calls, even putting the phone to my speakers so he could hear the newest raps. But in no time, he'd have to go and I'd do my best to start studying again (even though it never ceased to bug me out that here I was, studying at an Ivy League school, while part of my heart was behind bars, "flushing out" his nasty toilet so he could yell up to the girls a few floors above after they'd "flush out" theirs).

Now Deuce wasn't locked up at Union County Prison with Keell; he was at another prison in some remote part of Jersey. And the first time I drove to see him, it felt surreal as the correction officer lead him into the visiting room so we could sit face to face. By this point, it had been a couple years since we'd seen each other—both of us so busy trying to make a name for ourselves in our respective cities. But as we sat there now, our popular names didn't matter as years' worth of emotion came flooding back. Like it was only yesterday that we were sitting in my bedroom, listening to KRS-One's song about the destructive paradoxes of hustling.

"How's your mother and Brett?" The first thing he asked since we had always been like blood.

"Man, they're good. Brett's at New York University, and he's doing it big with his spoken-word poetry. Matter of fact, them poetry dudes, The Last Poets, been digging his stuff and invited him to start rollin' with them. So he's chillin'. And you know he's doing his little fashion model thing, too. The girlies still lovin' that fly cat. But yo, how's your mom, man?"

"Man, she's cool. She's been alright lately, you know?" (meaning she hadn't been getting high lately, which was great to hear.)

And from there, Deuce and I talked about everything—from cars, to clothes, to girls, to the "good old days." So sweet, it was like we were in Greg's backyard all over again—brown bags of candy and all. However, this was far from Greg's backyard; and how quickly we got yanked back into reality as that same correction officer came over and said "time's up." So sucking our teeth and rising to our feet, it was time to be thugs again. Time for him to swagger back to his cell, and time for me to swagger back to West Philly. Though we still hugged like brothers, and got teary-eyed too.

"Yo Aaron, come check me out again soon, man! Yo, take care of my daughter, too. Yo, you're her god-daddy, ai-ight. I never got to tell you this, but you're her god-daddy."

"I got you, man. I'll cut through the projects and put some loot in her little pocket right now."

"Yo, love you man."

"Love you back, son" What a mess this was. What a mess we were.

And by the way, I was now a "big senior" at UPenn. But again, amidst all the drama I was finding it hard to rejoice nearly as much as I should've been.

▲▼▲▼▲

So I still hit a few clubs in NYC here and there, but other than that, I was pulling away from much of the party scene—even getting rid of my beloved, big Rolex-link chain and bracelet. I mean, the profiling, the shiny cars, the crowds, it just wasn't "doing it" for me anymore. In fact, some nights when I did go to Newark's notoriously-wild Brick City club, I'd just sit outside on the bench, sipping brandy and giving love to people I knew as they were leaving the joint.

But don't get me wrong, I still had my crews who I adored being with, from NYC to Plainfield to D.C. And of course there was always Van' Puddin'. In fact, one summer night, as Van' Puddin' had decided to pop up in Philly for the big annual "Greek Fest," he anxiously surprised me with a phone call (though still cool as ever).

"Duke, where you at? I'm in Philly man. Right here on 40th Street."

"What! Man, you're right around the corner from me! Just chill right there and I'll be right over."

Spotting him on that street corner at the top of UPenn's campus as I approached, how good it felt to have Brooklyn's finest down here in Philly! We hugged, both knowing how rare and special this was. More so, it wasn't just me and Van' Puddin' standing there, because this was also the "Greek Fest" when every gangster he'd ever been locked up with had decided to meet for a big reunion. People I'd always heard about ("legends" even), but was now meeting for the first time. So we were "deep" for sure that night, with more than enough parked cars for everyone to lean on.

However, as deep as we were, Van' Puddin' and I still shared like we were all alone. Just as if we were standing outside of the Port's second floor bathroom.

"Duke, so you ai-ight down here, son?"

"Yeah, I'm chillin', man."

"Well, you know if you need some loot down here, man, I can set you up with a hustle."

"Yeah, I know. But it's cool, 'cause I got my own hustle going on already, and it's keepin' that cheddar in my pocket, too." And how good it felt telling my dad on the streets that my hustle was tight.

"Ai-ight, son, cool. But listen, man . . ." Van' Puddin' got serious now, flicking the blunt's ashes before passing it along to me next in the circle (since he never got high, himself). "Whatever you do, just make sure you still get that piece of paper, son. Ya' heard, man? Get that degree, kid!"

"No doubt, man!" I quickly replied like it could never be otherwise.

But at this point in my life—as the restless and increasingly risky person I was becoming—it sure could've been otherwise. I mean, who in the world was I kidding? And Van' Puddin' could obviously see that, as I'm sure he'd seen it with so many other young dudes. Matter of fact, this was the most deeply concerned I'd ever seen him.

"Yeah man, just get that paper." He said it to me one last time while staring off in the distance. And what surprised me was that there was even this sadness in his eyes. Something I couldn't quite put my finger on. I mean, was it because he somehow felt responsible for the fact that I was now so criminally minded? Not so much. Rather, I think I just caught him sighing at the craziness and emptiness of life—just as I had been.

Anyway, it still felt like an oasis standing there with Van' Puddin', and I could've leaned against those cars with him all night long. But out of nowhere, two of his reunion homies began beefing with these two other cats who were walking by. Then things started heating up. It was at this point that Van' Puddin' stopped his next sentence short, said "excuse me for a minute," and stepped right between the two arguing parties,— using his huge frame to force some space into the mix.

He tried addressing the two passersby in that calm, commanding way of his. The only problem was that they started yelling even more. Then they started yelling at Van' Puddin'. Wrong move.

"Oh, so y'all n*gg*hs tryin' to get Go-rilla?" A Brooklyn way of saying someone was beating their own chest like they wanted war. Van' Puddin' chuckled and then turned to the rest of us with indignant resolve.

"Y'all see that cop car right there? As soon as that &^^$### cop car leaves, bury these jokers right here where they're standin'!"

"Ai-ight, no problem." A few of his reunion homies responded.

And since Van' Puddin' was a born commander, everyone around me began popping the trunks to the cars we were leaning on, reaching for what everyone knew was there. Clearly some bodies were about to drop. Everyone just watching for that police car to move like the minute hand on a clock.

So what was I gonna do now? Run? Nope, I wouldn't. I mean, how could I? How often had Van' Puddin' stepped up like this for me over the years? Like with that razor-slashing, "rape you too" gang from the Meat Rack? Or even how he was so willing to hand me his favorite gun when I was scared after trying to crush that dude's legs with my van. Lastly, I realized that in this very situation, it could've just as easily been him taking up for me! Man, I loved Van' Puddin'. And man, he loved me right back. So that's why in a nano second's time, it was a no-brainer that I'd go down with him for attempted murder or whatever was about to befall us.

And to think, four years back, Aaron was this cheery-eyed, private school graduate, ready to give "success" a whole new definition—swearing he had the most ingenious master plan for life, with his University of Pennsylvania T-shirt underneath his janitor jumpsuit. And that master plan was actually succeeding! Then how quickly it was lobotomized. And now this . . .

However, nothing happened as we stood on that corner. Because the minute those two dudes saw how comfortable everyone was with pulling out guns in the middle of the crowded streets with a cop car a hundred feet away, they took off running.

"Man, 'dem cats was about to get it for real." I chuckled to Van' Puddin' while finishing off my twelfth or so brew for the day.

"Yeah, Fam," he chuckled right back. "But I'm glad they ran, though. 'Cause I ain't need that on my head tonight!" So we went right back to chillin', reminiscing about crazy stories in the Port, like we always loved to do.

▲ ▼ ▲ ▼ ▲

One of my favorite songs was "Take It Easy" by reggae-rapper Mad Lion, who began the song by saying that there were too many suckers and not enough time to shoot them all down. But the part that always jumped out to me was, "not enough time." Because while I was definitely quick to call someone a "sucker," I truly did feel there was not enough time to find what I was searching for.

For although I now had journals full of anecdotes from wisemen and sages from many eras and ethnicities, I still needed concrete answers—something I could sink my teeth into. Plus, I needed some real power to break these addictive cycles I was stuck in. And as for those blasted tarot cards? I tossed all of them in the trash (some I even burned in the fire)—sick and tired of feeling their evil energy.

And just like liquor and weed (along with hashish and "shrooms") had long since stopped giving me that all-fulfilling rush, so it was also with that "stealer's high" I got from boostin'. Not to mention that while UPenn once had me feeling like one of the smartest dudes on the planet, even that "high" was no longer high enough. Therefore, in my continued gropings after meaning and wonder, unbridled wildness became my next cup of tea. Though I never would've called it that. I would've just said that I was "living life to the fullest"! And Tash could sense it, which is why the night after I crashed her mother's car (pretty much on purpose), and then thought it was funny how I had managed not to spill any of my mixed drink in the process, she started crying (drunk herself), "Aaron, I don't get it! It's like you're not gonna be happy until you just kill yourself!"

But again, where were those big answers I was still hunting for—even more intensely than the bounty hunters who eventually nabbed Deuce? Where was true fulfillment and peace to be found? Like Mad Lion said, there was simply not enough time. And there didn't seem to be enough help, either. Because if this were a baseball game, Humanism, Hedonism, and Existentialism were far too poor a match for such intense "bottom of the ninth" pitches. More so, since I was getting bored with "subbing them" in and out all the time anyway, they were officially off the team!

Then one morning, I simply walked into Wistar, and quit right on the spot without even as much as a two-week notice. And here I had just been assigned to one of the biggest revolutionizing experiments in the lab, destined to appear in medical journals around the world. That's why Satya, the Indian doctor who I'd been partnering with, stood in utter shock—like I had just killed our very dream. And while it hurt to see his face like that, what could I say? My dreams were being frustrated and killed, too. And by the way, I didn't want to be a doctor any more. Because while my main motivation in that career path had been to make big money and thereby have that "stability," I now realized that money and "success" hardly guaranteed such.

Farewell, Wistar.

So what was left now? Well, other than having the best mom and girlfriend in the world, I didn't really know. But I still felt there had to be something out there, somewhere—some "Rock of Gibraltar" that I could build my everything on. And until then, as much as I loved the woods, I was still addicted to thug-life, just the same.

"Maybe jail would be the ideal place for me? A place where I can be left alone and continue this search without distractions?"

So as more time elapsed, and life with no concrete answers became more frustrating, I started not caring (Existentialism now forcing his way back onto the team). In fact, I became so reckless, that when my homie Shem, who worked for Continental Airlines, called me with an opportunity to fly to the Dominican Republic (and in the middle of my exam week, at that), I grabbed Sudanese Willis—a fellow UPenn student from my crew—and left like a fugitive with only fifty bucks to my name.

Then through a turn of bad events down there—revolving around us being way too cocky (even with the pimps' prostitutes)—as we found ourselves on a dark beach with guns aimed at us with Spanish threats, I actually thought the whole thing was quite funny. Just like I thought it was funny how I had managed to sneak that weed into the country— right under the nose of the sweaty-faced customs officer in the camouflage. (Even though it got real tense for a moment, as he stepped a foot away from me and screwfaced me like he wanted to knock my front teeth out with the butt of his machine gun.)

And speaking of getting stuff past customs, some rastas in Jamaica had just propositioned me about trafficking pounds of weed into the

U.S. for them, promising to treat me like a king while I stayed on their island. And of course I'd never see the light of day if I ever got busted. However, all I could think about was the thrill of getting away with it—never mind the money.

So with "carpe diem" in fullest effect now, I'd just keep burning my Native-American sage on hot coals to clear away all negativity. But the only problem was, if all negativity was supposed to be clearing away, then why was there such a part of me that still craved it? And more so, why did I keep having this recurring dream of a giant black bird trying to snatch me up with it's machete-sharp talons? So, until the next big thrill or irresistible "power move" came along (because best believe I still knew how to don a shirt and tie and play that part, too), you'd find me hitting my bong to the dismal sounds of British singing group, Portishead. My favorite song was "Wandering Star."

> Please could you stay awhile to share my grief.
> For it's such a lovely day to have to always feel this way,
> And the time that I will suffer less,
> Is when I never have to wake...

> Wandering stars, for whom it is reserved,
> The blackness of darkness forever.
> Wandering stars, for whom it is reserved,
> The blackness of darkness forever.

> Always doubled up inside,
> Take a while to shed my grief.
> Always doubled up inside,
> Taunted, cruel...

And while the lyrics were already dark, I had no clue that the hook to this song was actually a verse from the Bible.

So again, not enough time, as I sat on a dark front porch on the darker West Sixth Street, right off of Plainfield's Park Ave, sipping my brew as Keell served more of that crack to his customers. Man, I could be so "blah" about everything. Keell was, too. Both of us were too blah to even bother studying which "crackhead" might be another undercover, like the cop who nabbed Keell the first time. And ironically, here we were right down the street from the "Killer Clown's" cemetery—of which Remi had strictly warned us about playing around on, back when we were a bunch of innocent little kids, happy just to have a mouth full of Lemonheads.

Part III

Stepping
(into the light)

XX

THE MORALIST

First, human beings, all over the earth, have this curious idea that they ought to behave in a certain way, and cannot really get rid of it. Secondly, they do not in fact behave in that way. They know the Law of Nature; yet they break it.

These two facts are the foundation of all clear thinking about ourselves and the universe we live in.

—C.S. Lewis

Mary J. Blige said it so sweetly—all I really wanted was to be happy.

D idn't I somehow deserve it? I mean, wasn't I still a good person?
So what if the prostitute I "met" on that Dominican beach was now haunting my nightmares, and so what if my favorite rappers were from Brooklyn's forbidden Saratoga Ave., and so what if I drank, smoked, stole, and lied so much that I couldn't even keep track of my last lie. I still believed I was a good person, so that's all that really mattered, right? And I would gladly run my resume to any other "moralist" who felt they had good works to brag about.

For even though my life was chock-full of dirt, it was full of good stuff, too. Take my job at Wistar, for instance: even after hitting my maximum in work-study hours for the week, I'd plug away into the a.m. hours for free, not going home until the experiment was through. Then way before Wistar, there was my manager position at Plainfield Dairy Queen, which afforded me the privilege of helping Mom with bills. Good stuff, for sure.

And what about my studying such good stuff over these years? (That had to amount to something!) There were the literary classics (compliments of Wardlaw), lectures from some of UPenn's most famous profes-

sors, and even my worn-out erasers attesting to the longest, hardest physics problems. I mean, year after year, late night after late night (sometimes
even in New York City alleyways), it seemed like I was always at it. And
this wasn't even counting my voluminous personal studies.

Then there was little Eddie, my street-adopted little brother and son,
who I protected and nurtured while his mom blasted crack in the Port
bathrooms. And on top of that, one of the first things I did during my
freshman year was get involved in UPenn's "big brother program," where
I was introduced to Omari, an eight-year old from some of West Philly's
worst housing projects. His father was serving a long bid in prison and
his mother was on crack. Tash, who was a junior then, happened to be
the organization's chairperson (that's actually how she and I first met).
However, after I learned of the organization's rule of instructing students
to never giving money to the kids or their families, I ditched the program
altogether (not Tash, of course). I simply "adopted" Omari as my own,
giving him my word that I'd never leave him.

Well inevitably, I ended up adopting Omari's little brothers and sister as well, soon putting food on their dinner table like it was nothing
(as much as I could afford). Thus, Omari became my "little bro" for real,
just like my two actual blood brothers. Whenever I was at UPenn and
Omari rang me with an emergency, I was at his projects on the double.
When there was a suicide attempt in his apartment, I was there. When
their refrigerator was butt-naked and his family didn't have so much as a
25¢ pack of Ramen noodles on their counter, I was there. When Omari
just wanted to come and be with me, I was there, walking him back to
campus through his dark neighborhood.

Then as Omari got older and became conscious of his perpetually
dirty clothes and smelly sneakers (his mother couldn't afford to do laundry), I proudly transformed him into one of the best-dressed ten-year-
olds in his grammar school. He went from no-name "bo-bo" sneakers
to Polo riding boots, from stretched-out, soiled sweatshirts to Tommy
Hilfiger rugby tops. And just like Robin Hood, robbing the rich to give
to the poor, I loved how a good portion of my robberies were going to
great use.

So therefore, while there were scores of folk who judged me for my
evils (and as right as many of them were), I, in turn, felt that I could judge
them for some of their own "evils"—like the way so many at UPenn loved

talking about the plight of the inner-city, yet neglected the hundreds of other Omaris who could only dream of being adopted and visited as little as one hour a week! And yes, I could be more than a little self-righteous about this whole thing. But then again, couldn't we all when it came to our "strong points?" After all, wasn't moralism really nothing more than gauging one's righteousness subjectively, and generally at the expense of others (a man-birthed method bereft of any absolute standard)?

Then, as the last showcase of my "goodness," there was Momma, my amazing grandmother. One day, back when I was no older than twelve, Momma took Mom, Brett, and me to Catholic mass with her, where she broke the news to us that she had cancer. I'll never forget the overcast sky nor the somberness of the day. Cancer. Back then, I wasn't even too keen on that word. Unlike today, that was a time when not many were afflicted with it; though I still knew it was something real bad.

And of all people, did it have to be my own Momma? I mean, she was our "Momma bear" and "Poppa bear" combined. This five-foot tall, Cherokee and Jewish widow, who lead us with steadfast resolve like a Harriet Tubman. But within a matter of months, chemotherapy had "scalped" Momma's two long Indian braids, leaving her head bald and her skin itching and burning. But she still had the prettiest little bald head you could imagine. She was no quitter.

Momma had five grandchildren, but I was her firstborn, and we had a special bond that everyone could see. That's why, sometimes even when I was drunk or high, I would call her in the middle of the night, just to hear her sweet voice. And though she'd barely hear me over the music, it would still break her heart to hear me that way. But of course she'd never tell anyone else, because that's just the way Momma was.

Then years down the road, as her cancer came out of remission yet again—only this time in the "trickiest" part of her small intestine—my Uncle Andreas used his connections to get one of the best gastrointestinal surgeons in the world, some doctor from Europe. And then the minute I got that phone call saying Momma had miraculously made it through the procedure—against the odds of something like 1-to-1,000—I dropped everything and hopped the very next train for New York.

Entering her recovery room at Sloan Kettering Hospital that next morning, there my sweet Momma lay—so frail with tape all over her face and her forearms riddled with tubes and I.V.'s. And as she slowly turned her head and saw me there—her firstborn grandchild and "Ivy Leaguer" that she still believed in with all her heart—her mouth dropped in awe. Obviously, she had feared she'd never wake up to see me again. Plus, even in her groggy state, she somehow realized that I had just skipped my organic chemistry exam to be there.

"Momma, you know I'm always gonna be by your side," I whispered as I kissed her forehead with my Newport breath. Then, stepping away from her bed as my mom and two aunts quickly huddled around her, I stepped to the window overlooking Manhattan's East River and did something I hadn't done in years: I cried. The tears pouring down my extra-dry skin.

Man, it hurt seeing her like this. For while Mom was my "everything," Momma was Mom's everything, thus making Momma everyone's everything. That's why before Momma even came home from the hospital, I was already researching herbal remedies for her immune system and tummy pains. And Momma trusted me so much, that she'd take whatever I prepared for her, from poultices to fresh-boiled licorice root with "royal jelly" instead of honey (all courtesy of my personal studies).

"You're such a good person, Aaron." My Aunt Cecilia would say as I'd regularly troop up from Philly to check on Momma.

So simply stated, I just had to be a good person. Better yet, I most surely was. No doubt, about it! However, if I was as persuaded as I feigned to be, then why did I feel such a need to stress it, defend it, and prove it to myself? Because the unmitigated reality was that just like Shakespeare's Lady Macbeth—troubled in her sleep by the indelible stain of guilt—and just like those private school boys in Golding's *Lord of the Flies*, I still knew that I had serious issues: a cancer in my soul, leading me to liquor, weed, and other escapes as my own "chemo."

▲ ▼ ▲ ▼ ▲

Well, not only had I made the "righteous" decision not to drink myself insane anymore—as that's what had lead to me and that Dominican prostitute walking hand-in-hand to begin with—but after that trip to the Dominican Republic, I quit cheating on Tash altogether. And it was working, too! Even in the face of me now getting surprise phone calls from girls I had been plotting after for years. "Tash is the one for me," I proudly told everyone. But then again, I had known that all along.

More so, as the grim reality of Momma eventually dying began hitting me—and with me so wanting her to see me "jump the broom" more than anything (especially as she and Tash had fallen so in love with each other)—I even decided to pop "the big question." So late one night, as Tash and I were driving back to Philly on the New Jersey Turnpike after another great Easter dinner with Momma and the family, I just threw it out there.

"Hey, why don't we get married?" And I said it just as casually as I might've suggested us grabbing a bag of White Castle burgers. There was no bended knee, no romantic music playing, not even as much as an engagement ring.

"Okay!" She perked up and responded just as casually.

"Yeah, 'cause I really want you to be my wife." (She was beaming now.) "And also, I really wanna do it before Momma dies, ya know?"

"Yeah, that's true," she said. It was so beautiful how our two families had already become each other's families.

"So let's do it at the end of the summer, then?"

"Okay, kind of like the fall, right?"

"Yeah, or the cooler part of the summer, like the end of August."

"Okay, so let's do it on August 31st?"

"Cool. It'll be an evening wedding, then." By this point, I knew she had it all pictured out.

"Ai-ight, cool then . . . I love you, girl."

"I love you too, baby."

So it was settled. And although I was only twenty-two years old, and she still had one year of law school left, and I still had one extra semester at UPenn—I wasn't the least bit scared (and neither was she). Amidst life's uncertainties, "me and Tash" was the one thing that made absolute, perfect sense to me now.

However, some of my own family withheld their support of my wedding, feeling I was way too young. I mean, many of them were still in shock that I had just decided to no longer pursue medicine. But Mom sure was happy, as was Tasha's mom. And of course, Momma was tickled. In fact, when Momma saw that I didn't have an engagement ring, she immediately took the diamond ring off her own finger and put it right on Tasha's. Thus, the matriarch had spoken. And after that, the rest of my family kept their opinions to themselves.

The summer before my wedding was surreal, almost like slow-motion. (Wow, I was actually getting married!) This was also my first summer in four years not working at the Port. And since I only had two classes left at UPenn, which I could only take in the fall anyway, I basically spent my summer hanging in different hoods—from Washington D.C. to Newark—blazing my weed as always, while reading about government conspiracies, listening to Bob Marley, and despising a "Babylon System" where the elite continually subjugated the poor. And though by this point, I wasn't running nearly as wild as I had been, I was still drawn to where some of the wildest things happened. And the summer of 1996 was as wild as ever. That's why whenever I came across some random body gunned down in the streets, all I could do was shake my head and keep moving.

There was one night I could never forget. It was Harlem Week, that long-awaited time of the year when everyone flocked to Harlem's 125th Street—"buckwildin'" like there was no tomorrow. Well as Keell, Baby Grand, and I had arrived there and were walking up one of the dark side streets—bugging over how just days before, some dude had let his pit bulls loose on the entire crowd just for laughs—we noticed a small cluster of people ahead.

Arriving on the scene, it was a fresh "drive-by" that had left two dudes dumped over on the ground. And the craziest thing was that even though it had just happened, we hadn't heard any shots while walking up the street! Taking my place among the small circle, I could even see the deep red holes in the Puerto Rican dude's back as he just lay there, with one leg on the curb and the other in the hydrant's trickling flow along the edge of the street. His head buried in some girl's lap as she sat there sobbing and stroking his hair, he was most likely paralyzed now. Again, this shooting was so fresh that you didn't even hear any sirens yet. *"Man, if this was just a few minutes later, me and my homies would've been right here, too!"* I couldn't help but wonder. And oddly enough, some dude was standing right next to me, with Jay Z's, "Can I Live," blasting from his box.

"Yo man, I don't give a %$#@, man! As long as it wasn't me!" Some other Puerto Rican cat obnoxiously hollered and broke the somber silence. All I could do was shake my head, finish off my beer, and take more glances at the holes in the guy's back—the deepest red I'd ever seen.

As we then headed around the corner to get some more beer from the corner store, to our surprise, there lay the other shot-up body. Only this dude was dead, for sure. Dead and all alone, with nobody as much as smoking a Newport in sight.

"Dag."

So what did I do? Well, since the body was blocking my way to the liquor store, I just stepped around it like nothing. And at this point— in the twenty-second year of life—it was clear that I had seen way too much, too much evil. And utterly destitute of a philosophy or worldview that could process such recklessness and sickness around me, my heart had become rock-hard. So emerging with my next beer, I stepped back around the dead body without a second look and soon found myself on fully alive "one-two-five"—blazing another Newport while some random cats paused to ask me for a quick light. Motorcycle wheelies, the flyest cars (one cat even had an actual dune-buggy), and thousands of other cats who looked just like me—we were all just trying to maintain.

Existentialists with no answers. Sheep without a shepherd.

▲▼▲▼▲

The end of August finally arrived. Then came the eve of the big day, it-self! I noticed how my brother Brett and my homies couldn't wipe these sneaky smiles off their faces, so I knew they were up to something. Then sure enough, later that night, as we were all reminiscing and being silly at Shem's crib in Newark's infamous Colonnade Apartments, there was an unannounced knock at the door. And as everyone became so bent on me sitting in this one big chair in the most open part of the room, I knew the deal, as we had gone to many strip clubs in our day.

The door opened, and in strutted two girls with duffle bags slung over their shoulders. While they were both pretty cute, they were still every bit of "Brick City" rugged, and didn't seem the least bit phased about being in some dark apartment full of lustful thugs and weed smoke. I'm quite sure they had weapons in their bags, too. (Nas' "Shoot Outs" ironi-cally blasted through Shem's speakers.) So with the lights now dimmed, the girls were back out of the bathroom in no time, wearing high heels, but otherwise butt-naked.

"So, who here is the bachelor?" One of them asked like they were officially taking control from this point forward.

"This one over here!" My homie Kenny hollered, hovering over my back like a vulture. And while he was so excited for me, it was also obvious that he was looking forward to getting his own turn afterwards. But as I said, cats still couldn't fathom when I said I was "ready" to marry Tash, I really meant it. My mind more made up than when I had first hatched that illustrious master plan of mine.

Anyway, it was clear that the naked one who was doing all the talking had brought along the other naked one for what was more or less her first night. I mean, "rookie" was written all over her. So at the leading girl's nudge, the rookie began strutting towards me, almost in step with the music. She then stopped directly in front of me like a brand new sports car, turned around, and bent fully over, touching her toes while my homies cheered like mad. But little did this girl realize that I wasn't even looking. And with every bit of her personal business just a few feet away from my face now, I simply raised my Timberland, placed it flush against her bare backside, and slowly pushed her a leg's length away.

The whole room got silent on that one.

More than a little confused, I could tell that the rookie was hurt by my rejecting her. And here she probably was—"Brick City" rugged and all—yet still searching for some type of acceptance and identity. And was there really all that much of a difference between her search and mine? Nope. But of course I wasn't thinking nearly that deep at the time. My only concern was turning my chair away from the whole sex scene, now "rudely" facing the colossal window that looked over the dark city of Newark. And as my homies then did a great job pretending I no longer existed—swarming around the two girls with giggles and non-stop ventures to the bathroom—all I could do was sit there and daydream about how gorgeous my bride was gonna be.

Well, the next morning arrived. The phone woke me up as I slept on the apartment floor; it was Van' Puddin'.

"Fam, today's the day, n*gg*h! Yo, I'm proud of you, Fam. I'mma see you up at that wedding later on today, ai-ight!"

"Cool. See you then, man."

Wow, it really was the day. And with the sun already shining, how good it felt to wake up to Van' Puddin's happy voice. In fact, it was happier than I'd ever heard him.

So with me and my homies dressed and with our weed serving as breakfast, we hopped in the car and started towards the Palisades Interstate Parkway to take us up to Tasha's home in New York's Bear Mountain. Fast forwarding to the very hour itself, everything was decorated just the way me and Tash wanted it—elegant, but super chill, too. We had a giant tent set up on her three-acre lawn, white folding chairs on the fresh-cut grass, and even a makeshift altar with a golden arch, right in front of her pond. Needless to say, family and friends were shocked by the lay out—pristine, surrounding mountains included. (Though when one of Tasha's neighbors stopped by, she said it looked too much like a "gangster wedding.")

So with Brett and Shem as my best men standing at the altar with me now, and as Baby Grand—my old partner-in-crime and wedding DJ—threw on Sade's, "Cherish the Day," the ceremony was officially underway. And lo and behold, my bride emerged from the house. Now my eyes were hardly 20/20 by this point, but she still looked so beautiful in the distance that I didn't know what to do, except drop my jaw and start fighting back tears. Wearing a long, white lace gown that she refused to let me peek at all summer, she was so stunning that even men in the audience removed their shades for a better look. And beyond her beauty, what now had me so choked up was all the memories that started flashing before me. I mean, everything that she and I had been through together over these years—the good, the bad, the studying, the stress, the fast-life, the searchings. She truly was my best friend!

And as she continued towards me to the sound of Sade's voice—innocently staring at me, as if hoping that she was as beautiful as I had hoped—I could see the little girl in her like never before. Just like me, all this little girl ever wanted was to be happy. Then, in another flash, I saw her growing up in her own broken home, enduring her own drama, and crying her own tears that left her struggling with her own demons over the years. Yeah, I was ready for a life of continued healing with her, too. Then, coming back to the present, there she was right in front of me now—her slightly watery eyes and smile matching mine.

And honestly, all I remember about the rest of the ceremony was that when it came time for us to recite our vows, we both seemed to forget everything we had written. All we ended up telling each other was how much we adored each other, and how we were gonna take care of each other. Then, it was time to kiss my bride—which I most happily did—and the audience clapped like crazy. And that was that.

Then, after retreating into the mountains with our photographer to take tons of pictures in warm, sunny fields with perfectly shaded waterfalls, we returned to the celebration where my dad and uncles were already deep-frying chicken and Momma had been waiting on the edge of her seat to get a picture with me. And while we cut the cake and toasted the champagne under the moonlight, the day wouldn't have been complete without Baby Grand throwing on the Gap Band's "Outstanding"—so me and Mom could have our special dance together, just like when I was younger. And by the way, there was no need for us to dance "the Hustle" anymore, because Mom was now one of New Jersey's more noted adult educators. And far from those frozen-toed, mugger dodging bus days of ours, she even had her eye on the "triple black" Mercedes Benz she always wanted.

Well, since Tash and I didn't have money for a honeymoon (after being so broke from paying for our own wedding), one of Tasha's uncles graciously treated us to a hotel room in a neighboring town. So after a little more celebrating and thanking people for coming, Tasha and I disappeared. And we sat on the hotel bed and took the time to look at each other—wow, she was really, truly, absolutely my wife now!—she took our first private moment together to cry tears of joy.

"Cherish the day."

We couldn't wait to have kids, either. However, I began thinking: what was I going to teach my kids that life was all about? Would I tell them like Shakespeare said, that life was just a stage where we play our many parts and then exit into nothing? Most of all, what power could I give them so they wouldn't end up experiencing so much of what me and Tash had been through?

XXI

THE ANSWER

Truth fears no questions.

—Anonymous

HITTING THE REWIND BUTTON NOW . . .
(BACK TO THE BEGINNING OF THE SUMMER, WHEN I WAS
ENGAGED TO TASH, BUT NOT YET MARRIED.)

One night, I had this dream that rocked me like a volcano. I was zipping through UPenn on one of my stolen mountain bikes. In fact, I was zipping so fast, that as I raced over the campus' 38th Street bridge, I took off flying like my bike had wings. Man, it was cool. However, when I landed, I wasn't on campus anymore. I was suddenly in the middle of nowhere—in cornfields of North Carolina—still racing away, but now under the grayest sky. And as much as I tried to stop, the momentum was too powerful.

Within seconds, I crashed into a pool of quicksand that was hidden amidst the cornstalks, where I was immediately up to my neck. My stolen mountain bike was nowhere in sight, but I was hardly alone now. Countless vipers, in neon blues and greens like only the deadliest tree frogs, were slithering on top of the quicksand and began wrapping around my sinking head. I squirmed and fought as best I could, but my arms were stuck like in drying cement. Nothing was working. And as I continued fighting, the strain had my heart ready to burst. So sinking to my eyes now, I was dying for certain—those snakes just nanoseconds away from puncturing every part of my face with their agitated fangs.

However, just before sucking in that first lung-full of sand, this hand miraculously appeared. There was no face with it—no words even—it

241

was just a hand, reaching out to save me. Suddenly able to move my arm, I quickly grabbed hold and it yanked me right out. *"Whew."*

Dream over.

Jumping up in my own bed (with no snakes in sight), I was so relieved it was just a dream. However, I also knew right away that it was a sign—a real omen—something I needed to heed right away. Because even though I was engaged and "so in love," I was still yearning for that true change and peace within. And even with the volumes of "deep stuff" I had been studying, my lack of answers to life's biggest questions still had me vexed and heavy.

For starters, there was the question of man's origin: I mean, where did we all really come from? And legends or mere scientific theory passed off as scientific law just wasn't enough for me. Never mind the fact that as much as I had ingested everything my anthropology class offered, yet I still couldn't reconcile my being the descendant of some cannibalizing, feces-flinging monkeys. (Never mind the holes in the theory—from the inconstancies in radioactive dating methods, to the absence of transitional fossils, and irreducible complexity.)

Next, what was the meaning of life? I mean, beyond the endless strivings after popularity, pleasure, success, and "good deeds"—all things of which I had already tasted deeply enough to know they couldn't satisfy? Again, I wanted to know where true fulfillment could be found, and where true healing could be found—for the deepest part of me that no psychologist could possibly reach.

And why was there evil in the world? I mean, "devil," "demon," "666," darkness, or whatever one chose to call it, where did it all come from? And more so, why did it seem to prosper? Then lastly (and probably my deepest wonderings of all), what was gonna happen to me after I died, and why did we all have to die to begin with? I mean, was Death truly like some unfettered king, wielding its sovereignty so mightily, that people literally needed to "knock on wood" (or quickly switch topics whenever it came up), as if to "pay it off" until another moment—hopefully in the very distant future?

So with all these thoughts on my mind (and with a reckless lifestyle fueled by pride and lust), it was definitely time to heed this dream and get to the cornfields on the double. But not just any cornfields, mind you, for I knew my dream represented none other than the swampy farmlands of Lake Waccamaw, North Carolina—my dad's neck of the woods. And to think, I hadn't been down there since I was a teenager; because while I once spent a portion of every summer there as a kid—with my late grandmother and million-and-one cousins—by the time I had reached fifteen, I considered myself too much of a "city boy" to be driving around on the backs of dusty pick-up trucks. But now, however, the thought of doing that was actually quite relaxing.

So without delay, I called my Aunt Bev, my dad's baby sister who I hadn't spoken with in years. Her sweet, country accent hadn't changed a bit.

"Hey, Aunt Bev."

"Hey, how ya doin'?" After all these years, she still knew my voice.

"I'm doing good. Hey, if it's okay, I was gonna take an Amtrak down there to see y'all for awhile. It's been a long time!"

"Yeah, well c'mon! You know we'll make a bed for ya'."

"Okay! I'll be down there soon, then."

"Okay, love you." And for some reason, it felt especially good to hear her say that.

"Love you, too, Aunt Bev."

So in a matter of days, I was at the train station with my big duffle bag, my big Timberlands, my big $250 North Face pants (stolen, of course), and my big head of hair,(since I had just yanked out my cornrows). As I stood there in the Amtrak ticket line, lo and behold, one of Hip Hop's most famous rappers was standing a few places behind me. And as I noticed him, I could see that he noticed me too, as he suddenly began talking to his friend extra loud about his upcoming record. But little did he realize how little I cared. Because by this point, I had blazed weed with enough rappers in the game to know that many of them were inwardly frustrated by the monotony of it all (just like me) and on the same hunt for fulfillment (just like me).

So I boarded the train, and surprisingly, I felt better already. It was a bright, sunny day, and as the hours raced by with me staring out the window, the fondest childhood memories came rushing back. Thoughts of when things were so much simpler—when the biggest thing I ever coveted was some G.I. Joe action figure. However, as much as I was enjoying these thoughts, the stress was still heavy on my mind. (And I had a big bag of weed in my napsack.)

Well I finally arrived in Fayetteville, North Carolina, the closest stop to my family's community. And sure enough, as I glanced over the train station's small parking lot (looking every bit like some northern drug dealer), there was my Uncle Ronald, my dad's younger brother. He was sitting in a silver Ford sedan, with his big arm waving out the window for my attention. Uncle Ronald was always a favorite of mine and Brett's. He was a tall, very large, and extremely quiet man, who at the same time, was the anchor of the family. He was also the family preacher, pastoring the growing baptist church that my late great-grandmother had helped start, some decades before reaching her one hundred and third birthday.

Looking at Uncle Ronald now, he hadn't changed one bit.

"Hey there, now! H-h-how you d-d-doin'?"

"Good! Good to see you!"

We shook hands as I jumped into the air-conditioned car. Uncle Ronald always had a heavy stutter; yet miraculously, his speech became perfect whenever he stepped into the pulpit to preach. Smiling that shy smile, he was so happy to have me down there. And in keeping with true southern hospitality, the first place he took me was to eat some fried chicken with the sweetest ice tea and the strongest toothpicks afterwards.

My Aunt Bev got home from work later that evening—along with my Uncle Greg, her husband—and with the biggest of smiles, we all picked right-up like it had only been yesterday since we saw each other.

"Great day in the mornin'! Boy, look at all that hair on yo' head! Why don'cha lemme get some scissors and cut that off for you?"

We all laughed (though she definitely would've done it, had I agreed). And of course they could tell that I was "out there," most of all because my Uncle Greg and Aunt Bev were once "out there," themselves. They had lived up in Jersey back when I was little (my Uncle Ronald, too), but after getting sick of the "city life," they returned "down home." But I could still remember their big, Plainfield summer BBQ's like it was yesterday.

For starters, their cook-outs would draw people from all over. Since my dad and uncles were masters at frying chicken, hush puppies, and everything else, there'd be more women sucking grease off their fingers, more dudes chugging cans of Lowenbrau, and more decks of cards than there were tables. Now with my parents being divorced by this point, this was about the only time I'd get to see so much of this side of my family.

And how I loved it, convinced that I had the absolute coolest uncles and cousins on the planet.

However, there was usually a point where things would switch from "kid time" to "adult time." And as much fun as I might've been having, that's also when Dad would get up from one of the spades tables and say, "Hey, I'mma shoot the boys home and be right back!" And what was Dad's indicator that it was time? Well, I'm sure it was a bunch of things: the moon high in the sky, the Lowenbrau getting lower, and the loose lips getting louder. I'm also pretty sure it had a lot to do with my Uncle Greg and his rowdy crew making their second or third grand entrance for the evening—each time being more high and carrying more cases of beer.

Brett and I idolized Uncle Greg. He was the coolest, Sugar Ray Leonard-and Bruce Lee-imitating, sunglasses-and-afro-rocking dude we knew. "The Dragon" was his nickname; and not only was he good at martial arts, he was good at "crazy," too. One night, when Plainfield's Golden Gloves boxing champ tried to chump Uncle Greg at a local gas station, he simply grabbed the gas nozzle, put it directly over the champ's lap (as he posed in his car with his ladies), and held a cigarette lighter right at the spout, ready to flick if the champ said one more word. Thus, it was the champ who was chumped.

Well, back to the present, Uncle Greg no longer had the fro (or the Lowenbrau), but he still loved wearing his shades. He even had his own trucking company now, with two of his giant rigs sitting right in the yard beside the house. However, while I remembered him at least driving trucks seven years ago (the last time I was there), there was something else different about him. For starters, all Uncle Greg talked about now was "the Lord"—and by that, I knew he was referring to Jesus Christ. (A far cry from the way he used to talk.) And while I had already heard through the grapevine how Uncle Greg had started going to church a while back and had even become a deacon (whatever that was), I could now see for myself that he had truly changed. And the change looked good, too—just like when sitting in a restaurant and noticing someone so satisfied with their meal, that you just had to ask the waiter what they were having.

So I concluded my first day down there by driving around and surprising more of my family—from cousin Duckery, who could fry even some cow-stomach and have you licking the plate, to my Uncle Haines and his sixty-acre farm, with everything from cattle to protein-rich cat-fish that would snap your fishing line like nothing. Yup, I was in the country, for sure ("Indian country" as my family would say), tobacco and "butter bean" fields everywhere. And yes, there were plenty of cornfields, too—wasn't forgetting about my dream.

▲ ▼ ▲ ▼ ▲

Sitting at the swamps of Lake Waccamaw, smoking my weed, smacking monster mosquitos, and looking for eels and alligators in the murky wa-ter, it was nice to be reunited with my cousin, Snap. (Snap was my age and had also lived in Plainfield, until he got into trouble back in high school and got sent "down south," where he'd been ever since.) However, as great as it was to be with Snap and all my family, and even daydream about my big wedding day at the end of the summer, nothing was allevi-ating this burden of mine. I mean, things might have diverted me from it, at times, but nothing could alleviate it.

Burden: what a fitting word to describe it, too—the big gorilla on my back that I couldn't shake loose. And talk about the proverbial candle burning at both ends? Here I was with this big gorilla on my back and this obvious leak in my heart. Because along with that burden, almost everything I poured into my life always leaked right out—leaving me longing for more. That's partly why I always went so gung-ho with every-thing, in my fight for fulfillment (and what a fighter I had been). I was tired, and man, my soul needed some rest.

And as for Uncle Greg being a Christian and really loving God? That was rocking me, for sure. And he wasn't messing around, either. Never had I seen such transformation in someone (as by this point, I knew lots of people into lots of things). I mean, way beyond "turning a new leaf," "getting on the good foot," or "pulling himself up by his own boot-straps," this change was clearly supernatural. He had this glow, too. And with that big, servile smile, being around him was like having a cool glass of water on a hot day. (And man, I was parched!)

Nevertheless, hard-core skeptic that I was, I still had my issues with Christianity. For starters, I had seen too many hypocrites over the years. People talking that "Jesus stuff" one minute and then frolicking in the same pigpens where I was a ringleader the next. Talking holy while living lowly. And while I didn't really know much Bible, I at least knew the Bible taught that Christians weren't supposed to look anything like me! However, on the flip side, there was J.J., my roommate from freshman year. Now that was a guy who really lived it. And while he wasn't perfect (nobody was), even a blind man could see that God held the reins to his heart and mind. And then, along with J.J., there was this other "real deal" Christian named Joy, also in our same year at UPenn. Whenever I saw Joy, it was like pure sunshine, and I only gave her the most gentlemanly of hugs (flirtatious as I'd otherwise be)—even feeling the need to excuse myself whenever I bumped into her while drunk and high.

So as faithful as these two witnesses were, why was it still the hypocrites who shaped my final views of Christianity? Or, could it be that I simply chose to focus more on the hypocrites because it helped me justify living my life the way *I* wanted to? Meanwhile, all this "living the way *I* wanted to" had only succeeded in showing me that there had to be something more to life. Clearly, my mind was all over the place, by this point.

Then, last but not least, I had also entertained every attack imaginable against Christianity: from "them" not really being allowed to eat pork, to "them" worshipping on the wrong day of the week (Sunday instead of Saturday), to the Bible justifying slavery and Native-American genocide, even to Shakespeare supposedly writing parts of the Bible. So, while I was no doubt attracted to this whole thing Uncle Greg now represented, needless to say, I now had tons of questions. And with everything I had been studying over the years—from ancient, to "eastern," to street philosophies galore—Uncle Greg needed to be ready.

▲ ▼ ▲ ▼ ▲

So the rest of my stay followed much of the same pattern: eating like there was no tomorrow, talking with Uncle Greg for hours, and then retreating back to the swamps to smoke my weed and think. And even though one night, I came back into their house so high, that I just stood staring in their fridge like a zombie, my aunt and uncle never commented on it. They just kept loving on me—fully persuaded that what God had graciously done for them, He was more than willing to do for me.

"You see, Aaron, I was once just like this cup," Uncle Greg said as he held his morning mug of coffee. "And just like this mug is full of fatty cream and sugar, I was once full of all types of junk; I mean, everything the world could throw at me. Real full of myself, too. And it only got worse and worse, to the point where one night, I ended up doing the one thing I swore I'd never do: I tried a hit of that crack, man . . . But when I finally heard the Gospel: how the Lord loved little ol' Greg so much, that He died on the cross for all my sins, and then rose from the dead on the third day, conquering death and even the devil; and that He wanted to forgive me for everything, and come live inside my heart, too? Man, I was ready!" He laughed with childlike joy and continued.

"But before the Lord could move into my heart, I first had to empty all my junk out, which meant repenting of all my sins. Because again, just like this here cup, before I can pour anything new into it, I first gotta pour this old junk out . . . And man oh man, lemme tell you what! After that, God changed my life three hundred and sixty degrees by His power, and it's been a blast ever since. Most of all, when I die, I now know for a fact that I'm going straight to Heaven!" He chuckled some more and sipped of his "junky" coffee with joy.

The way Uncle Greg talked about Jesus, it was like He really knew Him and had a personal relationship with Him. How attractive it was how he believed this stuff so much that he'd be willing to die for it. (As even Dr. King once said that a man who wasn't willing to die for anything, wasn't fit to live.) And talk about God having a sense of humor? Here I had sat before some of the planet's most brilliant minds, yet the most immensely blessed I'd ever been was right now, by a truck driver with no college education.

"You see, Aaron. We can know for certain that the Bible is the very Word of God. Because you see, while there are lots of other books out there that claim this and that, the Bible does something that no other book does—it tells the future in advance! We call that prophecy."

Prophecy? Uncle Greg definitely had my attention now. Reaching for his Bible and opening it, he began showing me how every major world empire—Nebuchadnezzar's Babylon, Cyrus' Persia, Alexander the Great and Antiochus Epiphanes' Greece, and even Caesar's Rome (histories I had studied quite well)—had all been predicted way before they ever arose to power. (The Bible even mentioning Cyrus by name before he was born.) Then, turning to the books of Daniel and Revelation, he showed me how the Bible even spoke about the "revived Roman empire" to come. Lastly (and most importantly), Uncle Greg showed me how's God's reign over the ages was bigger than any one kingdom, tyrannical ruler, or government conspiracy that I might've been consumed with; and that ultimately, prophecy was given to us so that we might always know that God is sovereign, and caught off-guard by nothing.

Now with all the evils and injustices I had witnessed throughout my life (and all the indescribably sad histories I had studied), this was the sweetest song to my ears. So life wasn't just some arbitrary, impersonal game of lucky and unlucky, "good karma" or "bad karma," after all? I mean, to be learning how God was all-knowing (omniscient), everywhere (omnipresent), and in total control (sovereign), and that He proved all this to us by telling us things in advance? And while "higher criticism" did its best to attack the accuracy of such Bible prophecies—insisting they had been written after the fact and then fraudulently presented as "ancient"—the finding of the famed Dead Sea Scrolls confirmed with absolute certainty how these Old Testament books were written when they said they were (and by the way, millennia before William Shakespeare.) As the hard-core skeptic and formally trained researcher that I was, I so needed to hear and see all this.

Though Uncle Greg was just getting warmed up. Because he then showed me how the greatest of all the Old Testament prophecies were about the first and second comings of the Christ—hundreds and sometimes even thousands of years before their fulfillment. In rapid-fire fashion, he showed me where the Bible prophesied the Christ (the Messiah) being be born in Bethlehem[1], born of a virgin[2], healing the sick and giving sight to the blind[3], riding into Jerusalem on a donkey[4], betrayed by his friend[5], crucified and killed for our sins[6], and even rising from the dead[7] (and many others). Needless to say, when he was through, I was speechless.

And what I appreciated most, was how there was nothing Uncle Greg said without showing me exactly where it was, so I could read it for

---

1 Micah 5:2
2 Isaiah 7:14
3 Isaiah 35:4-6
4 Zechariah 9:9
5 Psalm 55:12-14
6 Psalm 22:16; Isaiah 53: 5, 7
7 Psalm 16: 8-10

myself and make my own conclusions. Because in my journeyings, I had come across so many cults (even joining a few for a season) who claimed to represent the Bible, but yet never interpreted verses in the context of the rest of the Bible (let alone allowing me to raise the hardest questions).

Plus, it bugged me out that Uncle Greg had his Bible all marked up with yellow highlights and notes in the margins. I didn't even know you were allowed to do that. Though one thing was for certain; while I had seen others open their Bibles like they were opening some antiquated refrigerator, when Uncle Greg did, it felt more like a cozy warm fire. More so, while fanning through his Bible's well-worn pages like a giant love letter, he dove head-first into topics that I'd seen even the "brightest of the bright" run from: the origin of man and purpose of life, the reason for the existence of evil (and the ultimate answer for evil), and why death came upon mankind (and the only answer for death). He even showed me how heaven was a real future place—the true answer for man's search for utopia. Yup, the Bible had it all, and the skeptic in me was being replaced by the curious and humble seeker.

"So Uncle Greg, why do Christians have church on Sunday instead of Saturday?" He smiled and patiently showed me what "the Scriptures" said.

"Why can Christians eat pork?"

He smiled and patiently showed me what "the Scriptures" said.

"Were slave-owners using the Bible correctly when they used it to support slavery and even all that was done to our Indian people?"

"Great day, no!" He got especially excited to show me what "the Scriptures" said on that hot topic.

So back at the swamps I was, puffing, pondering, and rehearsing all we had discussed, thus far (hours and hours of convo by this point). Still shocked at how the Old Testament spoke about so much way before it even happened, I realized most of all how the resurrection of Christ was huge—where Jesus repeatedly said He was going to do it, and then did it at just the foretold time. I mean, here was something we just glibly talked about on Easter Sundays, yet if it was really true its implications were bananas! I mean, who else could resurrect and conquer death but the true Savior of mankind? Not to mention how Jesus repeatedly said in the plainest of terms that He was indeed the Messiah and Savior of the world. And most of all, unlike some cryptic and whimsical Nostradamus stuff (so vague, it could be twisted to mean anything), this Bible prophecy thing was clearer than the mountain streams Tash and I once tried to purge ourselves in.

So basically, I had a serious decision to make: Was Jesus truly Lord, like He said? Or was Jesus just a liar, maliciously saying something that wasn't true? Or, was Jesus simply a lunatic, thinking He was something when He really wasn't—a megalomaniac? So, Lord, liar, or lunatic, which was it? Because the Bible also made it clear that I had a decision to make, and that even my indifference counted as an answer.

"Whoa."

▲▼▲▼▲

Sunday meant time for church. Waking up to Gospel music playing from the stereo, grits bubbling on the stove, and smothered meat and onions waiting to go on top of the grits, this was every bit of the loveliest environment. And as we finally made it to church, different family members insisted on me sitting in the pews with them (again, it had been seven years). However, as much as I loved being close to everyone—even recognizing some of the pretty Indian girls I used to scope out as a teenager—I still had tons to think about. So I just grabbed a seat in the back, alone.

In no time, the service was underway, and in came the choir through the back doors, in a single-file procession with the soloist at the front. The soloist was a single mother of three beautiful kids by different men, but when this single mom lifted up her sweet voice, it was obvious that she was free from all guilt and shame. She was free to worship her Lord, as the rest of the choir repeated her every line in that old-fashioned "call and response" style:

> Trouble in my way (trouble in my way)
> I had to pray some time (had to pray some time)
> LORD! So much trouble (trouble in my way)
> I had to pray some time (had to pray some time)
> I lay awake at night (lay awake at night)
> But that's all right! (that's all right!)
> 'Cause I know Jesus (Jesus is gonna fix it)
> And I know Jesus (Jesus is gonna fix it)
> After 'while! (after 'while)

The place was alive now. Way more than human emotion or "positive energy," there was something special going on. Inspecting everything, I watched as people sang. I looked over at my cousin Duckery, one of the hardest workers I'd ever seen, with hands so calloused (from years of metal work) that he could handle hot steel without gloves. Well, those calloused hands were now lifted in praise, his eyes closed with the sweetest tears flowing down his cheeks. And of course there was Uncle Greg, looking so happy and free as he danced in place up in the front row. And as the teenager drummed away and the piano player pounded away, this song was even sweet enough to make me want to bop my head a little. However, as much as I wanted to, I realized that I couldn't. For as sad as it sounds (but so real), here I was so shackled to this "beloved," calloused manhood thing, that the most I could do was lightly tap my finger on the pew in front of me. My pointer finger feeling like it weighed fifty pounds.

Man, I wanted to be free—free like everyone else.

As the choir made its way up the middle aisle and filled the rows at the rear of the stage, there stood my Uncle Ronald at the pulpit, already in a happy sweat and bursting with joy like he was thanking the Lord for every single thing—from his deliverance from that deadly colon cancer, to the new church building they had just finished building with their own hands. And as he began preaching, there wasn't a single stutter.

"I'd like to welcome everyone out this morning. It's so good to be here! Now we believe in lots of love here at Union Baptist Church, so get tighter together in them pews, okay? If you're cold, I'll let you borrow my sports jacket, and if your hungry, I'll fry you up a piece of chicken, afterwards." And as the church laughed, they could see that he really meant it, too.

I was all ears throughout the whole sermon as Uncle Ronald began preaching about the life, death, and resurrection of Christ. And I couldn't help but notice how he was hammering home the very same point Uncle Greg kept touching on: how God's salvation and forgiveness was actually a free gift, and that all of our "good deeds" and "good works" were utterly unable to earn it. Now obviously this news was like a comet from another world. Because all *this* world ever taught me was that good things *only* came by working, working, working, and earning, earning, earning, and that there was no such thing as a free lunch. Yet, after all this time (and all this tiredness, too), I was now learning of God's perfect, unconditional love as a free gift—all to be received strictly by grace[8].

I had been to church at least a few times before in my life, but this was the very first time I heard the true Gospel as laid out in the Bible. See, I always knew that Jesus "died on the cross" and that it was "for the world," but I always saw it as some general type of death for "mankind" in a general sense. Never did I imagine it to be so unbelievably personal: that while He did indeed love all of mankind, He actually loved Aaron W. Campbell in particular, suffering and even dying for Aaron W. Campbell, in particular.

More so, as I sat there—alive, healthy, and still in my right mind after all these crazy years—I could now see how God had always been with me, watching over me and preserving me every step of the way (even as I mocked Him and hated Him). I mean, just to think of all those times I should have died alone! (Even when I was terrified that I had contracted HIV from this freshman gal at UPenn.) Nothing was by good luck; everything was only because of His goodness. And this realization now had me wanting to know Him even more.

The bottom line was that God loved me so much that He gave His only begotten Son, Jesus, to pay the price for all my sins, so that I could be saved from the Hell I deserved[9]. More so, Jesus died and rose again so that I could be His in Heaven, forever. Wow, what amazing love! I mean, no human could've even invented all this! Prophecy, history, the resurrection—what truth! My anti-Christian, scientific scrutiny could do nothing but bow in the face of such variegated evidence. Yup, I believed it now. I truly did; and right in my pew, this sweet wave of relieving emotion started coming over me, far loftier than the superficial, contagious excitement like in a football stadium. No, this was something springing up from the depths of my heart—a real work of God.

So at the end of service, as Uncle Ronald gave the opportunity for anyone to come up and receive God's gift of salvation, did I venture up the aisle? Nope. Actually, I didn't even budge. Though I did watch as others chose to respond and walked up; men, women, and teenagers alike, some wiping tears away (looking just as tired as I was) as they looked more than ready to make peace with God Almighty.

---

8 Ephesians 2:8-9
9 John 3:16

Well after service was through, of course we ate tons of fried chicken. And as cousin after cousin was inviting me to do everything from fishing to hunting, lo and behold, my week down there was actually up now. The next day I'd be heading back to my fiancée. However, before I left the next morning, my Uncle Ronald handed me a brand new Bible. And on the inside cover he wrote me a simple message:

"This is the Word of God. In this you will find all the solutions to the problems of the world. 'Study to show thyself approved unto God; a workman that needeth not be ashamed, rightly dividing the word of truth. (II Timothy 2:15)'"

▲ ▼ ▲ ▼ ▲

HITTING THE FAST-FORWARD BUTTON NOW . . .
(BRINGING IT BACK TO MY WEDDING DAY.)

Needless to day, Uncle Greg and Aunt Bev were elated to learn that our wedding day was "coincidentally" the same day as theirs. Cruising up I-95 from Lake Waccamaw to upstate New York, they wouldn't have missed it for the world. And not only did Uncle Ronald come too, but he's the one who married us. Not only that, but right after the ceremony, he even changed clothes and fried his legendary chicken in the homemade "cookers" that cousin Duckery had just welded together for us.

Now by this point, Tasha and I still weren't Christians, but we had started reading the Bible that Uncle Ronald gave me and definitely took our wedding vows most seriously. And to now fill in some more details, when that stripper had exposed herself in front of me like that, not only had I pushed her away and turned my chair towards the window, but I actually began begging God to be merciful on my wedding day for even being in the same room with that stuff! See, I was beginning to develop a healthy fear of God Almighty.

So as I said before, with no money for a honeymoon, my wife and I simply headed back to Philly to our new two-bedroom apartment on the corner of 45th and Spruce Street—me still having that one semester left at Penn, while Tasha had that final year of law school. As newlyweds, life was sweet and quiet now. We shopped together, tried new foods together, studied together, took naps together, and as we soon had our first signs of her being pregnant, we got nervous and smiled real big together.

I had slowed down by now, too—even on my weed and my drinking. Tasha and I were bent on working hard and providing a great life for our future kids. She had just wrapped up a summer clerkship at a D.C. law firm, where she worked on projects for Bill Clinton's advisor Vernon Jordan, and was now looking at top law firms in Philly. And as for me (like I said, no longer seeing my life mission in Medicine), I was looking to do all that my talents were curious towards, and chiefly, there was this five hundred page book about my life that I had just written—simply feeling that my life's experiences needed to be penned.

And of course there was still much Bible reading going on. In fact, I now studied it so much that my eyes often got bloodshot. And then one day, the revelation just hit me: I could have "new life" in marriage, "new life" in Philly, and even some type of "new life" in respect to my wildest ways, and yet none of that equalled eternal life. Plus, I still didn't have that true change and peace that I was after. More so, I still didn't have forgiveness for my sins, and therefore could not boast that if I died at that very moment, I wouldn't go straight to Hell. So upon realizing how huge a difference there was between merely acknowledging Truth and submitting to it, one night in our West Philly apartment, I lowered my head (all by myself), repented of all my sins and received the resurrected Christ into my heart—fully confessing Jesus as "Lord" of every part of my life and asking Him to be my personal Lord and Savior.

So what happened next? Did fireworks go off in the sky? Did angels appear and sing in my room? Did I suddenly have the strength to do ten backflips? No. However, I will tell you what did take place: there was suddenly a light in my soul where before there had only been darkness, confusion, and fear. More so, there was now unspeakable joy in knowing I was truly forgiven by God for all that I'd ever done. Mind-blowing! Lastly, there was incomprehensible peace in knowing that He was living in my very heart now, never to leave me or forsake me.

And that wasn't all, because this salvation thing was like having the piñata of the universe busted wide open with the sweetest blessings raining all over my soul. And speaking of piñatas, no longer was I "blindfolded," either. Because now, I finally saw life for what it was—a gift from God. And now, I finally saw people for what they were—no longer mere acquaintances or resources who only existed to fulfill my selfish ends, but creatures who were made by God and adored by God with inestimable worth. And as for Christ's resurrection, I even believed that like never before—because my life had just been changed, just like Uncle Greg's. And lastly, as for death—that big, pale elephant in every room—for the first time I now had great boldness in facing it, knowing that when I died I would surely go to heaven to see my Savior face to face.

So, I was born again now, and my soul finally had that rest it so desperately craved. And the world could mock the "folly" of the cross of Christ and being born-again all it wanted. I didn't care, one bit. Besides, I was once a bigger mocker than them all. That is, until I took the challenge and read Jesus' words for myself.

▲ ▼ ▲ ▼ ▲

Now as for my wife, as she watched my new life, she couldn't help but notice my unspeakable joy and supernatural change. Most of all, my deliverance from Newports, weed, and liquor—as what I had tried to do so many times on my own and failed, Jesus did with just one touch! Not to mention how I was quick to tell a homie from Plainfield, "no thanks, I'm a Christian now," when he called me with this golden opportunity to run bank scams for thousands of dollars (something I would've dominated just months earlier). So therefore, just as Uncle Greg had me more than curious, I now had "my baby" more than curious, and one day, I sat her down and explained the Gospel (her mind just as blown away by the biblical concept of "grace" as mine had been).

Then about a month later, as I was reading and relaxing one day, Tasha suddenly emerged from our guest bedroom with a look on her face like I'd never seen. There was such a peace, such resolution, and the biggest, happiest little-girl smile.

"Well, I did it!" And seeing her Bible in her hand, I knew just what she meant. "I got on my knees in there, and took my time repenting of all of my sins and asking Jesus into my heart!"

"Awww, man! C'mere, girl."

She came over to me for the biggest hug, and we hugged for a while. Both of our sordid "pasts" now forgiven and erased, everything was new for the both us[10].

---

10 II Corinthians 5:17

Well, word began spreading like wildfire that "Aaron gave His life to God," and everyone marveled. Some even said they refused to believe it until they saw it with their own eyes. However, as I even gave away everything I had ever acquired through crime—my most expensive clothing and accessories—slowly, people began believing the unbelievable.

And guess what? My phone and doorbell went from ringing around the clock, to almost never ringing at all now. (For the ever-popular Mr. Hyde had just been transformed into Mr. Christian.) But that was quite all right, because while I still loved all my homies—even praying for every one of them—I hadn't really lost anything. Only gaining the Answer to everything, and that Answer was a Person—the very "helping hand" in my dream who yanked me from the quicksand, just in time.

Matter of fact, looking back over my entire life now, I could see that He had always been with me! In a fallen world stained with Lucifer's rebellion, Jesus was "my Lock" holding our little back door together. He was "my Sanity" during that night with Big-fat-Ron. He was "my Angel" protecting me at the Port, and "my Brains" at UPenn. In fact, He was even my "J.J. the roommate!" More so, He was "my Physician" for my drunk liver and drugged lungs, and "my Mercy" for all the nights I should've died. To sum it all up, He was my "All in all." For the Bible declares that every single blessing comes from God's gracious heart, and that while God is never the author of evil, He sovereignly reigns over it and may even use it to show us that He's the only thing that makes sense in a senseless world. And lastly, it was also the Bible that finally showed me what being a man truly was—walking with God in reverence and keeping His commandments.

So life made perfect sense now. That indescribable burden (the gorilla) was now gone, and that perpetual hole in my heart was now filled. And like King David once exclaimed, how great it was to be forgiven for all I'd ever done[11]! No guilt, no shame, plus a best friend, too! The very same One who even touched my little heart that day, when I was just a lonely, misunderstood kid walking down Liberty Street:

"And I'm so happy, so very happy,

---

11 Psalm 32:1

I've got the love of Jesus in my heart . . ."

Back then, I knew the beautiful words, but now, I knew the beautiful Person, Himself. That's why true Christianity isn't a religion—it's a personal relationship.

▲▼▲▼▲

"Hey Momma, guess what? Tasha's having your first great-grandbaby!"

And of all the places we could've been when we first found this out, we were at Momma's. And of all the days that pregnancy test could've come back positive, it was on Father's Day.

Yeah, I was definitely ready to raise some beautiful kids with my Tasha. Ready for a life of ministry with her, too. And if you had told me back then that I'd one day be pastoring a "live" church, with outreaches stretching from the rough waters of southeast Alaska, even to post-quake Haiti, where I'd hold kids who had lost legs and arms while helping others escape from human traffickers, I would have told you that God would never use someone with as troubled and crazy a past as mine. But by His matchless, amazing grace, He most surely did (and still does).

ACKNOWLEDGEMENTS

With "eyes that seen plenty," I've come across countless people who have touched my life! So I'll first start with my pastor, Joe Focht, of Calvary Chapel of Philadelphia. Thanks for being who you are and sharing everything with me, from your favorite commentaries even to half your sandwich—I love you. Damien Kyle, pastor of Calvary Chapel Modesto, thanks for that three-hour chat as we discussed our lives and the art of sharing our lives publicly; I love you for that. "Uncle Carl" and "Aunt Barb" Westerlund at Calvary Chapel Costa Mesa . . . thanks for making family an action word!

To my assistant pastor, Johnny "Biscuits" Bell. Johnny, I couldn't have done this without you, period. And the day you stepped between that potential gang fight at West Philly High with me, I knew you loved me. Maybe one day I'll get the pleasure of stepping in the line of fire for you! You're my dearest friend like words can't convey.

Dr. Jeff Black. You're another one I couldn't have done this without. The way you were used in this project was supernatural; nobody could've had that much insight into what another person was attempting/needing to put on paper. I forever tip my hat to your inestimable value to the Kingdom. Cheryl Black, thanks for not thinking your husband and I too crazy for texting each other like mad. Stacey Murrell, you're one of the greatest encouragers and quite the editor! Steve and Nancy Tuttle, thanks for your edits, as well (along with your delicious quiche and apple thing-a-ma-jiggy). Mike and Kim Allen, the same to y'all; and Brett D. Allen (a.k.a. Baby Helga), you're one of the most faithful and dearest friends I've ever had ("cousin" is the only way to describe it).

My Antioch family. Thank you for being a praying church that doesn't want to "play church." Whether I'm in Alaska, Haiti, or wherever in between, thanks for always having my back. I love you all. To my other assistant pastor, Talib, and my deacon and right-hand-man, Chris, I don't think I'd be alive without you guys (as far as the day-to-day goes). We lock shields forever! Todd and John Allison, you are men I've come to love and respect deeply. Monica, thanks for being a true sister; Erika, you too. Quanah, my true "brother from another mother;" it's like we were raised in the same crib. John "Espo," my family has never been the same since you've walked into our lives (glad my kids call you "uncle"). Lee and Mariella . . . I love you like the family you are! Kevin Kologinsky, thanks for being who you are—brotherhood is fun with you!

Plainfield, N.J. Best city on the planet! Whut?! Now if I even start naming names, I simply won't stop. So I'll just give a special shout to the Dunns, the Allens, the Fowlers, and the Sanders, and tell everyone else, "I love you, for real." Big thanks to my god-parents, Aunt Bonnie and Uncle David, and my god-bro's, and all my family on my step-mom's side. Uncle Mike and fam! Cousin Kimmy!

The Wardlaw-Hartridge School. Thanks for a great education (way more than books)! Class of 1992: Jen Blackman, Vic Sarkaria, and Nick Zagorski (best doubles-partner in tennis). Mrs. Gubelman: thanks for always believing in me. The Masones.

My New York crew. Brooklyn, Uptown, Queens, you know who you are! And when I see y'all again, we'll pick up reminiscing right where we left off. Love is forever!

UPenn. Currently, number three only to Harvard and Yale, yeah, I'm a "Quaker" for life (and I've got a ton of loan-payment receipts to prove it). Much love to the class of 1996. Man, we were crazy. Crazy about those books, too. I enjoyed laughing with so many of you. Disco Biscuits, you guys shouted me out on your very first record, so here it is, right back at you. Much love to all of CREW—you know who you are. DJ Baby Grand: we learned how to cook together, marinating wing-dings in forty juice. Dr. Chaz Howard, thank you! We've got lots to do my friend! Professor Walter McDougall, you've been a great encouragement and a friend.

Much love to my crew from Newark, New Jersey ("Brick City"). Shem, Pathfinder, George "the Wookie," Rob, Mike, Spencer, Will Boone, and Hass from Hawthorne.

Acknowledgements

Much love to my South London family. Redbeard and H.M.S.S., Jahaziel and Nadine, Robert, Efrem, Patrick, Chenoa, and Calvary Chapel South London.

My native family in Angoon, Alaska! My Tlingit ("klink-it") tribe, the Beaver clan. Most of all, the George family. Martin from Yakutat, Marti Fred, Levi and Stefan, Marcus ("my son"), Lillian, Guy, Robert, and all my nieces and nephews, Kenny Johnson's family (R.I.P. "Phantom"), Gold Medal Basketball Champions 2010 and 2011. Albert Howard and Frank III. Chenera and Kyle. Regina Jack.

My family in Port-au-Prince, Haiti. Maria Andre and "the babies" (never to fear those human-traffickers again), Lucia, Betty and Denis, little Juanito, Marvince and Robinson, Sebastian, Yvner, Jean-Joel—it was just me and you walking though the chaotic aftermath, brother, I trusted you with my life, I love you, always.

My brothers, Brett and Kyle. Thanks for letting me be a big brother to you guys. I love you both so much. Raymond and Joyce, thanks for everything and love you! Aunt C.C., Aunt Carol, Uncle Andreas, thanks for helping my mom raise me and Brett. I love you guys, always (Alexis, Panos, and Eleni, too). Uncle Greg and Aunt Bev, and my millions of cousins, aunts, and uncles "down home." Aunt Mary made the best comfort food, and Uncle Haines is still the best farmer. Uncle Clyde, Aunt Karen, and Aunt Delphia . . . thanks for everything!

To all my adopted little brothers, sisters, and "god-kids," I love you all.

And last but not least, on the technical side of the book: Julian and Ed (Eggtoapples.com), Esso and your video camera, Jeffrey Kranz, and Andrew at Bethany . . . thank you. Eileen Scott, Lou Flores, Dr. Cornel West and his personal assistant, Lili Polluck . . . thanks a million! Patty and Steve Bulack—way to come through in the 4th quarter @ "4th and goal." My own daughter Anni, thanks for all your insight in this project from beginning to end (you're gonna be a better writer than me one day soon!) My sons, Josiah and Jonah, for your understanding and excitement. My "Mash" (Tasha), your A-to-Z support for this endeavor was so sweet that this book is just as much yours . . . most of all, thanks for always believing!

In loving memory of Momma, Omari, and Uncle Ronald

ABOUT THE AUTHOR

Aaron Campbell is the founder and senior pastor of Antioch of Calvary Chapel (www.antiochphilly.org), said to be one of the most ethnically diverse churches in Philadelphia. The church's outreaches—including free "fish fry's," food and clothing drives, carnivals, and "street" basketball tournaments—have gained them city-wide recognition and respect, from the projects to the colleges.

Aaron is the founder and CEO of Angoon Alive Project, Inc., a non-profit dedicated to helping Alaska natives (and natives at large) become economically self-sufficient (www.angoonaliveproject.org). Along with Alaska, he also does extensive work in Port-au-Prince, Haiti.

Besides enjoying each day with his amazing wife, Natasha, his other hobby is laughing with their three super kids, and wiping the drool from their Sicilian mastiff, Agapé. *To contact him for a speaking engagement, email contact@kaatenapress.com*